# ADVANCES IN QUALITATIVE ORGANIZATION RESEARCH

# ADVANCES IN QUALITATIVE ORGANIZATION RESEARCH

Series Editor: John A. Wagner III

Previous Volumes:    1 & 2

ADVANCES IN QUALITATIVE ORGANIZATION
RESEARCH    VOLUME 3

# ADVANCES IN QUALITATIVE ORGANIZATION RESEARCH

## EDITED BY

### JOHN A. WAGNER III

*The Eli Broad Graduate School of Management,
Michigan State University, USA*

### JEAN M. BARTUNEK

*The Wallace E Carroll School of Management, Boston College, USA*

### KIMBERLY D. ELSBACH

*Graduate School of Management, University of California, Davis, USA*

2001

JAI
An Imprint of Elsevier Science

Amsterdam – London – New York – Oxford – Paris – Shannon – Tokyo

ELSEVIER SCIENCE Ltd
The Boulevard, Langford Lane
Kidlington, Oxford OX5 1GB, UK

First edition 2001

Library of Congress Cataloging in Publication Data
A catalog record from the Library of Congress has been applied for.

British Library Cataloguing in Publication Data
A catalogue record from the British Library has been applied for.

ISBN: 0-7623-0772-2

∞ The paper used in this publication meets the requirements of ANSI/NISO Z39.48-1992 (Permanence of Paper).
Printed in The Netherlands.

# CONTENTS

vi

# ADVISORY BOARD

# EDITORIAL STATEMENT

*Advances in Qualitative Organization Research* is an annual series that publishes qualitative research relevant to the interests of organizational scholars. Included in this volume, the third of the series, are eight articles. The first, by Murnighan, Cantelon, and Elyashiv, examines ethical dilemmas faced by agents in the residential real estate market in Vancouver, British Columbia. In one of these dilemmas, realtors are caught between the legal requirement of according primacy to the interests of sellers, even when providing primary service to purchasers, and their own desires to retain the confidence and business of the purchasers. In the other, realtors must cope with regulations requiring disclosure to sellers of complete information about purchasers while at the same time seeking to protect purchaser interests. Revealed are varied instances of bounded personal ethics, in which moral decisions are made without complete awareness.

The second article, by Kurke and Brindle, is an historical analysis of the life and military strategies of Alexander the Great. Recognizing that the concept of enactment has grown to become central in the field of organization theory, yet is not yet fully understood within the field, Kurke and Brindle suggest that enactment processes involve reframing problems, using symbolism, forming identities, and building alliances. Analyses of several of Alexander's campaigns produce illuminating examples of each of these aspects of enactment, thus rendering more tractable this important concept.

Third is an article by Elsbach that examines how individuals working for organizations with hybrid identities – identities that are stigmatized in some respects and non-stigmatized in others – develop positive professional identities for themselves. Data from staffers working for the California State Legislature suggest that such individuals develop split identifications, or schizo-identifications, in which they actively identify with some dimensions of the organization's identity but just as actively disidentify with others. Elsbach concludes that schizo-identification enables individuals to reconcile the conflicting demands of hybrid organizational identities, on the one hand, and desires to validate or enhance one's image of oneself, on the other.

In the fourth article, by Brindle and Stearns, the authors survey the recent history of management faddism in the United States and France, describing how 20th century fads, developed mostly in the U.S., have met with open resistance in France and yet have influenced French management practices in countless ways. Brindle and Stearns' study indicates clearly how cultural context can influence the interpretation and adoption (or rejection) of management and organization practices, despite seeming indifference on the part of many management consulting firms and "gurus" to national distinctions and indigenous routines. Also substantiated is a combination of distinctive elements and imitative adaptation in French management practices which indicates that cultural proclivities and business necessities both play parts in shaping managerial behavior.

Biggart's article on rotating savings and credit associations – roscas – follows next, and describes a type of communal lending arrangement that can abate the effects of poverty. Roscas typically arise when traditional lending institutions refuse to extend credit, and are especially likely to involve women and small businesses (often owned by women) as participants and beneficiaries. Biggart's analysis indicates that success is especially likely when five contextual characteristics – forming a "situational logic" – are present and provide support for the social influence structure of rosca arrangements.

The sixth article in this volume, by Clair and Pearson, is a case study of an organization's attempts to deal with employee fraud. The organization, a medicare carrier for the U.S. government, is subject to attempts by employees to submit fraudulent claims and receive illicit medicare payments. The authors note various points in claims processing that are especially vulnerable to employee fraud, and describe how the organization detects and investigates fraudulent behaviors. Proposed is a model of factors though to affect the likelihood of success in dealing with employee fraud.

Seventh is an article by Porter that analyzes responses to open ended queries on a questionnaire about managerial diversity administered to employees in a U.S. manufacturing facility. Findings of the analysis indicate that most respondents viewed diversity among management personnel in a favorable light and expected that it would yield positive benefits ranging from broadened business perspectives to a richer organizational culture. Other respondents, however, expressed concerns about quotas, communication difficulties, and similar issues or problems. Porter's results suggest the emergence of both sympathetic and ethnocentric viewpoints when managerial diversity is encouraged through supportive company policy.

Finally, Wilson and Sankaran report the results of a case study of vendor-manufacturer relations conducted in a forestry products company located in New Zealand. Examined in the case are processes through which the company selected and managed relationships with the network of suppliers that comprised the firm's supply chain. Analyses confirm previous findings that have shown trust to be critical in maintaining effective vender-manufacturer partnerships, and substantiate the importance of mutual dependence in supporting the development of trust-based relationships. Wilson and Sankaran's study also allows the authors to gauge the extent to which the findings of prior research, conducted most often in mass production facilities, are relevant to firms and manufacturing operations in process industries.

As in Volumes 1 and 2 of *AQOR*, the eight articles appearing in this volume cover a broad array of issues amenable to qualitative research. While common themes of contextualized meaning and social sensemaking bind the articles together, differences in topics of investigation – from the dilemmas and significance of trust in buyer-seller negotiations to the effects of history and culture on emerging business practices – are readily apparent. In all instances, data drawn from sources ranging from interviews and transcripts to questionnaires and historical accounts provide the sense of "being there" that is such an important feature of qualitative investigation. Findings have both theoretical relevance and pragmatic significance, holding implications and insights for scholars and practitioners in all areas organizational.

John A. Wagner III
Series Editor
Jean M. Bartunek
Kimberly D. Elsbach
Editors

# BOUNDED PERSONAL ETHICS AND THE TAP DANCE OF REAL ESTATE AGENCY

J. Keith Murnighan, Debra A. Cantelon and Tal Elyashiv

## ABSTRACT

*This paper begins by reporting the results of a study investigating how a small sample of successful real estate agents reacted to two ethical dilemmas. Agents first had to decide whether to reveal to purchasers that their legal responsibilities were actually to owners. Even though they provided considerable service to purchasers, the agents were legally required to represent the owners. Agents believed that revealing their responsibilities, however, increased their chances of losing clients. Their second dilemma was whether to comply with regulations and reveal to owners the information they had about purchasers, violating any implicit personal connections they had established with them. Interviews indicated that agents tended to hide their responsibilities to owners but still protected purchasers' interests. In essence, they acted illegally on both issues. These findings were used as the foundation for a new model, called bounded personal ethics. The latter part of the paper, then, uses the specifics of the first half to move to the general issue of ethical decision making. The model suggests that, although many people have a well-developed sense of ethics, decisions that must be taken quickly, often with seemingly small consequence, rarely generate ethical concerns. Thus, many moral acts are taken without complete awareness, and many of these*

Advances in Qualitative Organization Research, Volume 3, pages 1–40.
ISBN: 0-7623-0772-2

*decisions might be considered unethical. Reanalysis of additional data from the real estate agents' interviews revealed many instances of bounded personal ethics. The paper concludes with a discussion of the dynamics of agency relationships and the implications of bounded personal ethics.*

# INTRODUCTION

The inevitable lack of expertise that people experience when their endeavors diversify encourages them to seek the services of localized experts and avoid the trials, errors, and costs associated with learning and implementing new skills. The recent, worldwide explosion of the service industry attests to the importance of such activities. According to Pratt and Zeckhauser (1985: 2), the need for agents is "pervasive in business" and "helps explain a great deal about how business is organized." Duska (1992: 151) claims that "it is not only pervasive in business, but pervasive everywhere."

Although theories of principle-agent relationships (e.g. Eisenhardt, 1989; Jensen & Meckling, 1967) provide models of the contractual and economic interactions of service providers and their users, few papers have addressed the demands and dilemmas faced by individuals whose job title describes them, literally, as agents. In addition, although a central focus in agency theory might be characterized as rational, Mitnick (1992) describes agency as "fundamentally relational." Yet even fewer studies have addressed the interpersonal, relational consequences of agents and principals' contractual interactions.

Even without considering the consequences and influence of relationships, the data on agency theory tends to be basic, sparse, or inconclusive. Prendergast's (1999) recent review of the effects of incentives, for instance, concludes that agents clearly and consistently respond to incentives but that they also are able to act in ways that benefit themselves rather than their principals, with efficiency being sacrificed in the process. He also concedes that much of the literature deals with agency statically and cannot accommodate the possible impact of extended relationships.

Thus, this paper focuses on the dynamics of real estate agency, including structural elements like the creation of formal and informal agency contracts and interpersonal elements like the relationships that develop between agents, owners, and purchasers. Our particular focus is on the interactions between agents and purchasers in the residential real estate market in Vancouver, British Columbia. This research began with a specific purpose in mind: to investigate how these agents handled two inherent ethical dilemmas in a system that parallels those in many other areas in North America. Our study investigates whether agents conformed completely to regulations, whether they shaded their actions to serve their own self-interest, or whether they worked to serve the interests of their clients, in this case purchasers, with whom they often established strong personal connections, even when legal strictures made such service difficult to deliver.

During the course of our investigation, we realized that agents' actions, and possibly those of people in general, seem to be bounded in a limited way by a sense of personal ethics. As a result, this paper also moves from the specific to the general, presenting a broad model of ethical decision making, called bounded personal ethics. We return to the data to ascertain whether the model is consistent with a more detailed analysis of the agents' responses. Rather than addressing major decisions like ethical dilemmas, the bounded personal ethics model focuses primarily on individuals' everyday decisions – decisions that can nevertheless have inadvertent, cumulative moral consequences on others. As such, it extends considerably beyond this project's original issue, ethical dilemmas.

The paper begins by describing the study's context, the real estate system in Vancouver at the time of the study. Subsequent sections describe methods and results, a model of bounded personal ethics, additional data, and the model's implications.

## REAL ESTATE IN VANCOUVER, BRITISH COLUMBIA

Vancouver is one of Canada's largest cities and experiences its most temperate climate. Surrounded by mountains and sitting on Canada's Pacific coast, its cosmopolitan nature and small town feel combine to lead one-third of all Canadians to express a desire to live there (Real Estate Weekly, 1995). The economy centers around three well-established industries, tourism, fishing, and lumber, as well as emerging industries like international banking.

In the early 1980s, when interest rates rose dramatically, real estate values in Vancouver dropped precipitously, with many homes losing half their value in less than a year. The median price of homes in Vancouver was $150,000 in 1981 and $100,000 in 1982. Soon thereafter, however, values began to rise. The World's Exposition in 1986 (Ross & Staw, 1986) helped bring international attention to Vancouver and, in particular, attracted Asian investors. Real estate values soon skyrocketed, and from 1983 to 1993 home values in the desirable west side of Vancouver quadrupled. By 1988, the median house price on the west side of the city was $275,000; in 1994, it had risen to $578,000. As one top agent put it, "W" (indicating the west side) was the most expensive letter in the alphabet.

The number of licensed real estate agents[1] also rose dramatically. There were 10,638 licensed agents in 1983; by 1990, there were 15,163, and by 1993, their number rose to 19,099. Although sale values rapidly increased, the average earnings of Vancouver real estate agents increased far less: mean earnings in 1983 were $24,137; in 1988, they were $38,896; and in 1992, they peaked at $55,074 (dropping to $48,492 in 1993).

Higher selling agents typically associate with an agency office. These offices operate as either traditional or 100% houses. Agents at traditional offices keep a percentage of the sales commissions; the office pays many if not all advertising and office expenses. Traditional offices tend to start agents at 50 or 60% commissions and increase their percentages as their sales increase. Some offices start all of their agents at the same rate at the beginning of the year and allow them to increase the percentage of their take as their sales accumulate during the year; others boost an agent's percentage permanently when the agent's sales hit certain milestones.

The 100% houses allow agents to keep all of their commissions but charge them a fee for every transaction (e.g. $150), as well as requiring them to pay a monthly desk fee and many or all of their expenses. Depending on their sales, this is comparable to a 90% commission rate from a traditional house. After considerable turnover from traditional to 100% houses, many if not most of the top agents in Vancouver either worked for 100% houses or had arrangements with a traditional office to keep all or almost all of their commissions.

Unlike the relatively flat rates in other areas, an agent's typical fees in Vancouver are 7% on the first $100,000 of property (5% for new construction or very expensive homes) and $2\frac{1}{2}$% on anything more. (As a point of comparison, agents in the northern suburbs of Chicago typically receive 6% on the first $100,000 and 5% on anything more.) As a result, commissions do not increase proportionately with increases in a property's price. Especially for the more numerous, less expensive homes, sizable changes in the price (e.g. $30,000) have much less sizable effects (e.g. $750) on commissions. Because these commissions are typically split between two agents, it is not particularly important for agents to sell a house for a higher price. Numerous sales increase agents' outcomes more than bigger sales. As one agent put it, "low price deals are as good as high price deals; 80 or 800 (thousand) doesn't matter." Thus, the system establishes incentives that encourage agents to recommend that owners set low (but not unrealistic) prices to increase the likelihood of a quick sale, more commissions, and smaller carrying costs (e.g. advertising, etc.). As two agents put it, succinctly, "ask less, get more" and "by pricing on, you get good, quick offers." Even when commissions are a flat percentage of the sale price, agents' desires to close deals conflict with sellers' desires for a high price (Valley, White, Neale & Bazerman, 1992).

Agents' preferences for quick sales are directly opposed to sellers' preferences for high prices; they have compatible preferences as far as the sale of the house is concerned, but conflicting financial interests on price. The inclusion of purchasers, who want to buy the best house for the lowest possible price, increases the complexity of the real estate system, complicates agency relationships, and increases the likelihood of conflicts.

During the time that we were conducting our interviews, agents in Vancouver had clear legal obligations to owners who contracted with them to help sell their homes: the training manual for agents prepared by the Real Estate Board of Greater Vancouver indicated that listing agents were obliged to provide owners with "good faith, full disclosure, obedience, competence, and full accountability." Good faith means, "to place the interests of the principal above all else except the law" (Ontario Real Estate Association, 1990: 185). In other words, they must reveal all relevant and material information, i.e. all offers or expressions of interest in the property. Obedience means to strictly follow the principal's lawful instructions. Competence means that agents must make all of their skills and best judgment available to the principal. For instance, they must keep damaging information about the vendor, like impending bankruptcy, confidential. Full accountability means that they must handle all money and properties related to the sale with great care and scrupulously avoid any hint of personal use. In addition, agents are legally required to keep the vendor updated on all relevant facts, like changes in market values. Known defects in the property, however, must be disclosed to anyone who asks. Agents are also ethically bound to tell the truth when they are asked direct questions.

The agency contract stipulated that selling agents, those who worked with purchasers, acted as sub-agents of the listing agent, with duties that were identical to the listing agent's: "Like the primary agent, the sub-agent must act solely for the benefit of the principal" (Waller & Waller, 1989: 33). Thus, when a selling agent met with a seller and the listing agent to present a purchaser's offer, they were required to work together to get the best deal possible for the seller, even to the extent of revealing information that purchasers may have thought was privileged.

For purchasers, agents had "a legal duty not to misrepresent, a moral and ethical duty to be fair to all parties, and to take care in answering inquiries or giving advice or information so that the information is complete and accurate". The fact that their first duty identified what they should *not* do rather than what they *should* do implicitly indicates the limited nature of their responsibilities to purchasers. Their limited responsibilities to purchasers, however, were not implicit: agents clearly understood that their only legal responsibility to purchasers was to answer direct questions truthfully (e.g. about known defects in the property).

Although these minimal limitations satisfied the formal agency contract, they conflicted with *the common law of agency*: unless agents disclosed that they were actually sub-agents of the listing agent before they established a relationship with purchasers, working with purchasers established an implicit agency relationship that required that agents protect purchasers' interests. These two guidelines often conflict, putting selling agents in an ethical dilemma: do they work solely for the sellers or do they act to support purchasers whom they have been working with and whom they may have come to like? In many (if not most) cases, the result is unintended and undisclosed dual agency, that is, a formal sub-agency contract with the seller and a common law, implicit agency contract with the purchaser (Schneider, Tune & Bain, 1992).

Purchasers, however, are generally unaware of agents' obligations to sellers and, instead, feel that "their" agent is working for them: 72% of U.S. home purchasers in a survey by the Federal Trade Commission (Schnieder et al., 1996) believed that the agent who worked with them represented them. In British Columbia, 19% of a survey's respondents realized that agents working with purchasers were actually obligated to the seller; 88% did not know that realtors were supposed to divulge their sub-agency commitment (Real Estate Weekly, 1994). Although purchasers understood that they did not pay the agents' commissions, few realized that agents were obligated to work for the person who did pay the commission (the seller).

Because the agency contract also stipulated that selling agents were required to volunteer any information they had about the purchasers to the seller, purchasers who mistakenly assumed that the agent they had been working with was working for them might have been surprised to discover that the information they shared with the person they thought was "their" agent might actually be used against them during the negotiation process leading to a sale. In particular, purchasers who openly revealed information about the highest price that they would pay for a house might end up paying more than they needed to.

In addition, when purchasers found a house that they were interested in, they might expect to get information from "their" agent[2] about how much they might offer. Real estate training materials, however, recommended that agents' respond to "How much do you think we should offer?" by saying, "If you offer them what they are asking, you will probably be able to purchase the house." Needless to say, this kind of response is far from helpful for a purchaser.

## *The System's Inherent Ethical Dilemmas*

At the time of this study, real estate agents in Vancouver found themselves enmeshed in a formal, legal system that provided them with no easy actions. In fact, the dilemmas that the system imposed on them were the impetus for this study. In particular, we asked ourselves before we began this research how agents could possibly handle these dilemmas. How would they solve what we called 'The Agency Dilemma'? More specifically, would they protect purchaser's interests by *not disclosing* potentially relevant information about them, in opposition to the best interests of the seller, or would they freely volunteer any information they had, fulfilling their sub-agency responsibilities to the seller, in opposition to the best interests of the purchasers?

A large literature on relationships (e.g. Clark, 1984; Miller, 1990) suggests that agents will be seriously affected by their relationships with purchasers. On the one hand, they would clearly understand the long-run possibilities of good service: happy purchasers might want to use them to sell whatever house they might buy. But more than that, we reasoned that the intense personal nature of looking for a home would lead to personal attachments that would be hard for real estate agents to ignore. From our perspective, then, The Agency Dilemma appeared to be particularly compelling. In essence, it asks selling agents to choose between the sellers and the purchasers, and between the two forms of the agency contract, the formal and the common law.

The Agency Dilemma also contrasts the classic agency problem – whether agents really are working to achieve principals' interests (Bowie & Freeman, 1992) – with a concept of relational ethics, that is, that a personal relationship and the natural expectations that grow as its evolves might influence agents' sensitive actions. For real estate agents, The Agency Dilemma documents the potential conflict between the requirements of the formal agency contract and the fact that, over time, trust tends to grow between people whose interactions are benevolent (Mayer, Davis & Schoorman, 1995).

To probe this dilemma, we asked agents whether they provided any and all information they had about the purchasers when they were presenting an offer, i.e. when they might be torn between their fiscal, legal obligations and any personal connections they had established with the purchasers (whom they may have been working with for some time). Agents typically told purchasers that, to make their offer more personal, they would provide descriptive information about them to the owner. The real issue was whether they told owners more than this.

Agents could circumvent this dilemma by acting as a purchaser's agent, that is, an agent who had a contract with and was paid by purchasers to help them purchase a house. At the time of this study, however, purchasers' agents were extremely rare in the residential real estate market in Vancouver.

Agents could also circumvent this dilemma, to some degree at least, by conforming to legal and ethical regulations. That is, they could inform purchasers of their responsibilities to sellers and follow this with advice that purchasers should not give them information that they didn't want the seller to have. This solution, however, presented agents with another ethical dilemma: agents were reticent to reveal to purchasers the exact nature of their responsibilities because they felt that doing so might lose them a client. Thus, revealing their responsibilities was the agents' second ethical dilemma, which we call 'The Revelation Dilemma'. It asks agents to choose between revealing their responsibilities (as required by law), thereby increasing the chances of losing a client, or not revealing their legal responsibilities, thereby keeping their clients but violating the law and creating a relationship of undisclosed dual agency.

Since all of the agents in the system had the same legal responsibilities, it might seem that agents could conform to the law, reveal their obligations to purchasers, and add that it applied to all of the agents in the area. Given the competition among agents in Vancouver, however, the possibility that a purchaser could find an agent who would pledge to work for their interests was probably not small. Revealing their obligation included considerable risk of losing potential purchasers and the selling agent's portion of a commission.

At the time of this study, the Real Estate Board published a "soft disclosure form", which is reproduced in Fig. 1. In less than simple English, it informed purchasers about agents' responsibilities. Some of the agents in this study gave this form to purchasers they were working with; whether purchasers understood its message is not clear.

To probe The Revelation Dilemma, we asked agents whether, when, and how they informed purchasers that their primary responsibilities were to the seller. We also collected archival data on sales from the previous eight years to determine whether the agents' handling of these two dilemmas was related to their financial and performance outcomes.

The agents' possible responses to the two dilemmas fit a simple $2 \times 2$ matrix: protect/not protect purchasers' information (the Agency Dilemma) by reveal/ not reveal responsibilities (the Revelation Dilemma). Not protecting purchasers favored sellers and conformed to the formal agency contract; protecting purchasers favored purchasers and conformed to the implicit, common law of agency and to our conceptualization of relational ethics. Revealing their responsibilities protected agents legally but might lose them clients; not revealing served their short-term financial purposes better and exposed them to

In every real estate sale, there is a seller and a purchaser. If a real estate agent is involved, he/she has a relationship with each and obligations to both. However, the obligations and responsibilities that the real estate agent has are not the same to both the seller and the purchaser.

\* \* \*

The real estate agent with whom the property is listed is the listing agent and, as a result of the listing contract, owes the seller a certain set of responsibilities.

An agent working with a prospective purchaser is normally a sub-agent of the listing agent and therefore owes the seller the same level of responsibility.

This means that the listing agent and sub-agents owe the seller the following duties:

*Loyalty;
*Obedience;
*Disclosure;
*Confidentiality;
*Reasonable Care and Diligence; and
*Accounting.

The listing agent and sub-agents are required to protect and promote the seller's interests as they would their own.

\* \* \*

While the listing agent and sub-agents usually act for the seller as a result of the listing contract, they owe the purchaser the following responsibilities:

*To present all offers to the seller promptly.

*To respond honestly and accurately to questions concerning the property.

*To disclose material facts the agent or sub-agent knows or reasonably should know about the property.

*To offer the property without regard to race, creed, sex, religion, or national origin.

The listing agent and sub-agents are obligated by law to treat the purchaser honestly.

In addition, the listing agent and sub-agents are able to provide the purchaser with valuable market information and assistance.

\* \* \*

In some instances, a purchaser may desire the level of service offered under an agency agreement. Should the purchaser elect to have full agency representation, he/she should enter into a written contract with the agent that clearly establishes the obligations of both the purchaser and the agents.

The existence of such an agency relationship between a potential purchaser and a selling agent would be disclosed to the seller and the listing agent.

\* \* \*

If you have any questions regarding the roles and responsibilities of real estate agents, please do not hesitate to ask.

*Fig. 1.* Responsibilities of Real Estate Agents to Sellers and to Purchasers.

only minimal risk of legal ramifications, as this issue almost never led to professional or legal recriminations.

*Disclosing and not protecting.* This strategy meets agents' legal requirements, is what agents are trained to do, and serves owners extremely well. Institutional and legal models (e.g. Scott, 1995) would predict this outcome. From the agents' point of view, this approach makes eminent sense since it reduces their vulnerability to charges of illegal behavior and to civil suits from wronged owners. (Unless they disclosed immediately, they remained open, however, to the less likely event of a civil suit from wronged buyers who worked under the common law assumption that the agent was working for them.) Also, because agents had strong preferences toward working for listings rather than with purchasers, their primary allegiances should have been with owners, making compliance with these standards easier.

*Disclosing and protecting purchasers.* If agents take a long-term view of their business, as many of the agents in our sample acknowledged, they should reveal their legal responsibilities but protect their purchasers' interests. Having purchasers find that "their" agent was really working for an owner rather than for them – a likely event when purchasers become owners – provides little prospect for them continuing to work with an agent when they decide to sell their home. A few agents did note that revealing their legal responsibilities was also relatively costless because they could simultaneously indicate that all other agents had the same responsibilities. In addition, although protecting purchasers may be illegal, it may increase potential future outcomes when purchasers become sellers.

*Not disclosing and not protecting.* Agents in this category act almost completely in the best interests of the seller. They also seem to be driven by their own short-term self-interest because they increase their immediate chances of retaining their purchasers but do not protect their information in final negotiations. This works even more in the agents' own favor when they act as a dual agent for both the seller and the purchaser.

*Not disclosing but protecting purchasers.* According to the agency contract, this strategy is illegal twice over. But agency theory suggests that self-interested agents might try to attract purchasers, or not lose them, by not disclosing. At the same time, while they don't tell purchasers everything, they might protect purchasers in the negotiations. They may assume, possibly naively, that when purchasers become owners, they will value the agents' personal loyalty to them and will not penalize them for not telling them the whole truth when they were purchasers. Particularly if purchasers bought a house that appreciated (as was typical of Vancouver homes at the time of the study), agents may expect that purchasers continue to value their psychological bond with the agent and continue to employ them. Agents who are in the business for the long term may protect their purchasers in the hopes of being hired by purchasers who become sellers, but the average turn-around time for a house (between 11 and 12 years) or for a condominium (7 to 8 years) in Vancouver exceeds the expected length of time that many agents stay in the real estate business. Thus, agents in this category may be myopic in terms of both purchasers' and sellers' subsequent reactions.

In some sense, agents who act primarily in the owners' interests satisfy their legal requirements; agents who act primarily in the purchasers' interests are likely to be responding to their psychological connections with people they have worked with for some time (and to the hope of working with these people again); and agents who act primarily in their own interests support the predictions of agency theory.

These ethical dilemmas occurred within a system of three or four parties (seller, listing agent, purchaser, and selling agent) rather than the frequently considered two-party principal-agent system (Dees, 1992; DeGeorge, 1992). In addition, because agents often had a formal contract with sellers and an informal agency contract (and possibly personal connections) with purchasers, the dynamics of this system are based on asymmetric connections among the parties. Finally, although agency theory typically assumes that agents are simple, self-interested actors, this study addresses how they grapple with potentially difficult ethical questions that might limit a singular, unidirectional (i.e. financial) pursuit of self-interest.

## METHODS

Participants were 24 of the highest selling residential real estate agents in Vancouver, British Columbia. We obtained a preliminary list of agents' names and phone numbers from a personal contact who was a top agent herself. Interviewees recommended other names. Thus, the sample was derived from a combination of informant information and snowball sampling. We initially contacted agents by letter and scheduled interviews by phone. One agent refused to be interviewed; two others failed to return repeated phone messages.[3]

We focused on top sellers rather than a random sample of all agents for several reasons. Many people move into and out of this profession; as a result, a random sample would likely have included many agents with little experience, limited knowledge of real estate transactions, and less investment in ethical concerns. Many agents also worked only part time; our sample included only agents who worked full time. We wanted to focus on full-time, experienced professionals who had encountered many negotiations and had had the time to consider the ethical dilemmas of their profession seriously. Also, by studying this very successful group, we hoped to gain the insights that can be obtained from studying extreme cases (Pondy & Olson, 1977).

All of the respondents focused on residential sales; some also worked in commercial real estate, managed or owned their office, or marketed and sold condominium projects. Seventeen had worked either for the same office their entire careers or had made at most one or two office changes. The sample included 12 men and 12 women who ranged in age from their early 30s to their early 60s, averaging approximately 45. They had worked in real estate between 7 and 25 years, averaging 14. Ten worked in 100% houses; 14 worked in traditional houses (with most receiving 90% to 100% of their commissions). They worked in a total of 16 different offices. Seventeen used an assistant to help with paperwork, showing homes, and other less desirable tasks; two had more than one. Most worked long hours, with typical workdays starting early and running into the evening six days a week, plus a half-day on the seventh.

Most of these agents were award winners. The Real Estate Board, which administers the multiple listing service, presents Medallion Club awards to the top 5% of the agents each year and President's Club awards to the top 1%. Twelve of these agents had achieved President's Club status at least once in the past 8 years; 10 had been Medallion Club winners for 10 consecutive years.

The first two authors[4] jointly conducted 1- to 2-hour semi-structured interviews that included general questions about their interactions with purchasers and sellers as well as directly addressing the two ethical dilemmas. Following our informant's suggestions, we did not use recording devices. Midway through the interviews, we addressed the two ethical dilemmas. We tried to ask these questions as we had asked all of our other questions – with interest but not undue interest in these particular answers. We had consciously probed deeper when we asked other questions and agents had been vague or unclear in their answers. This allowed us to probe deeper on these two questions as well.

We broached the Revelation Dilemma by saying, "Do your purchasers know that you are required to act as a sub-agent of the listing agent?" We then asked if they had informed purchasers of this fact, and if so, how. We posed the Agency Dilemma question by asking the agents to describe the process of making and delivering an offer. This allowed us to probe the offer delivery process. In particular, we asked agents what they said about their purchasers, how they answered questions about them, whether they revealed information like the purchasers' hoped-for final prices, etc. Both of us took separate notes and transcribed them as soon after each interview as possible, providing an opportunity to check the reliability of our reactions and ratings and to record as many quotes, verbatim, as possible.

We obtained data published by the Real Estate Board on sales (number of agent's listings and sales and total dollars in sales) and awards for the 8 consecutive years immediately prior to our interviews. The data reflect sales that were listed by the multiple listing service; sales of properties that were not multiply listed were not available.

The two interviewers independently rated solutions to the two ethical dilemmas. Agents either protected information about purchasers or disclosed it to sellers or listing agents; they told purchasers about their legal responsibilities to sellers voluntarily only if they were asked, or avoided the question by saying, "The seller pays my commission." Due to the size of the sample, responses to The Revelation Dilemma were collapsed into two categories, whether they avoided revealing and only revealed if asked (combined) or they voluntarily revealed their responsibilities.

## RESULTS

Each of the agents described many of their actions as being consciously orchestrated. Most described the first contact, the first visit, and the subsequent meeting to discuss listing a seller's house (and for how much) in very similar terms. Everyone uniformly noted that sellers valued their houses highly, sometimes to an extreme degree.

The agents also had well formulated scripts that described their dealings with purchasers, but these varied from one agent to another. Thus, some agents had purchasers look at 60 homes in a day or two to narrow down their interests. Others explicitly quizzed their purchasers to make sure that they understood current market values. Still others had their assistants do all of the showings and only came into the process when purchasers wanted to make an offer.

Our post-interview ratings of agents' responses to The Agency Dilemma and The Revelation Dilemma questions were highly reliable: 95.3% of The Revelation Dilemma ratings and 90.5% of The Agency Dilemma ratings were identical. The few (3) discrepancies were resolved via discussion, after referring back to field notes.

## The Revelation Dilemma

Most agents were quite uncomfortable when we asked them whether they told purchasers about their legal responsibilities to sellers. One agent paused, looked at the floor, and finally said "No." An office manager (who was not in the sample) became immediately distant when we described the issues we were studying. She was not willing to explain her position and tried to divert the discussion to another topic.

A clear majority of these agents admitted that they did not voluntarily reveal (see Table 1): of the 21 who worked with purchasers, 71.4% did not. The statements of four non-revealing agents are typical:

"I make light of it".
"They have no idea that I work for the seller".
"If I'm asked a direct question, then I am obligated to answer".
"They feel that I am working for them".

Others indicated that they had never said anything before, but "these days" they were more attuned to this issue.

Of the 15 agents categorized as non-disclosers, the most frequent reaction ($n = 11$) was for agents to admit their responsibilities only if purchasers asked

***Table 1.***    Frequencies of Top Agents who Disclosed or Protected Information about Purchasers and/or Told Purchasers about their Obligations to Sellers.

|  | The Revelation Dilemma: Whether Agents Told Purchasers about their Obligations to Sellers | | | |
|  | Only if Asked/ Seller Pays | Freely Disclosed | Un- classifiable | Totals |
| --- | --- | --- | --- | --- |
| The Agency Dilemma: Protected Information About Purchasers | 9 | 5 | — | 14 |
| Disclosed Information About Purchasers | 5 | 1 | — | 6 |
| Unclassifiable | 1 | — | 3 | 4 |
| Totals | 15 | 6 | 3 | 24 |

Note: Of the 3 agents who could not be rated on either issue, one avoided working with purchasers, another tended to work on large condominium projects where prices were usually fixed, and the third worked almost exclusively with builders rather than purchasers. The fourth agent, who could not be classified for his/her handling of purchaser information, was one whose interview had to be terminated prematurely, before this information was obtained.

about it. Four agents told purchasers that "the owner pays my commission" and let purchasers make their own conclusions. One agent said that she never mentioned the word commission.

Their rationales varied. On one hand, they tried to emphasize, sometimes negatively, that their intentions were good. Two agents' responses were typical of these kinds of rationalizations:

"Top agents don't chop people's legs off . . . . Keep in mind that we are not trying to do damage to anyone"
"If you buy something from a department store, the clerk represents the company yet she represents the customer, too".

On the other hand, they often deflected our questions by indicating that purchasers were knowledgeable about real estate, implying that they did not need to be told. For instance:

"Clients are more educated (about the market) than they have ever been".
"The west side is made up of sophisticated people. They know".

One agent presented the nature of their undisclosed and unintended dual agency succinctly:

"You want to take good care of the purchaser but work for the seller".

Many of their responses reflect the justifications, excuses, and accounts of impression formation strategies (e.g. Elsbach & Sutton, 1992).

Agents who indicated that they told purchasers about their obligations to sellers were quite open about it; they typically provided purchasers with the "soft disclosure" form (Fig. 1). One agent included it in a packet of other materials; four indicated that they explained the rules so that purchasers understood the system. One agent indicated that, prior to the publication of the form, she was writing her own version so that she could give something tangible to purchasers.

The agents clearly realized that this was an ethical dilemma, e.g. "revealing has made some people uncomfortable." A few indicated that if they told purchasers about their obligations, they might push them to another agent, but they rarely connected this with the fact that they could also explain that other agents would be bound by the same legal requirements. One agent told us that, if any agents in our sample said that they fully explained the rules to purchasers, they were certainly lying and that their whole interview was probably garbage.

One agent used a unique, devious, but seemingly effective strategy: She explained the rules, indicated that she did not agree with them, and suggested that she could fulfill the letter of the law while "doing a tap dance around them." Thus, when purchasers asked her how much they should offer on a house, she responded by saying that, if they were to make an offer on a similar property with similar characteristics a little way down the street, she would recommend that they offer $X (the amount that she felt was strategically best for the purchasers). By not providing information about the exact house the purchasers were interested in, she did not violate the letter of the law. In her own words, however, she was tap dancing around the rules and clearly violating their intent.

### The Agency Dilemma

Sharing information, about purchasers or in general, was a delicate topic. All of the agents shared some information as a normal part of their interactions. They all shared the same general outlook:

> "You don't have to spill everything, only the relevant information".
> "Too much information can complicate the situation . . . . I give all parties the information they need to make the right decision".

A clear majority – 70% – indicated that they protected purchasers by withholding information about them (see Table 1). One agent was both representative and voluble, and highlighted his relational approach to the business:

> "Who is this person (the seller)? I've never met them before. Why should I tell them anything about my purchasers?"

Several agents became uncomfortable after this kind of admission and followed it with claims that they also served the sellers, e.g.

> "The seller needs to feel that the best possible job is being done . . . . I rely on the listing agent to protect the seller".
> "My commitment is to be the best for the seller; the real estate act states this".
> "You work for the seller; this is drilled into your head".

Agents who indicated that they disclosed everything about their purchasers (30%) often reiterated the legal language that their responsibilities were primarily to sellers. Some said that they not only disclosed this information, they volunteered it. These "canned" responses seemed less genuine than the statements made by agents who admitted keeping information to themselves.

Agents who did not protect purchasers often tried to reassure us that they still served purchasers well. One fell back on his general, relational approach, saying,

> "You are their friend . . . . They have to like you . . . . I tell everyone everything . . . . You have to give the client what they want".

Another non-protector revealed her long-term self-interest,

"I want them to like the deal in the future".

She also blamed them for not keeping information to themselves:

"My purchasers better not tell me anything they don't want me to say".

Several agents tried to avoid the dilemma, telling purchasers not to tell them everything so that they wouldn't have information if the seller asked them questions.

Agents who did not reveal everything acknowledged that many purchasers openly discussed sensitive information in their presence. Many indicated that they pretended that they had not heard it.

Agents occasionally went to great lengths to protect purchasers. One agent told a story about showing a condominium with a recently reduced price. Another agent was also showing it, to clients who seemed quite interested. One of our agent's two clients openly criticized the place, much to his surprise, since this was just the kind of place his clients had been seeking. After leaving, both clients revealed that this was the place for them and that their comments were only meant to discourage the other purchasers. The agent recommended that the new price was reasonable, so the couple decided to offer $1,000 more than the asking price to make sure that they would still get it even if the other couple also made an offer. As things developed, the other couple did not submit an offer. The agent then reduced the offer to reflect a full price offer and marked the change with his clients' initials. The offer was accepted, the purchasers got the condominium they wanted, and they saved $1,000 from what they were willing to pay. The agent, however, was guilty of forgery and other legal infractions.

In sum, most of these agents reported that they did not reveal sensitive information about their purchasers. Most also did not reveal to purchasers their responsibilities to sellers. In essence, they were constantly violating the law. Unlike the expectations of agency theory, however, overall financial data suggests that these strategies did *not* maximize their financial returns.

## Financial Outcomes

Data were available on the overall volume of the agents' sales and the numbers of their listings and sales for 8 consecutive years (from 1986 to 1993, inclusive). Although the numbers varied from year to year (probably due to economic factors), each agent's volume, listings, and sales were highly intercorrelated. For instance, correlations among volume, listings, and sales that were separated by only 1 year were extremely high (correlations typically exceeded 0.85 and often approached 1.0) and uniformly significant. Data across longer time periods led to smaller sample sizes but still produced many high, significant correlations. For instance, the correlations of agents' outcomes from the first to the last of the 8 years ranged from 0.39 to 0.78, with six of the nine correlations significant at $p < 0.05$. Clearly, these agents were consistent performers.

The small sample size and considerable yearly variation may have contributed to the fact that analyses of these data by categorizing agents on the two dimensions of ethical dilemmas were uniformly non-significant. Nevertheless, the data suggest some consistencies (see Table 2) that should be interpreted with considerable caution. For instance, the data suggest that, for each of these 8 years, agents who avoided revealing their obligations to sellers sold more than the agents who revealed. This supports the logic that forms the foundation of The Revelation Dilemma, that is, that revealing may be financially risky. In addition, agents who did not protect purchasers sold more than agents who protected purchasers, again for each of these 8 years. This suggests that relational ethics and the protection of a trust may be costly.[5]

Table 3 shows each agent's average annual volume, sales, and listings for the period. The five agents who did not reveal voluntarily and did not protect

***Table 2.*** Dollar Volume as a Function of Telling Purchasers About Agent's Responsibilities to Sellers and Protecting or Disclosing Information about Purchasers.

| | The Revelation Dilemma: Whether Agents Told Purchasers their Obligations to Sellers | | | The Agency Dilemma: How Agents Handled Information about Purchasers | | |
|---|---|---|---|---|---|---|
| Year | Only if Asked/Voluntarily Seller Pays | Revealed | Un-classifiable | Kept Information | Told Everything | Un-classifiable |
| 1993 | 13,190,240 | 7,029,091 | 9,429,250 | 9,966,675 | 13,619,760 | 8,644,136 |
| 1992 | 12,896,647 | 8,063,173 | 6,667,900 | 9,897,715 | 18,545,261 | 7,763,400 |
| 1991 | 11,182,272 | 5,658,053 | 8,379,650 | 7,557,308 | 13,737,928 | 9,518,575 |
| 1990 | 7,796,528 | 3,883,413 | 9,152,000 | 6,194,851 | 7,869,389 | 9,152,000 |
| 1989 | 10,312,768 | 6,263,438 | 7,714,013 | 7,754,118 | 14,218,581 | 8,208,008 |
| 1988 | 6,494,111 | 4,777,882 | 5,441,175 | 5,612,664 | 6,793,893 | 6,530,000 |
| 1987 | 4,315,036 | 3,552,240 | 2,579,812 | 3,572,308 | 5,970,757 | 3,158,708 |
| 1986 | 3,578,359 | 2,743,900 | 4,493,875 | 3,334,655 | 4,125,627 | 3,266,063 |
| *n* | 15 | 6 | 3 | 14 | 6 | 4 |

purchasers performed better financially than the other agents. The means, however, are skewed by the presence of one very strong seller. As a result, we converted these data to rank orderings, which are unaffected by outliers. The findings remain unchanged. They indicate that the agents who did not reveal voluntarily and did not protect purchasers had an average ranking of 6.6 compared with average rankings of 10.7, 12.6, and 18 for the agents in the other three categories. These data suggest that the most frequent reaction to the two ethical dilemmas – protecting purchasers but not revealing responsibilities

***Table 3.*** Average Outcomes for Agents (1986–1993) as a Function of Whether They Told Purchasers about their Obligations to Sellers and How They Handled Information about Their Purchasers.

| | The Revelation Dilemma: Whether Agents Told Purchasers about their Obligations to Sellers | | | | | | | |
| --- | --- | --- | --- | --- | --- | --- | --- | --- |
| | Only if Asked/Seller Pays | | | | Clearly Revealed | | | |
| | Mean $ Volume | Mean Sold | Mean Listed | No. of Years | Mean $ Volume | Mean Sold | Mean Listed | No. of Years |
| The Agency Dilemma: | | | | | | | | |
| Kept Purchaser | 2,603,273 | 10.90 | 17.40 | 5 | 3,601,888 | 11.50 | 18.75 | 4 |
| Info from Seller | 4,889,827 | 10.93 | 19.43 | 7 | 4,845,333 | 7.67 | 14.20 | 5 |
| | 4,901,144 | 13.06 | 15.75 | 8 | 5,757,645 | 5.17 | 13.42 | 6 |
| | 5,577,127 | 5.50 | 13.08 | 5 | 5,845,689 | 17.31 | 56.56 | 8 |
| | 6,029,256 | 18.63 | 28.25 | 8 | 9,728,767 | 16.00 | 83.50 | 2 |
| | 6,306,375 | 8.50 | 20.50 | 1 | | | | |
| | 8,110,188 | 22.17 | 39.14 | 7 | | | | |
| | 11,328,156 | 11.42 | 20.92 | 8 | | | | |
| | 12,383,339 | 13.93 | 24.21 | 7 | | | | |
| Unweighted Mean | 6,903,188 | 12.78 | 22.07 | 6.22 | 5,955,864 | 11.53 | 37.29 | 5 |
| Told All | 5,629,579 | 26.94 | 30.81 | 8 | 4,517,638 | 9.38 | 9.63 | 4 |
| to Seller | 6,595,720 | 9.67 | 15.29 | 7 | | | | |
| Seller | 7,864,459 | 9.81 | 26.50 | 8 | | | | |
| | 10,086,514 | 8.79 | 17.79 | 8 | | | | |
| | 23,837,850 | 72.60 | 192.79 | 8 | | | | |
| Unweighted Mean | 10,802,823 | 25.56 | 56.64 | 7.8 | 4,517,638 | 9.38 | 9.63 | 4 |

Note: The standard deviation for each agent's volume sales exceeded all but two of their mean volume figures. For number of units sold, standard deviations exceeded means for all but three agents. For listings, standard deviations exceeded means for all but six. For the most part, means and standard deviations were comparable. Also, "no. of years" refers to how long they had been working as a real estate agent in Vancouver.

to sellers – was not related to maximum financial performance, as agency theory might expect. This finding also fits our analysis of the four possible reactions to these two ethical dilemmas (protect/not protect purchasers' information by reveal/not reveal responsibilities). That is, the not protect/not reveal combination satisfies agents' self-interests more than their principals'.

The logical analysis of an agent's possible responses to these ethical dilemmas does not depend on deep, complicated logic.[6] Thus, it is striking that most agents did not choose the set of responses that both logic and empirical evidence suggest is most beneficial financially. Essentially, this means that many of these agents may have been able to increase their income by changing their strategies by not protecting their purchasers. Thus, these findings suggest that relational ethics may have been an integral and possibly a conscious part of these agents' ethical decision making processes, even though they were costly.

## DISCUSSION

The major results are quite clear: most of these agents violated one or the other of the regulations surrounding the two ethical dilemmas that we have investigated here. Most did not disclose their responsibilities to sellers and most protected purchasers' interests during contract negotiations. Although we may be naïve, it seemed to us that there were at least two surprises here: first, that so many agents did not conform to legally established guidelines, especially when it appears that it was not in their financial best interests to do so; and second, that so many agents were willing to admit this in our interviews. In addition, given the potentially damaging nature of these revelations, if any of these agents did not describe their behavior accurately, then these findings are conservative and underreport the actual number of agents who violated these regulations.

The findings suggest that relational ethics become important in agents' interactions with their purchasers. The Agency Dilemma presents them with two choices. On one side of the coin are their purchasers, with whom they have interacted intensely. They have seen many properties together and experienced a tense and emotional purchase process (or two or three). On the other side of the Agency Dilemma coin, their legal and professional requirements as well as the potential for greater financial income push them to reveal the information they have about purchasers. The fact that most chose to protect their purchasers indicates that they solved this troubling ethical dilemma relationally.

Although several agents literally squirmed when we asked questions about these ethical dilemmas – only one raised the issue before we did – we were struck by how unconcerned they seemed about other equally, if not more potent, ethical issues, such as dual agency, i.e. acting as the agent for both the purchaser and the seller, simultaneously. Part of the reason for their seeming comfort is that intended (in addition to unintended) dual agency was not uncommon. One agent, for instance, indicated that as many as 30% of his deals were completed with him acting as the agent for both parties.

Only two agents acknowledged that dual agency could pose problems. (They were much more uncomfortable with questions about whether they would cut their commissions to close a deal.) This runs counter to all of the material that was published by the industry and its observers. Rather than being an ethical quagmire, the agents in our sample treated dual agency as a normal course of affairs. As one agent put it, "somehow the situation works."

The differences between industry strictures and the agents' comfort with what looked to us like ethical minefields seem to have been caused by two additional factors. First, because this group of agents was so consistently casual about issues like dual agency, it appears that implicit norms developed among them to support their positions. Clearly, if all of a person's contacts in a profession are comfortable with intended dual agency, any concerns that a particular agent might feel are likely to diminish and possibly even disappear, particularly on a day-to-day cognitive basis. The second factor is more individually oriented and multi-faceted, combining three issues that boil down to a concern for self-interest. Although these agents expressed a mixture of motivations, they all expressed considerable pleasure in: (1) being in control throughout the process, (2) playing the game well, especially the endgame when they went "in for the kill", and (3) working hard for a good living. They could all be characterized by their love of the deal and their pride in how they controlled the process. Also, although some denied their monetary self-interests, one agent was particularly clear: "Where else could someone like me, with a limited education, earn so much?"

Contrary to a bedrock assumption of agency theory – that they would be strictly self-interested – these agents seemed to be genuinely affected by the relationships that they established with purchasers. The agents often talked about the fact that one of the fascinating and rewarding parts of their job was that they had the opportunity to meet many people. Many had a background in volunteer or other social service occupations and saw their work in real estate as a natural extension of their interests in helping others. They often mentioned that dealing with purchasers allowed them to "become intimate with people very quickly," much like Meyerson, Weick and Kramer's (1996) concept of swift trust. They frequently developed personal relationships with purchasers. Although they acknowledged the need to establish a positive relationship so that they might later represent purchasers who became sellers, the relatively slow turnover of homes in Vancouver makes this a curious strategy, at least from the perspective of strict self-interest.

The consistency of the agents' responses to both dilemmas also suggests that they might be acting in line with localized social norms (Birenbaum & Sagarin, 1976). In other words, these agents might be simplifying their lives (i.e. acting as cognitive misers; Bazerman, 1998) by doing what other agents also did to resolve these ethical dilemmas. There are several difficulties with this explanation, however. The first is the fact that all of the agents were aware of their legal and ethical requirements. The real estate profession is exceedingly clear about agents' responsibilities. As one agent indicated, these requirements were drummed into them constantly. For instance, when we showed our findings to a lawyer who taught courses on ethics for aspiring and continuing agents in the Vancouver area, she was horrified. Thus, if an implicit, or even an explicit norm existed among the agents, they were aware that they were putting themselves at considerable legal and professional risk by complying.

In addition, there is no clear mechanism for promulgating such illegal, normative guidelines. Many of these agents were acquainted but they knew *of* each other more than actually knowing each other. Most worked at different offices and many of the agents who worked at the same office were 100% agents who rarely came into the office at all. In addition, if they were sued, they were on their own, as if they were acting solo. Thus, the structure of the profession makes the transmission of strong social norms difficult. Instead, the data suggest that the agents' allegiances were to their customers rather than to their professional peers. As salespeople, they competed with each other –even within the same office. In addition, all of their language in the interviews was focused on their own actions and those of their clients. They never referred to what other agents did (except to ask about our other interview data).

DiIulio (1994) presents another case in a markedly different context that also shows how relationships can dampen strict self-interest. He studied a group of "workers who do not shirk, subvert, or steal on the job even when the pecuniary and other tangible incentives to refrain from these behaviors are weak or non-existent". He eloquently describes the everyday and extraordinary actions of employees in the U.S. Federal Bureau of Prisons and shows how "rational choice theorists who discount the possibility of public-spirited bureaucratic behavior are wrong." Among the most picturesque of his examples were "middle-aged, gun-toting secretaries" who, during a major uprising at an Atlanta prison, "stood watch on the perimeter". The case describes how these government agents identified with each other and their organization and how pride and personal contacts influenced them to do much more than the minimum required on the job. Where DiIulio's (1994) data suggest relational ethics among these employees, the current data document relational ethics between agents and purchasers. The largest group of real estate agents in our study had strong, consistent responses to the personal relationships they had established with purchasers. Both this study and DiIulio's, then, provide important cases where strict monetary self-interest seems to have been blunted by non-pecuniary, interpersonal connections.

# BOUNDED PERSONAL ETHICS

From a broader perspective, the findings in this study suggest that these agents, and possibly people in general, are influenced in many of their everyday decisions by a system of *bounded personal ethics* (akin to Simon's [1976] notion of bounded rationality). A model of bounded personal ethics begins with the idea that people are influenced by a concern for ethics and by self-interest, assumptions that have long had a central place in philosophy and the study of human behavior (e.g. see Plato's *Republic*). On one hand, we tend to be morally responsible in our actions: we usually tell the truth, we often consider fairness as a criterion when we choose how we will act, and we both understand and espouse the golden rule. In fact, individuals in most cultures seem to be driven by an underlying desire to live up to moral standards (Lewis, 1947). On the other hand, we are naturally influenced by self-interest, which can, depending on the circumstances, interfere not only with our desires to act morally but even with whether we are aware that ethics are relevant. When we experience conflict between these two motivations, we face ethical dilemmas.

Recent models of ethical decision making (e.g. Rest, 1986; Trevino, 1986; Jones, 1991) assume that ethical action requires awareness and cognitive effort. In contrast, bounded personal ethics assumes that many people are often not aware of the ethical nature of their actions, and this lack of awareness leads them to act self-interestedly (as Jones, 1991, alludes in an example, on page 380). To resolve ethical dilemmas by acting morally, actors must make a conscious, reasoned choice: they must understand and be aware that they are facing a moral decision. If they are unaware, however, this does not mean that their decisions are not moral. They can still benefit or harm others. Instead, the bounded personal ethics model assumes that, for many decisions, people make moral decisions without being aware of the moral consequences of those decisions. They act without thinking, or without thinking deeply. This favors the selection of self-interested action for the simple reason that, for most people (particularly people whose moral development may have progressed less;

Trevino, 1986), self-preservation and self-interest are easy, relatively immediate choices.

The bounded personal ethics model paints a picture of people being only occasionally attuned to their ethical values. Most of our actions and most of our decisions have no ethical consequences. When actions or decisions do have ethical implications, they may not be immediately obvious. This suggests that people will often act as if no ethical implications exist, and this automatic calculus lends itself to self-interested action. This is not to say that people are most often unethical. Instead, following Wicklund (1979), it suggests that ethical values may need to be prompted before people will normally consider them in their decision making processes

In the case of Vancouver real estate agents and their ethical dilemmas, it appears from their statements that they consciously addressed these two dilemmas at some point prior to our interviews. The preponderance of their choices suggests that they decided to act relationally rather than to conform to legal strictures. We suggest that they consciously chose how to act once and, after those actions played out successfully, they built them into their repertoire. Thus, they did not appear to be confronting the Agency and the Revelation Dilemmas repeatedly. Instead, it appears that they formulated a plan of action, possibly explicitly, and their subsequent actions became habitual and automatic.

The bounded personal ethics model suggests that, once ethical values have been raised to the level of awareness, they will be a significant force in an individual's decision making. The model suggests that often this awareness comes after a decision has been made. When this occurs, people often experience feelings of regret (e.g. Bell, 1982; Loomes & Sugden, 1982). When awareness precedes decisions, the expectation of potential regret can be incorporated into the decision making process and avoided (e.g. Larrick, 1993).

Some individuals have such well-established ethical philosophies that they are almost always aware of their actions' ethical consequences. These people may be related to that small subset of individuals who consistently make cooperative choices even in decidedly competitive situations (Organ, 1988). (After these decisions, they will tell you that, regardless of what others might do, they themselves must choose cooperatively. They choose to uphold their own image of themselves rather than for any other reason.)

Jones' (1991) model of ethical decision making is similar in some ways to the bounded personal ethics model because it focuses on awareness in terms of moral intensity. It suggests that, as moral issues become more intense, they have more impact on the ethical decision making process. In Jones' model, moral intensity depends on six components: (1) the harm or benefit that an act can have on people; (2) the degree of social consensus concerning whether an act is evil or good; (3) the joint probability that an act will occur and will actually cause the harm or benefit predicted; (4) the time between the act and its consequences; (5) feelings of attachment to the people involved; and (6) the number of people the act will affect. As an action can have greater potential harm or benefit, it is clearly understood as good or evil, its effects are more likely, its effects happen quickly to many people who are important to an actor, and its moral intensity increases and becomes a more salient decision criterion.

Bounded personal ethics follows Jones (1991) and suggests that, as the moral intensity of an issue increases, awareness will also increase. Bounded personal ethics suggests that awareness is the critical causal antecedent of ethical behavior and that increased moral intensity is one of many possible instigators of awareness.

The flip side of awareness from the perspective of bounded personal ethics is that many unethical actions will be unintended. Due to the enormity of stimuli that people must continuously manage, their ability to appreciate the potential ethical consequences of their actions is limited. Thus, they may act in ways that, after some awareness-induced reflection, they would change if they could. Derry's (1987) findings are consistent: she found that a third of the people she studied claimed that they never encountered moral conflicts at work, even though independent observations suggested otherwise.

Jones' model (1991) does not add the decision makers' own outcomes as a causal factor in ethical decision making. As own outcomes increase, attention is also likely to increase (e.g. Vroom, 1964). Whether this attention will stimulate awareness of a decision's moral consequences is an open empirical question. Table 4 displays the possibilities without assuming any connection between ethical awareness and the expectation of own outcomes.

When minimal outcomes are expected and people have only minimal awareness of their actions' moral consequences, the model is quite clear: people will act with little concern and little contemplation. These are the kinds of decisions that people make many times every day. Paying too much attention to them would be debilitating.

When expected outcomes are sizable and moral awareness has not been stimulated, the model would expect purely self-interested action. Should these actions actually have moral consequences, the potential for subsequent regret increases.

***Table 4.***  The Motivation of a Person's Decisions as Moral Awareness and Their Expectation of Their Own Potential Outcomes Vary.

|  |  | Moral Awareness | |
|  |  | Minimal | Complete |
| --- | --- | --- | --- |
| | High | Pure Self-Interest | Enlightened Self-Interest |
| Expectations of Own Outcomes | Low | Lack of Concern | Altruism |

When expected outcomes are small and a person is fully aware of their moral consequences, ethical action is highly likely. In fact, it may even be interpreted as altruistic. At the same time, such action is easy, as it is relatively costless in terms of the person's own outcomes (Radner, 1981).

Finally, when moral awareness is strong and expected outcomes are large, individuals may be aware that they are facing a moral dilemma. If others' and own consequences are inconsistent, the pressure of an approach-avoidance conflict increases (Lewin, 1951). Both self-interest and a sense of enlightenment come into play. The balance of own and others' outcomes need to be juggled to determine a final decision. For sufficiently large consequences, self-interest will dominate ethics (e.g. Dawes, 1980).

The bounded personal ethics model is based on assumptions concerning the development of self-interest and moral values. We assume that self-interest is innate, that people are born with the motivation for self-preservation, and that self-interested reactions are therefore likely to be automatic. In contrast, we assume that moral values are learned (e.g. Kohlberg, 1976), that they are often situationally specific, and that, following John Stuart Mill, they fail the test of absolutism, i.e. there are few inviolable ethical positions.

These assumptions drive the notion that awareness is a critical antecedent of ethical action. Without ethical awareness, people are likely to act automatically and self-interestedly. With awareness, people can weigh the dynamics and the consequences of different actions that have ethical implications.

Admittedly, this is a simple model. It does not begin to specify all of the particular circumstances that might favor moral versus self-interested action. Like Koford and Penno (1992), we assume that such differentiating criteria are likely to vary from one person to another, depending on the salience of their ethical values. Agents provide a particularly appropriate starting point to determine whether a notion of bounded personal ethics might be relevant because they must frequently choose between their interests and those of their principals. Duska (1992), for example, argues that the agency relationship requires agents to set aside their own utilities to serve their principals. In direct contrast are the economic approaches to agency theory, which expect that agents will uniformly and explicitly pursue their own self-interest first and foremost, even if their actions are counter to the interests of their principals.

Bounded personal ethics, however, suggests that many of an agent's actions (or anyone else's) have only minimal consequences for the agent and are therefore somewhat unlikely stimulants of moral awareness. In other words, most of our decisions reside in the lower left quadrant of Table 4, where our conscious concerns, for either others or ourselves are minimal. Thus, these actions are unlikely to be taken with any moral concern – even if they do have moral consequences for other people. Yet an accumulation of such actions can have important effects on other people.

The early part of this paper addressed the opposite quadrant in Table 4, that is, actions that might have serious personal consequences that prompted moral awareness. In the next sections of this paper, we return to the data to determine whether our sample of Vancouver agents engaged in a set of seemingly innocuous actions that, in toto, could have clear moral consequences for their principals (homeowners and purchasers). These observations provide preliminary data on the character and frequency of actions that fall directly within the domain of the model of bounded personal ethics.

## OBSERVATIONS OF BOUNDED PERSONAL ETHICS: ANOTHER LOOK AT THE DATA

Many of the agents in our sample seemed either completely unaware of or simply did not attend to many of the informal aspects of the real estate system in Vancouver. From an outsider's perspective, these taken-for-granted actions appear to be uniformly slanted toward the interests of the agents rather than toward the interests of the sellers or the purchasers they represented (cf., Messick & Sentis, 1983). Many of these actions, taken alone, appear relatively harmless. In combination, however, they portray a system that serves agents more than their principals.

One rather potent example occurred frequently when a purchaser made an offer on a home. After writing up the offer, the selling agent typically met the listing agent and, together, they presented the offer to the seller. After the presentation, the listing agent discussed the offer with the seller while the selling agent waited in another room for the seller's counteroffer. This seemingly innocuous procedure put tremendous pressure on sellers to quickly decide how they would respond, exposing them to considerable influence from their agent. When selling agents asked the purchasers to wait close by – often in a car parked outside – they put similar time pressure on the purchasers to also counteroffer quickly. Thus, by keeping the parties in close proximity to each other and by acting as the couriers of each party's offer or counteroffer, they could keep both parties under considerable time pressure and, in all likelihood, make them more susceptible to persuasion.

On its own, this process might seem innocuous. It gets sellers and purchasers relatively close together and encourages them to strike a deal. In essence, however, it serves the agents' primary interests – to close the deal – extremely well. It puts tremendous time pressure on both parties when there is no need for them to feel so pressured, in what is usually the biggest personal transaction they have ever made. It plays on their emotions and makes them hurry more than they need to, or should (from a rational point of view). And it increases the probability of a quick deal, which fits perfectly with the agents' interests.

This is just one example. Halpern (1996) reported that real estate agents in Berkeley, California also acted as if they were oblivious to the ethical consequences of many of their actions. She reported, for instance, that 30 experienced agents had monthly meetings to "discuss transactions, houses, clients, other agents, and the market generally". Although the meetings were discontinued (because too many uninvited agents began to attend), none of these agents "even hinted that there might be some collusion occurring."

Although many of the agents in our study described their roles as messengers or couriers and emphasized the service they were providing, they constantly tried to keep control (e.g. "It is important to be in control of the situation"), admitted being manipulative, and tended not to trust each other (e.g. "I don't think everyone is honest all of the time"). In essence, they "played the game" *amongst themselves*. Their roles as agents, with primary concerns for their principals' interests, soon became subordinate in the home-buying process.

Many agents argued that they worked for both parties, especially when they worked with a purchaser; they implicitly acknowledged undisclosed, unintended dual agency. As three agents put it:

"I am not there to bargain for the lowest price. I am there to facilitate a sale for both parties".
"I'm hired to get the purchaser and the seller together, to pay market value for the place".
"I know the seller is paying me but I want to be fair across the board".

They concentrated on pushing sellers and purchasers to reach the fair market price. Yet they acknowledged that the market price is determined by the emotional act of a single purchaser. Thus, determining a house's market value is essentially impossible. Even though comparable sales suggest a range for the final price, they cannot accurately predict what one person will pay. Northcraft and Neale's (1989) perceptive research on the relative inability of agents to predict the sale price of a house accentuates this point. Thus, it seems probable that these agents – conceiving of themselves as couriers or servants who were nevertheless in control – pushed for deals that favored their own interests over their principals'.

To investigate this premise, we coded the frequency of seven acts of potentially bounded personal ethics by agents. They included whether the agents: (1) indicated that dual agency was not a problem; (2) indicated that they would list a house for a price that they felt was too high given the market; (3) pushed to "price a house tightly," i.e. close to their estimate of the market value; (4) restricted themselves to listing houses with sellers who were "motivated"; (5) counseled potential purchasers that an offer was too low; (6) relentlessly sought the completion of a deal; or (7) argued that purchasers and sellers were aware of the real estate system and didn't need it explained. Although none of these actions seem particularly severe when considered alone, each violates their roles as agents.

Before describing each of these responses in more detail, it is important to emphasize that the real estate agents in this study were experienced professionals with long, successful track records in this industry. Rather than being a condemnation of real estate agents – which has never been our intention – our observations and suppositions point more toward the implicit, subtle choices that these agents often made. Most of the actions we outline here seem innocuous on their own and possibly not worthy of much attention. In fact, we are confident that the agents themselves would discount their gravity. Nevertheless, it appears that a combination of three factors – lack of awareness, the possibility that implicit norms developed within the profession to support these actions, and innate self-interest – have led to outcomes that are clearly disadvantageous to purchasers.

*Dual Agency.* In many instances, agents represented both the seller and a purchaser who wanted to buy a particular property. When the deal was completed, dual agents received both halves of the commission, which could be quite lucrative. Personal relationships with the purchasers were less likely in dual agency, as agents rarely had worked with the purchasers for any length of time.

The conflicts of interest that dual agency creates, in Bowie and Freeman's (1992) terms, undermine loyalty to formal principals.[7] As the National Association of Realtors in the United States put it, "Dual agency is a totally inappropriate agency relationship for real estate brokers to create as a matter of general business practice . . . . The disclosures and consent necessary to make dual agency lawful are so comprehensive and specific that a typical real estate broker cannot undertake them as a matter of routine". Similarly, the Canadian Real Estate Association states, "The obligations and legal ramifications (of dual agency) are so onerous that it is not a recommended real estate practice."

*Buying Listings and Pricing Tightly.* Most agents preferred to act as a listing rather than a selling agent (by a 5-to-1 ratio, according to several agents). They all realized that they could increase the likelihood of securing a listing by giving sellers inflated estimates, i.e. "buying listings." Paradoxically, agents also had an incentive to suggest a low price so that a home would sell quickly, even though this would not maximize the seller's returns. While a higher price was more likely to secure a listing, a low price, "tight to the market," was more likely to lead to a quick sale. Bounded personal ethics, then, can arise in listing negotiations when agents either: (1) recommend unrealistically high prices to secure a listing, with the unexpressed intent to pressure the sellers to reduce the price when their home doesn't sell quickly, or (2) convince sellers to set a low price, "tight to the market," so that the house does sell quickly because it is priced too low.

*Pushing Deals.* Many agents viewed their role as "securing the property" once an offer had been made. Almost everyone pushed and pushed to get the parties to reach an agreement. No agent mentioned that, even after making or receiving an offer, a purchaser or a seller might not want to concede as much as was needed to agree. There was no recognition of agreements that would serve one or both badly. Because reaching agreements was a positive outcome for agents, they tended to push for deals, almost regardless of their clients' real interests.

*Motivated Sellers and Low Offers.* Several agents indicated that they would not list a home for a seller who wasn't really motivated to sell. If all agents took this position, however, sellers would never be able to test the market to see whether they could get a premium for their home. Similarly, when purchasers wanted to probe the resolve of a seller, they might make a low offer. Many agents discouraged these, even though one agent reported that he "had never had a seller refuse to work with someone who made a low offer." Either of these two constraints put agents' interests above clients'.

Along with believing that sellers and purchasers know more about the real estate system than data indicated, each of these actions, on its own, is low in moral intensity (Jones', 1991) and should therefore have less impact in ethical decision making, even to the point of not prompting awareness. These instances of bounded personal ethics only evoke one of Jones' (1991) criteria for moral intensity, i.e. proximity, a close relationship between the agent and the principal. All of the other indicators are weak: (1) the magnitude of the consequences (harm or benefit to others) is low; (2) social consensus that the acts are evil is low (especially among agents); (3) the probability of any one of these acts having harmful effects on its own is low; (4) the time between acts and effects may be long; and (5) the acts' effects are not particularly concentrated. In addition, in the presence of implicit norms that support these acts, their ethical implications are likely to be ignored. The bounded personal ethics model, however, assumes that each of a series of small unethical acts like these can accumulate and have a potent biasing effect.

# RESULTS

Every agent revealed that at times they were more motivated by self-interest than by their responsibilities to their clients or to the ethics of their profession. Frequency counts of each of the instances of bounded personal ethics indicate that all of the agents in this sample engaged in them. Most were boundedly ethical in several categories; overall, there were 76 examples of bounded personal ethics (out of 168 possibilities). Half of the agents, or more, reported that they pushed relentlessly for a deal ($n = 16$), agreed to list a house at a price that they knew was too high ($n = 15$), felt that dual agency was not a problem ($n = 13$), and/or pushed for tight pricing ($n = 12$). Fewer indicated that they told people when an offer was too low ($n = 8$), that people knew about the agency problem ($n = 7$), or that they would list a home only if the sellers were motivated ($n = 5$). These numbers are almost necessarily underestimates, however, as we did not raise all of these issues in every interview.

The agents' comments provide further clarification. Many agents, for instance, indicated that dual agency was not a problem; as one put it,

"No worries; I have control."

Another said that,

"My job is the same as that of a single agent – to make a deal."

One agent was both gleeful and reflective, saying,

"Double ending is like Christmas; . . . somehow it works."

Agents expressed almost as much delight in closing deals as in the prospect of dual agency. One agent said,

"When I write an offer and a purchaser asks if they will get the house, I say 'Yes!'"

Most agents encouraged purchasers to write offers and encouraged sellers to make counter-offers. They understood the risks involved in closing a negotiation, but often expressed them in terms of their own outcomes (e.g. missing out on the deal) rather than in terms of their principals' outcomes. For example:

> "I won't push for an extra 5,000 for a seller if it risks losing the deal."

They took great pride in being "closers":

> "My duty is to keep the ball rolling."
> "My job is to put the deal together."
> "The bottom line is they want the house. My job is to secure the deal."

One agent who worked primarily with builders used this rationale:

> "If sellers do not get their price, they may not sell, but builders must sell – that's why it's great to work with builders."

Two agents summed things up well:

> "Our ultimate goal is to do the deal"
> "I must keep pushing. I try to think of all possible ways for it to work."

Most agents wanted to price a house tightly, close to what they thought the market price would be, although one agent admitted:

> "What's the right price for a house? What someone will pay."

As noted earlier, they encouraged sellers to "ask less, get more" and "by pricing on, you get good, quick offers." The question is whether these prices are good for the principals or good for the agent.

With respect to low offers, agents cautioned that sellers might be upset by such low offers and they should therefore be avoided. One agent argued that purchasers should:

> "Make an offer so that you won't lose the house; if the first offer is close, then the counter will not be as tough. If you like the house, what is $10,000 over 5 years? Not much per week."

Another used what she called the "highest/lowest offer":

> "Come in at the highest possible price you are comfortable with."

One reasoned that:

> "A more reasonable response will lead to a more reasonable reaction."

Given the unpredictability of the other party's responses, however, this advice seems particularly self-serving.

Agents also provided a series of idiosyncratic comments that suggested the influence of bounded personal ethics. One agent, for instance, said:

"I try to help if it's something I like and can sell in the future."

Another colluded with other agents before they brought an offer to his seller by agreeing privately that they would be honest and work together until the deal was done. When we asked one agent when he worked hard for a purchaser, he said:

"When an important lawyer has given me the client and is looking over my shoulder."

In response to questions about telling the truth, one agent indicated that:

"It's important . . . how you tell the truth."

Another indicated that he told the truth at the right time.

Even the agents who revealed their responsibilities to the seller downplayed this issue, saying that:

"People are sophisticated: they understand."
"Purchasers are more educated these days."

However, one agent said:

"People are much more aware now, but in some ways they are still at your mercy."

Another agent expressed the duality of bounded personal ethics by saying:

"We are here to work for the public. Today's purchaser is tomorrow's seller."

In addition, the agents' concerns about information, presented earlier, also attest to the notion that they not only wanted to be in control but that their own outcomes frequently superseded their principals. These responses, freely provided in our interviews, represent an impressive accumulation of admissions, with no apparent consideration of their moral consequences.

## DISCUSSION AND CONCLUSIONS

The final piece of data in this study is systemic. On January 1, 1995, the Real Estate Association of British Columbia changed their standards and allowed selling agents to work completely on behalf of purchasers, even though the sellers were paying their commission. The change became law on June 8, 1995.[8] In doing so, the Association implicitly acknowledged that agents had been breaking the rules for many years. Now it is perfectly legitimate for an agent in Vancouver to protect purchasers and work with them to determine the size of their offers.

The agents, however, faced true ethical dilemmas in the system as it was structured prior to 1995. Even after the change, they still faced a variety of conflicts of interest. Although many people have questioned their ethics, the agency and revelation dilemmas had no easy solution: regardless of their choices, some people in the system might view them as unethical. One central, underlying reason was their susceptibility to the lures of self-interest. Like many people, these agents made "an ungainly compromise, neither pure greed nor pure altruism (Messick & Sentis, 1983)." Although one agent claimed that, "Top producers can still be decent, nice people," it is also likely that the broader, professional system contributed to their dilemmas and how they handled them (cf., Trevino, 1986).

Another recent study provides evidence that supports the assumptions of bounded personal ethics; it also investigates gray areas of behavior that are not strikingly immoral or permanently damaging. Goldstone and Chin (1993) found that, in a university department that used self-reports to determine photocopying charges, most people (59% in their sample) accurately reported the number of copies they had made. A third of the underreporters reported making no copies; two thirds reported making less than they had actually made. Larger jobs led to more underreporting, as did charges to personal rather than to departmental or research grant accounts. As Goldstone and Chin (1993) noted (page 25), however, "When patrons do not report the correct number of copies made, they are not generally completely dishonest." In fact, among the underreporters who reported making some copies, no one reported less than 50% of the copies that they had actually made.

Similarly, in Van Avermaet's (1974) study of the distribution of task payoffs, only two of the 94 participants who had control over $7 (a sizable sum for a student at that time) mailed nothing to their counterpart. Instead, those who had done less were inclined to keep an amount that approximated an equal split of their joint pay; those who had done more were inclined to keep an amount that approximated an equitable split. From a strictly economic point of view, when choices are anonymous, massive underreporting of photocopies is more self-beneficial than partial underreporting (Goldstone & Chin, 1993) and keeping all of the money is more self-beneficial than keeping just part of it (Van Avermaet, 1974). Both studies provide neat portrayals of bounded personal ethics and the kinds of outcomes we would expect when moral values and self-interest conflict. In both instances, awareness and temptation may have led to strange compromises.

As with any empirical project, this study suffered from a number of limitations. The small sample size reduced the power and the sensitivity of our statistical analyses. The study was also restricted to a single location and focused on successful, experienced real estate agents. Although these issues raise concerns, the data paint a complicated picture of how these agents handled difficult ethical dilemmas and how their resolutions related to their own economic outcomes.

A ready set for potential generalizability are other obvious agents, like lawyers, stock brokers, and sports agents. But many organizational actors take the role of agents, even though we might not always think of them that way. For instance, chief negotiators in collective bargaining interactions act as agents for both the union's members and for the stockholders of a company. Their actions are critical for many important outcomes for both sets of principals. Yet they also negotiate for themselves (Walton & McKersie, 1965). Jockeys in horse races provide a similar example. In fact, many, many examples of agents who may face conflicting ethical pressures exist (see Prendergast, 1999). The bottom line is that many people act as others' agents in many different organizational and social situations – often with the potential for effecting serious consequences for the principals. Whether the current findings apply in all of these contexts is an open empirical question. The possibility that these agents may face ethical dilemmas, and that their resolution might affect their principals, seems obvious. Whether bounded personal ethics applies only to agents or, more generally, to most people, is another open empirical question, but one worth addressing.

Unlike agency theory, this study actually focused on agents rather than on how principals might deal with self-interested agents. Unlike models of ethics, it focused on the benefactors and victims of ethical decisions and behavior as well as on the decision makers and actors themselves. The findings provide the basis for a model of bounded personal ethics, which we suggest may have broader applications than simply to agents. Exploring the conceptual and empirical complexities of how the motivational force of ethical values and self-interest interact clearly seems to be a particularly worthy topic for future research. In particular, the current findings suggest that, although the moral hazard problem is serious, people are clearly affected by their relationships. How they are affected, how much they are affected, and how tempted they are to shirk or act only in their self-interest in any particular situation is bound to be contextually embedded, but we would expect that these tense dynamics are nevertheless likely to operate.

The agents in our study reflect a complex mix of behaviors that are sometimes self-interested and sometimes other-oriented. From the point of view of the bounded personal ethics model, it is not surprising that their less consequential actions are primarily self-interested and that their more consequential actions – which prompt awareness and ethical consideration –

are more often other-oriented. Whether this same pattern plays out system-atically for agents and actors in other domains is an important theoretical and practical question.

### Some Implications of the Bounded Personal Ethics Model

New models provide an opportunity for cautious speculation. In that spirit, we present a few preliminary ideas about the potential implications of the bounded personal ethics model. The first, consistent with Markus and Nurius's (1986) concept of multiple selves, concerns the likelihood of seemingly inconsistent behavior: people are both self-interested and ethically motivated. When the two motivations do not conflict, a person's ethical values may seem particularly strong. When put to the test in an ethical dilemma, however, people reveal how easily they can be influenced by self-interest, especially when they do not acknowledge the importance, or even the existence, of a dilemma.

Another, practical implication of the bounded personal ethics model suggests that ethical behavior will be more likely for people facing ethical dilemmas if they have time and/or encouragement to think about the dilemma. Pressure to make a decision quickly when self-interest and ethical values conflict should lead to more self-interested choices. Delays between the perception of a dilemma and the time to make a choice may allow people to construct ethical justifications that they may not otherwise consider if pressed for an immediate decision.

A third, straightforward implication is also practical: predictability increases when people consider choices that simultaneously affirm their self-interest and their ethical values. By providing people with these kinds of choices, managers might be more confident that their employees will behave ethically. In contrast, presenting people with ethical dilemmas makes their choices more difficult and gives them an opportunity to succumb to self-interest.

Finally, it seems clear that research on the implicit norms of various professions would provide a particularly appropriate arena for investigating bounded personal ethics. The model clearly suggests that implicit norms are likely to be in line with the actors' self-interests. In contrast, the model also suggests that explicitly stated norms are less likely to be so blatant in their underlying motivation. The investigation of implicit and explicit professional norms might also provide an interesting venue for investigation independent of the bounded personal ethics model. Such investigations could have tremendous practical applicability, especially if the model is supported, as people who become aware of their actions' ethical consequences may well act more ethically in the future.

New models should offer many avenues for new research directions. The bounded personal ethics model certainly meets that criterion. More specifically, we hope that it can contribute to the explanation and understanding of a wide array of individuals' moral choices. We present it as a theoretical foundation for ethical choice. We also hope that research on its tenets might actually hold the prospect for increasing ethical action. More generally, we hope that it provides a foundation for an increase in the research on the ethics of organizational decision making.

# NOTES

1. There is an important difference between real estate agents (sometimes called brokers) and real estate sales people. Agents receive considerably more schooling; licensed salespeople are only required to complete a 6-month course and the licensing exam. For the purposes of this article, and because salespeople work with homesellers and homepurchasers, we describe them all by using the general term "agent." At the same time, we apologize to agents for taking such license with their hard-earned credentials.

2. We hesitate to say that this was *their* agent, as the agent was still legally bound to the seller. This was emphasized, strenuously, by one of the agents in our sample when we mistakenly referred to an agent as representing a purchaser.

3. Since we promised participants complete anonymity, references to agents in this paper as "he" or "she" were chosen randomly and do not necessarily correspond to a particular respondent's gender.

4. One author was not able to attend three of the interviews due to schedule conflicts and our desire to fit the agents' schedules rather than our own.

5. The results for listings and sales are similar; all results (correlations and other data not included here) are available from the authors.

6. Lack of knowledge and the difficulty of successful litigation limit the likelihood of agents being sued. Thus, their actions were more likely to lead to professional censure than to legal liability. But even this likelihood was small.

7. These conflicts of interest are similar in many ways to those identified in investment banks. Hayward and Boeker (1998) note that securities analysts evaluate the same companies that their firm's investment bankers may be working with; providing negative evaluations of those companies hurts the firm's abilities to work with them on mergers and acquisitions. Because investment bankers had more power than analysts, they often tried to dampen negative securities reports. One major firm went so far as to advocate "no negative comments about our clients." Most of these conflicts of interest are so sensitive that firms deny their existence. Nevertheless, Hayward and Boeker's (1997) macro analysis provides strong evidence that they do exist and that they bias analysts' reports.

8. Interestingly, the same changes occurred in the Chicago area as well, in January of 1995.

## ACKNOWLEDGMENTS

We gratefully acknowledge the financial assistance of the Social Sciences and Humanities Research Council of Canada and the Division of Urban Land Economics at the University of British Columbia, and the encouragement and information provided by Stan Hamilton, Bob Helsley, Robert Laing, David Moore, and Deborah Nelson. We thank Kevin Au for his help with the data analysis. We also thank Dafna Eylon, Kevin Gibson, Jennifer Halpern, David Messick, David Moore, Greg Oldham, Madan Pillutla, and Tom Ross for their constructive comments on earlier versions of this manuscript.

## REFERENCES

Bazerman, M. H. (1998). *Judgment in Managerial Decision Making*. New York: John Wiley.
Bell, D. E. (1982). Regret in decision making under uncertainty. *Operations Research, 5*, 960–981.
Birenbaum, A., & Sagarin, E. (1976). *Norms and Human Behavior*. New York: Praeger.
Bowie, N. E., & Freeman, R. E. (Eds) (1992). *Ethics and Agency Theory: An Introduction*. New York: Oxford University Press.
Clark, M. S. (1984). Record keeping in two types of relationships. *Journal of Personality and Social Psychology, 47*, 549–557.
Dawes, R. M. (1980). Social dilemmas. *Annual Review of Psychology, 31*, 169–193.
Dees, J. G. (1992). Principals, agents, and ethics. In: N. E. Bowie & R. E. Freeman (Eds), *Ethics and Agency Theory: An Introduction*. New York: Oxford University Press.
DeGeorge, R. T. (1992). Agency theory and the ethics of agency. In: N. E. Bowie & R. E. Freeman (Eds), *Ethics and Agency Theory: An Introduction*. New York: Oxford University Press.
Derry. R. (1987). Moral reasoning in work-related conflicts. In: W. C. Frederick & L. E. Preston (Eds), *Research in Corporate Social Performance and Policy* (Vol. 9, pp. 25–49). Greenwich, CT: JAI Press.
DiIulio, J. D. Jr. (1994). Principled agents: The cultural bases of behavior in a federal government bureaucracy. *Journal of Public Administration Research, 4*, 277–318.
Duska, R. F. (1992). Why be a loyal agent? A systemic ethical analysis. In: N. E. Bowie & R. E. Freeman (Eds), *Ethics and Agency Theory: An Introduction*. New York: Oxford University Press.
Eisenhardt, K. M. (1989). Agency theory: An assessment and review. *Academy of Management Review, 14*, 57–74.
Elsbach, K. D., & Sutton, R. I. (1992). Acquiring organizational legitimacy through illegitimate actions: a marriage of institutional and impression management theories. *Academy of Management Journal, 35*, 699–738.
Goldstone, R. L., & Chin, C. (1993). Dishonesty in self-report of copies made: Moral relativity and the copy machine. *Basic and Applied Social Psychology, 14*, 19–32.
Halpern, J. J. (1996). The effect of friendship on decisions: Field studies of real estate transactions. *Human Relations*, in press.
Hayward, M. L. A., & Boeker, W. (1998). Porous Chinese walls? Power and conflicts in professional firms. *Administrative Science Quarterly, 43*, 1–22.

Jensen, M., & Meckling, Q. (1976). Theory of the firm: Managerial behavior, agency costs, and sellership structure. *Journal of Financial Economics, 3,* 305–360.

Jones, T. M. (1991). Ethical decision making by individuals in organizations: an issue-contingent model. *Academy of Management Review, 16,* 366–395.

Koford, K., & Penno, M. (1992). Accounting, principal-agent theory, and self-interested behavior. In: N. E. Bowie & R. E. Freeman (Eds), *Ethics and Agency Theory: An Introduction.* New York: Oxford University Press.

Kohlberg, L. (1976). Moral stages and motivation. In: T. Likona (Ed.), *Moral Development and Behavior.* New York: Holt, Rinehart, and Winston.

Larrick, R. P. (1993). Motivational factors in decision theories: the role of self-protection. *Psychological Bulletin, 113,* 440–450.

Lewin, K. (1951). *Field Theory in Social Science.* New York: Harper.

Lewis, C. S. (1947). *The Abolition of Man.* New York: MacMillan.

Loomes, G., & Sugden, R. (1982). Regret theory: an alternative theory of rational choice under uncertainty. *Economic Journal, 92,* 805–824.

Markus, H., & Nurius, P. (1986). Possible selves. *American Psychologist, 41,* 954–969.

Mayer, R. C., Davis, J. H., & Schoorman, F. D. (1995). An integrative model of organizational trust. *Academy of Management Review, 20,* 709–734.

Messick, D. M., & Sentis, K. (1983). Fairness, preference, and fairness biases. In: D. M. Messick & K. S. Cook (Eds), *Equity Theory: Psychological and Sociological Perspectives.* New York: Praeger.

Meyerson, D., Weick, K. E., & Kramer, R. M. (1996). Swift trust and temporary groups. In: R. Kramer & T. R. Tyler (Eds), *Trust in Organizations: Frontiers of Theory and Research.* Thousand Oaks CA: Sage.

Miller, L. C. (1990). Intimacy and liking: mutual influence and the role of unique relationships. *Journal of Personality and Social Psychology, 59,* 50–60.

Mitnick, B. M. (1992). The theory of agency and organizational analysis. In: N. E. Bowie & R. E. Freeman (Eds), *Ethics and Agency Theory: An Introduction.* New York: Oxford University Press.

Northcraft, G. B., & Neale, M. A. (1987). Experts, amateurs, and real estate: An anchoring-and-adjustment perspective in property pricing decisions. *Organizational Behavior and Human Decision Processes, 39,* 84–97.

Ontario Real Estate Association (1990). *Real Estate as a Professional Career.* Phase 1. Ontario Real Estate Association, Don Mills. Ontario.

Organ, D. W. (1988). *Organizational Citizenship Behavior: The Good Soldier Syndrome.* Lexington MA: Lexington Books.

Pondy, L. R., & Olson, M. L. (1977). *Theories of Extreme Cases.* Unpublished paper, University of Illinois, Champaign, IL.

Pratt, J. W., & Zeckhauser, R. (1985). *Principals and Agents: The Structure of Business.* Boston: Harvard Business School Press.

Prendergast, C. (1999). The provision of incentives in firms. *Journal of Economic Literature, 37,* 7–63.

Radner, R. (1981). Monitoring cooperative arrangements in a repeated principal-agent relationship. *Econometrica, 49,* 1127–1148.

*Real Estate Weekly* (1994). A fundamental change in how we do business. August 19:1.

*Real Estate Weekly* (1995). Long term demand expected to stay high. April 17:1.

Ross, J., & Staw, B. M. (1986). Expo 86: An escalation prototype. *Administrative Science Quarterly, 31,* 274–297.

Schneider, J., Tune, B., & Bain, N. (1992). *Who's my Boss? Seller, Purchaser, Both, Neither.* (Canadian Edition.) Burnaby, BC, Canada: Press Sure Publications.

Scott, W. R. (1995). *Institutions and Organizations.* Thousand Oaks CA: Sage.

Simon, H. A. (1976). *Administrative Behavior.* New York: Free Press.

Trevino, L. K. (1986). Ethical decision making in organizations: a person-situation interactionist model. *Academy of Management Review, 11,* 601–617.

Valley, K. L., White, S. B., Neale, M. A., & Bazerman, M. H. (1992). Agents as information brokers: the effects of information disclosure on negotiated outcomes. *Organizational Behavior and Human Decision Processes, 51,* 220–236.

Van Avermaet, E. (1974). *Equity: A Theoretical and Experimental Analysis.* Unpublished doctoral dissertation, University of California, Santa Barbara.

Vroom, V. H. (1964). *Work and Motivation.* New York: John Wiley.

Waller, N. G., & Waller, T. H. (1989). Protecting the rights and interests of home purchasers in cooperatively brokered sales. *Real Estate Issues,* Spring/Summer, 32–37.

Walton, R. E., & McKersie, R. B. (1965). *A Behavioral Theory of Labor Negotiations.* New York: McGraw-Hill.

Wicklund, R. A. (1979). The influence of self-awareness on human behavior. *American Scientist, 67,* 187–193.

# THE PROCESS OF ENACTMENT: EVIDENCE FROM ALEXANDER THE GREAT

Lance B. Kurke and Margaret Brindle

## ABSTRACT

*This paper enriches contemporary understanding of the process of enactment by examining the historical case of Alexander the Great. We preface our analysis with the suggestion that enactment involves reframing problems, using symbolism, forming identities, and building alliances. We then illustrate through our historical case analysis how a leader can manipulate the environment, enact a new reality, and thereby change the environment and reality to which the leader then responds. Our analysis of Alexander's actions provides evidence that effective outcomes during his military campaigns had as much to do with the process of enactment as with mere resource advantage or military prowess, as is sometimes asserted.*

## INTRODUCTION

He was one of the supreme fertilising forces of history. He lifted the civilized world out of one groove and set it in another; he started a new epoch; nothing could again be as it had been (Tarn, 1948: 145).

Pondy and Mitroff (1979) suggested that people in organizational life often produce part of the environment they face. More specifically, organization

Advances in Qualitative Organization Research, Volume 3, pages 41–57.
Copyright © 2001 by Elsevier Science Ltd.
All rights of reproduction in any form reserved.
ISBN: 0-7623-0772-2

members in general and leaders in particular at least partially *enact* the surrounding environment. Weick (1979: 131) defined the concept of enactment as:

> . . . a punctuated and connected summary of a previously equivocal display. It is a sensible version of what the equivocality was about, although other versions could have been constructed. We have used the term enacted environment and cause map to refer to retained content.

Later he added: "Enactment is the social process by which a material and symbolic record of action" is laid down (Smircich & Stubbart, 1985: 726). The process, he suggested, occurs in two steps. "First, portions of the field of experience are bracketed and singled out for closer attention on the basis of preconceptions. Second, people act within the context of these bracketed elements, under the guidance of preconceptions and often shape these elements in the direction of preconceptions . . ." (Weick, 1988: 307).

Weick's definitions are considered by some to be difficult to grasp, rendering both theoretical extension and practical application similarly difficult to execute. Acknowledging this difficulty, in the present article we provide evidence supporting the broad theoretical and practical significance of enactment by presenting an historical case analysis that reviews about thirteen years of the reign of Alexander the Great. In so doing, we attempt to improve current understanding of the concept of enactment. To accomplish this purpose, we begin by breaking down the enactment process into four distinct activities: reframing problems, manipulating symbols, building alliances, and establishing identity.

## Reframing Problems

To reframe a situation is a manipulation that changes what people pay attention to or deem important. As Goffman (1974) highlighted in his work on decision making, the meaning given to problems and the manner in which they are defined is critical. By transforming an unsolvable task into another solvable one, the world to which one responds is essentially changed.

As will be recounted in the following historical analysis, Alexander the Great did not accept perceptions of his environment as limitations to be accommodated. Perceived problems were reframed into alternative problems, which were then solved. The solution often was to redefine the situation and then to act in accord with the newly constructed reality. The recast solvable problem became the solution to the original problem.

## *Manipulating Symbols*

People attribute actions to leaders (Meindl, Ehrlich & Dukerich, 1985; Meindl & Ehrlich, 1987). Symbols are important because through them a leader can create sustained meaning, shared interpretation, and joint action (Mead, 1934). A leader can manipulate symbols and thus manipulate follower's attributions, due in large part to the salience of the leadership role and the cognitive response elicited by symbols.

Manipulate is from the same root as manage – the root is maun. To manipulate is to align, to control, and to bring into control. Using symbols and the cognitive attribution assigned to these symbols was critical to Alexander, who viewed symbols as part of tactics. By blurring the distinction between the environment and the organization (Meyer & Rowan, 1978; Weick, 1979) and between problem and solution (Goffman, 1974), Alexander reframed problems and used symbolism to alter the environment.

## *Building Alliances*

Building strong alliances via reciprocity has become a critical strategy for modern managers (Cialdini, 1986). Yet, the effective and deliberate construction of alliances was also extremely important to ancient leaders. Alexander formed alliances throughout his life – seamlessly building important relationships with individuals, organizations, cities, and peoples. These alliances changed the world to which he subsequently responded.

## *Establishing Identity*

Identity has been defined as a critical process by which members of organizations arrive at a shared understanding and attach a shared meaning to their activities (Thomas, Clark & Gioia, 1993). Many scholars have demonstrated that identity is a socially constructed phenomenon. The process of forming an identity creates a unity where there was not one before. Identity can be built among individuals (turning strangers into a coherent unity), cities (turning enemies into a League), or peoples (creating an empire). As will be shown, Alexander often manipulated the development of identity among his own troops and even among his conquered subjects.

# THE CASE OF ALEXANDER THE GREAT

Few non-historians realize how seminal Alexander the Great was to the development of the western world. It would be hard to overstate. The histories of Alexander are so numerous that it would be impossible in this paper to categorize exhaustively the incidents in his life.[1] Our discussion is admittedly superficial, intended to pique curiosity more than sate it. It is organized by the four enactment processes described above and follows a rough chronology of Alexander's campaign under each process.

## Reframing Problems

### Greece and Asia Minor

After unifying Greece, Alexander crossed the Hellespont to invade first Asia Minor, then Persia itself. He could not conquer every town in what is now coastal Turkey, because his resources were so limited. Accordingly, he had to reframe the campaign in Turkey from one of conquest to one of co-optation, wherein cities would capitulate without a fight. Alexander approached every town in Asia Minor, many of which were originally settled by Greeks, as the Hegemon of the League and propounded a policy of conciliation. He offered to allow local governance and no increase or a reduction in taxes in exchange for capitulation of the city and execution of the local Persian overlord. In this manner he was able to co-opt most cities without a battle. In essence, Alexander reframed the problem from one of conflict to one of cooperative alignment.

### Middle East and Egypt

After the battle at Issus, Alexander pursued his strategy of securing an Asian base. He could not venture into the Asian interior without supply by sea. However, his communications and supply would not be secure while the Persian fleet ruled the Mediterranean Sea. Alexander faced the formidable problem of destroying a vastly superior navy with his minuscule navy. His solution is one of the most important lessons for admirals throughout history. He had to destroy a navy on land. He succeeded by depriving the Persian fleet of their bases on the Mediterranean coast, so they would have no place to resupply and would become ineffective. This incident is doubly interesting, because to successfully reframe the problem he had to reframe the solution. In particular, the island of Tyre sold water to the Persians and had successfully withstood a thirteen-year naval siege. Being impregnable by sea and holding the key to rendering the Persian navy ineffective, Alexander redefined the situation. He declared that this island should no longer be an island – and induced his engineers and army to bring land to island. That is, he filled in the ocean between the mainland and the island and besieged it like any other city.

After seven months of building a mole out to the island, his army successfully conquered it in two weeks.

*Asia and India*
Once Alexander got his army across the River Hydaspes, he faced an impossible task. The Punjab king, Porus, who opposed him had a much larger army and two hundred war elephants. These elephants warrant additional attention.

Any reading of the literature surrounding Alexander indicates that his cavalry – horse-mounted forces – were the key to his military prowess. However, horses and elephants have a strong, natural antipathy. When a horse smells an elephant it will throw its rider and gallop wildly until it has escaped the scent. To behave comfortably around an elephant, a horse must be trained by putting the straw from an elephant's stable in the horse's stall, from birth. Only by becoming thus acclimated will a horse develop tolerance for elephants.

All of Porus' horses were acclimated to elephants, but none of Alexander's were. So, to compound the problem of defeating a superior army, Alexander did not appear to have use of his cavalry, which was central to his strategies. Military prowess alone did not offer a feasible solution. Reframing was required.

Alexander marched his exhausted army from the northern-most crossing point south to meet Porus' army. Porus reasoned that his army was fed and rested whereas Alexander's was tired from marching all night, fighting a small battle at the crossing, and now marching through mud to meet him. He picked a broad level plain and waited. Alexander met segments of his army at prearranged crossings and provided them with secure passage from his side of the river. By the time he met Porus, he had managed to get almost his entire army across safely.

The ensuing battle would have made a choreographer proud. In preparation to meet Porus' larger army, Alexander had drilled his troops to spread themselves out to be the expected width of Porus' lines. He thinned his ranks to about eight men deep. Porus' army was on the order of thirty or more men deep. However, they were of about the same width. Porus had reasoned that Alexander's ferocious cavalry would be the demise of his fine army, so he carefully organized his infantry so that the elephants were interspersed among the foot soldiers. This protected them from the cavalry who would not operate around the elephants.

To explain what happened next in this battle, we must digress and consider mahouts, sarrissas, military police, Sogdianian mounted archers, and javelin throwers. Elephants are enormous, intelligent mammals. They can be trained, but to do so, a person has to form a very special relationship with each animal. These trainers with special relationships to a certain elephant are called mahouts. At birth, baby elephants are separated from their mothers, if need be by killing the mother. From then on, the mahout provides all food the baby elephant receives, gives it daily baths and brushings, changes its straw in its stable (taking it to the horse stables), and eventually rides it. Because elephants live so long and because people in Alexander's era did not, mahouts were selected for this lifelong job at a very young age – typically as young as five. If a mahout was killed in an elephant's youth, the elephant was usually destroyed because no one else could control it. As the elephant grew to its four to six thousand pound maturity, the mahout was still able to exercise control because of the special life-long relationship. Each mahout was wedded to each elephant.

The Greek phalanxes were equipped with a long pike-like object called a sarrissa. This pole could be of varying lengths, such that men, staggered in ranks of eight, could present a front of all their sarrissas. By doing so, the front of Alexander's army was an impenetrable wall of steel.

Because the Indian army was primarily lightly trained peasants who only served when needed, there typically was a great deal of desertion during a pitched battle. To combat this untimely departure of troops, it was almost certainly common practice to station military police in the back row of the army. These would likely be somewhat disabled veterans who trained others during slack periods. They would lock arms to keep desertion to a minimum. In the heat of battle, being as many as thirty rows back from the fray, they were probably oblivious to how things were going.

As the infantry battle began, with the two armies separated by just over one hundred yards, the Sogdianian mounted archers that Alexander had hired came forward through passages in the infantry ranks. A good archer with a long bow could hit a two-inch target at about one hundred yards nine times out of ten. Sogdianian mounted archers could do this while riding. These archers rode to inside the edge of their range and systematically fired at their assigned targets. The first target was the heads of the mahouts. Given the numbers involved, the statistics, and the range, it must have been very few seconds before all the mahouts were dead. The second target was elephant eyes. The elephants were now driverless and blind, and the Sogdianians left the battlefield.

Next came the javelin throwers. These men probably had a quiver of sorts to hold a number of javelins- – perhaps as many as ten or fifteen. They were accurate at up to one hundred yards. Once in range, they released their load of weapons upon the hapless elephants directly in front of them. The javelin throwers now ran from the field. At this precise moment, the front of Alexander's army arrived at the front of Porus'.

The Indian soldiers were now hemmed in by the Greeks in front, the military police in the back, hundreds of yards of fellow soldiers to the sides, and in their midst were the elephants – two hundred blind, driverless elephants wounded by foot-deep javelin injuries. As might be expected, the elephants stampeded amongst the Indians, leading to extensive casualties in one of the two most lopsided victories in history (the other was probably Agincourt). Alexander lost about two hundred and twenty cavalry, ten mounted archers, and an insignificant number of infantry. Porus lost about twenty *thousand* casualties (nine thousand killed outright, twelve thousand captured injured).

Clearly, the military strength of Alexander's forces was not the primary contributor to this victory. Alexander carefully constructed and choreographed a reframing of the situation so that the Indian army destroyed itself.

## Using Symbolism

### Greece and Asia Minor

When Alexander defeated the city of Athens he uncharacteristically spared the city. By sparing Athens (a symbolic statement of the highest order) the Greeks saw that Alexander was magnanimous to his allies. An unharmed Athens was a potent symbol of his magnanimity and helped build a critical alliance.

Elsewhere in Asia Minor, when a town did not voluntarily capitulate, Alexander's army besieged and captured it, looted the town, destroyed the city walls, burned the city, brutalized the women and children in front of their male kin, killed all the men in front of their female kin, sold the women and children into slavery, and salted the fields to preclude subsequent inhabitation. News traveled fast of the consequences of capitulation or resistance. As he redefined citizens' reality, most cities without Persian garrisons opened their own gates freely. Alexander seldom needed to use his army again in Turkey.

He heightened his symbolic power by visiting the site of the Gordian Knot, where legend held that he who untied it would rule the world. He took credit for untying it. Whether accurate or not, the attribution is what matters. As Meindl and his colleagues (Meindl et al., 1985; Meindl & Ehrlich, 1987) have argued, attributions are one of the most important hallmarks of successful leadership. Their work on attribution shows clearly that saying it is so, often makes it so. Within the Middle East and Egypt, Alexander's actions demonstrated the power of effective symbolism.

After a straightforward defeat of the Persian satraps at Granicus, Alexander redefined his opponent's reality and thus enacted his environment by employing additional symbolism at his second great battle (Issus, November 333 BC). He leisurely held games and tournaments. The symbolism was probably to affect scorn for the nearby Persians. This enraged their generals into a tactical blunder. He further enacted his environment by redefining his opponent's reality with the symbolism of his showmanship and disdain. (Because the Persians were inland away from supply ports and were exhausting their supply, whereas Alexander was on the coast and receiving supply by sea, he forced the Persians to meet him in battle at a geographical position tactically inferior.) Symbolic disdain enacted defeat.

*Asia and India*

Another example of symbolism in action occurred at his third great battle in Mesopotamia in the spring. He confronted the Persians near a town we call Gaugamela. The battle was complex, and guaranteed Alexander's fame as one of the greatest generals of all time.

His officers were nervous to the point of being incapacitated. Alexander enacted confidence. He slept peacefully until well past dawn, the symbolism of which was not lost on his now confident officers. No small feat – Alexander's army was vastly outnumbered (five or more to one). The Persian front was easily double the length of Alexander's army and thus threatened to surround or outflank him. Accordingly, Alexander initially avoided battle, taking a defensive stance on the battlefield. When the battle began, he caused a gap to form in the Persian line, personally led the charge to exploit it, and chased the Persian king Darius from the field for the second time in their two meetings. Alexander had put himself at grave peril in front of all of his soldiers (he wore ostentatious armor and a plumed helmet to be easily visible to all). To the Persians, the symbolism of their leader's flight from the field was too much. The Persian army collapsed at the sight of their retreating leader. Darius escaped but was later murdered by his own generals.

Another example of enactment was exhibited at the battle of the River Hydaspes. Alexander faced a swollen river (by itself difficult to cross), and an opposing army larger than his own that included numerous elephants carrying archers on nearly impregnable armored platforms from which to shoot safely. Further, the elephants could crush infantry without even knowing it (which speaks for itself).

How did Alexander cross the river and deal with the elephants? The answer is awe-inspiring. First, he deceived the Indians into thinking he would wait until the river level fell in the autumn. He made it appear that he was drilling and exercising his troops. Each day Alexander would take a large contingent of his army (both cavalry and infantry) and march up (or down) the river. Porus (the Punjab king previously discussed) was of course forced to follow on the opposite side of the river with part of his army, to oppose any attempted crossing. At the end of each day, Alexander simply returned to camp. After months of this, Porus relaxed his vigilance, sending only a small contingent to keep track of Alexander's whereabouts. He eventually believed that Alexander was merely keeping his troops disciplined and fit. Alexander was able to get his army across the river at night in a thunderstorm by his deceptive maneuvers, life jackets, and collapsible boats. He hid his army during the march and had trained his men to march silently. As described in the previous reframing section, he then drew the Indians into battle and caused their elephants to stampede.

Symbolism served to enact unusual victories on the battlefield, even when greatly outnumbered. Moreover, Alexander turned to symbolic action to enact and strengthen loyalty internally with his troops. His sharing and extreme, genuine concern for his soldiers enabled him to save his army in the Gedrosian desert on the return to Babylon. He was fooled by local guides into believing that his admiral could provision the army with water by sea. But sheer cliffs precluded doing so. Many men were dying of thirst and the remainder were so demoralized that they had given up hope of surviving. To save their king, all of the soldiers sacrificed their remaining water, poured it into a helmet, and presented it to Alexander. They offered him life even at the cost of their own death. Alexander's problem was to save his dehydrated army, even without benefit of water. To solve that problem – to change his environment without benefit of water – he had to enact in thousands of men a will to live. In this spirit and in full sight of all, he poured the water offered him into the sand, saying that he would share their fate. The symbolism of that act redefined the army's reality. Since they could not let their king die, they would have to live to save him. Many more survived the remainder of the trip than would have otherwise (Engels, 1978). Such symbolic enactment was Alexander's hall-mark.

## Building Alliances

Without alliances, Alexander could not have conquered the Persian Empire. We offer here several examples of how the process of building alliances enacted his world.

*Greece and Asia Minor*

This first example of alliance building is a critical one, for it was the basis of all else that Alexander would accomplish. Before Alexander could invade Persia, he had to secure his home borders of Macedonia and pacify Greece. Since Greece was just a loose collection of city-states, he had to unify them and make them his allies, not his subjects, so they would not subsequently rebel.

Having displayed his magnanimity at Athens, he demonstrated that his aspirations were in all of Greece's interests. As Philip's (his father) successor, he had become Hegemon of the League of Corinth, a loose alliance of Greek city-states. When Darius (the Persian king introduced earlier) instigated a revolt in Greece (particularly in Thebes), Alexander redefined the perceptions of the Greeks, treating it as a revolt against the League rather than against his own aspirations. In other words, many Greeks thought Alexander would be a tyrant, and would intervene for what was in his own interest. Instead, however, he acted only through legitimate alliances. He thus reframed the problem and solution. He immediately subdued Thebes before other city-states joined the rebellion. He convened the Synhedrion, the supreme council of the League, to determine the fate of the Thebians. The verdict of the council was to destroy the city. Alexander accepted the decision, not only to eliminate Thebes as a power within Greece, but to teach all the Greeks not to revolt against the League. Alexander was merciful to the rest of Greece, so he could invade Persia promptly. He was thus accepted as the symbolic as well as military head of the confederation of Greek city-states. Consequently, Alexander built or fostered a deep and abiding loyal alliance with the remaining Greek city-states.

*Asia and India*

Immediately after the battle at the River Hydaspes, in a highly unusual move, Alexander gave sections of the Punjab back to Porus. Imagine defeating a king, then letting him keep his kingdom, later enlarged! The logic of enacting security through the symbolism of allying oneself with the foe you have just defeated, however, was impeccable alliance building. It made clear to everyone that Alexander could defeat any army under any circumstances, but that he was magnanimous – a king with whom any ruler would be proud to be allied. By imposing a truce between Porus and another Indian king, Taxiles, Alexander preserved the power structure in the Punjab and secured the eastern border of the Persian Empire with extremely loyal local rulers. The Persians themselves had never succeeded in doing this in hundreds of years of war. Thus, Alexander built abiding alliances in circumstances where the norm was to conquer and destroy.

## Establishing Identity

As we have argued, Alexander's success was not a product of mere resource prowess. Indeed, in most situations he was outnumbered, resource poor relative to his enemies. This was certainly the case in terms of numbers of soldiers. Building an identity with and among his troops was thus paramount.

### Greece and Asia Minor

Throughout his campaigns, Alexander built a rapport with his army through establishing an identity one on one with them. Unlike Darius, who had traveled with his complete entourage and maintained a "kingly" life style on campaigns, Alexander shared his soldiers' hardships. There are numerous examples of this. Alexander, who was trained as a physician, insisted on treating his soldiers' wounds before he permitted his own to be tended (if he was conscious), and he was wounded numerous times himself, sometimes seriously. Indeed, at times he would treat soldiers himself while his own gaping wounds went untended. It is said that he knew the names of thousands of his soldiers and called them by name, often inquiring about details of their lives. He never slept warm: even in winter he used only a light cotton cover. On the march, he ate what his soldiers ate. When the army had accumulated too many wagons, which limited mobility, he insisted that all wagons except communal ones and ambulances be burned – beginning with his own! These actions caused a level of loyalty heretofore unknown in professional armies.

### Middle East and Egypt

After the conquest of the island of Tyre, he liberated Egypt (they hated their Persian overlords and welcomed Alexander). He visited the sacred oasis of Siwah, at great personal risk, in part to further his role as one of liberator. Throughout his campaign, Alexander sacrificed to the local gods alongside his own, which he did at Siwah. This symbolically based his sovereignty upon divine sanction. At Siwah, it further established his unification of the far-flung empire.

### Asia and India

Alexander marched on to Babylon, Susa, and Persepolis, consolidating his hold on the administrative heart of the empire, acquiring the royal treasuries, and declaring himself King of Persia. He took on all of the symbolic trappings of the Persian King, including the humiliating (to the Greeks) gesture of genuflection. He sought now to unify the empire by integrating Greeks and Persians: intermarriage was encouraged, the armies were consolidated, and the cultures borrowed ideas freely. He even adopted Persian garb. One simple act, wearing pants instead of a toga, visually defined unification.

# DISCUSSION

Through effective enactment, Alexander's kingdom grew from a minuscule dominion in the north of modern day Greece to one of the largest empires the world has ever known. From his early actions of reframing intractable problems into solvable ones and thus securing his Asian base, to the formidable unification of Greece into a cogent identity, Alexander illustrates the process of enactment in dramatic fashion. His conquests had at their core not mere military might, but instead the reformation of problems, the effective use of symbolism, alliance building, and fostering of identity. Indeed, we argue that these processes proved more pivotal to his success than military prowess, as extraordinary as his generalship was.

As Alexander engaged in symbolism, by adopting garb of the Persian king, he sought and was mostly effective at unifying and integrating Greeks and Persians, their armies, and cultures. And as Alexander demonstrated concern toward the details of his soldiers' care and treatment, he fostered extraordinary loyalty among his troops, which served him well even when outnumbered by enemy troops. Returning to our four specific tools of enactment – reframing problems, manipulating symbols, building alliances, and identity – we can see in each the micro-level actions that determined large scale or macro-level effect on cultures, nations, and sustainable political boundaries.

As Alexander's wagons were burned, for example, at the Far East assembly, Alexander reframed the problem from one of severe limitation to a positive situation that promoted his own army's mobility. Concerning symbolism, Alexander and his troops adopted the very atypical practice of sacrificing to the local gods rather than the more typical pattern of looting and burning cities, although he was occasionally guilty of doing so for symbolic effect. This encouraged acceptance by the local populace and reduced Alexander's need to expend resources on garrisons.

*Limitations and Need for Further Studies*

While the case of Alexander provides a longitudinal illustration of the theoretical concept of enactment, we recognize certain limitations of our study. Most importantly, to explore enactment via history obviously takes us quite far from the controlled observation typical of the most unequivocal organizational research and into a realm of retrospect that is subject to interpretive analysis. While the events of Alexander's life and the impact of enactment processes are of the past and thus are open to a variety of interpretations, we offer that the vitality of the subject has lent itself to a vast array of study by reputable historians, many of whom have devoted a lifetime to painstaking review of sources, and comparative analysis. We can know with relative certainty that events transpired, that outcomes were real, and that actions were sustainable, as witnessed by many centuries of analyses.

Yet still, the historical method holds limits. We acknowledge that the passage of time and the obvious inability to engage in typical methods for review of enactment processes are real limits that cannot be erased. For instance, the dazzling display of leadership and enacted environment demonstrated in the Alexander case could be critiqued as the coincidence of historical events. History unfolds rather than merely happens and we believe we have demonstrated that history did not happen to Alexander, but was enacted by him. "His-story" is the story not of response to an environment, nor to defense, but of a truly constructed environment.

Our illustration of enactment is also in danger of being dismissed because it took place within a wildly different context than that which presents to modern organizational leaders. A less tamed environment may be perceived as more open to construction than today's "civilized" environments. Here, we remind that despite the modern viewpoint of some that ancient history was uncharted territory, the civilizations into which Alexander trod were indeed structured habitats, resplendent in norms, rules, hierarchies, and structures as well as in the military capacity to repel the unwelcome. In short, the tendency to accept the status-quo norms of ancient civilization would have been as formidable a constraint to a man such as Alexander as they are to any modern leader.

In addition, there is the argument that Alexander's success is not relevant because of the military capacity that supported it. While military prowess is not a tool of today's managers, resource prowess or control is generally assumed to be the pivotal component to success. We have argued that for Alexander, enactment processes often outweighed the mere display of military might. Numerous times, Alexander defeated nations that far outranked him in the resources of manpower, military capacity, and control. The analogy here is that resource access and control does not necessarily make the leader, predetermine the conqueror, or predict organizational survival.

As we have acknowledged, there is need for comparative work to explore the processes of enactment against a wider array of contexts. What is the balance, for example between environmental forces and enactment? What environmental factors might overcome the saliency of the cognitive reconstruction of problems, symbolism, alliance building, and identity formation? What is the role of context in shaping enactment, and the relative impact of leaders against competing enactments? These are questions that could be addressed in additional comparative analyses aimed at the examination of contextual variables. What is needed we believe are further historical studies to compare the events that leaders enacted as test and support of the theoretical underpinnings of enactment.

## The Power of Enactment

In limited scope, we have argued that the concepts and tools of enactment hold promise for managing in today's complex environments. Although contemporary managers face business competition rather than armed enemies, and employees rather than troops, the application of processes of enactment is nonetheless critical. Alexander, despite the obviously relevant contextual differences, offers an insight-provoking model for modern management and managers.

Enactment is an alternate paradigm for managers to use in thinking about their worlds. For many years, strategic management has been captive to the notion of analysis and response to environments. Yet, increasingly entrepreneurial behavior has been popularized, and we now suggest that the most successful entrepreneurs enact rather than merely respond to their environments. People in all walks of organizational life construct their environments, at least in part. Managers and leaders, in particular, do so with wider reaching implications. In any case, an environment is not a static, nor a given to react to, but instead is a constructed reality. Leaders and managers can benefit from the application of enactment theory, conceptualizing the environment as malleable and at least partly responsive to their actions.

Even as Alexander demonstrated the vitality of enactment, today's leaders and managers have similar resources at hand. Effective framing of problems, the use of symbolism, coherent alliance building, and the shaping of meaning and identity are very real tools with practical application. To take each in turn, in framing problems, leaders create and shape environments. How they reframe problems is critical toward acquiring support. As in the well-known example of Apple computer, for example, CEO Steve Jobs decided not merely to react to IBM, which at that time totally dominated the computer industry. Jobs and his partner Wozniak didn't want to create a better mainframe. Instead, they reframed the problem or need as one of putting personal computers on people's desks. Rather than building a better mousetrap, so to speak, they redefined the industry, by first reframing the problem.

Symbolism, too, is increasingly vital as a tool of building recognition and identity. The use of symbolism has long been widely accepted by marketing experts, and has been considered by organization scientists as useful for creating and sustaining organizational culture and for producing identity. Along with the promotion of symbolism, organizational identity is argued by some to be as relevant as resource control for sustaining organizational life. In the case of the telephone industry, for example, when Ma Bell broke into less centralized entities, the new organizations accepted being called "Baby Bells" as some evidence of the deeply entrenched identity fostered by the symbolic use of name (Thomas et al., 1993).

Finally, the building of effective alliances, as Alexander demonstrated vividly, is widely understood as an effective managerial tool against environmental uncertainty. We need only witness the prolific waves of merger and acquisition activity, and seemingly endless discussion of the creation of networks involving leveraged strengths, to appreciate the practical implication of this facet of enactment. For Alexander, building effective alliances both internally and externally was pivotal. He built rapport with his army which reciprocated with unwavering loyalty; he build alliances with the Persians, breaking down natural barriers; and as we discussed above, he returned a defeated king's territory to the king, as a means of building alliance for his longer range goals.

In closing, the concept of enactment enriches management theory and practice by suggesting that environments are not static and that organizations and their members need not simply react to them. Enactment is a non-linear, cyclic process whereby individuals act upon their environment to produce real change and then respond to the changed environment. Within the larger process of enactment, the process of reframing problems permits the reshaping of organizational and environmental realities. Likewise, the use of symbolism can reinvent an organizational culture and the response to a competitor as effectively as any resource. Identity building can create unity and common vision even within the discord that characterizes the current-day business world. And, effective alliance building, as a tool of enactment, is essential for success in today's climate of joint ventures, acquisitions, and mergers. Alexander's actions, analyzed as an historical case, validate each of these statements, and thus contribute toward improved understanding of the concept of enactment.

# NOTE

1. All major original works were consulted for this article as were prominent secondary sources, including: Arrian (1958 [circa 90AD]), Curtius (1984 [circa 40AD]), Diodorus (1933–1967 [first century BC]), and Plutarch (1959 [second century BC]), and the modern works of Tarn (1948), Fuller (1960), Fox (1973), Wilcken (1967), Lloyd (1981), May, Stadler, and Votaw (1984), Bosworth (1988), Green (1991), and O'Brian (1992).

# REFERENCES

Arrian (1958) [circa 90 AD]. *The Campaigns of Alexander* (trans. A. de Selincourt). Hamondsworth, U.K.: Penguin Books.

Bosworth, A. B. (1988). *Conquest and Empire*. Cambridge, U.K.: Cambridge University Press.

Cialdini, R. (1986). *Influence: Science and Practice*. New York: Harper & Row.

Curtius (1984) [circa 40 AD]. *The History of Alexander* (trans. J. Yardley). Hamondsworth, U.K.: Penguin Books.

Diodorus (1933–1967) [1st century BC]. *Diodorus of Sicily*, 12 Volumes (trans. C. H. Oldfather). London, U.K.: G. P. Punam's Sons.

Engels, D. W. (1978). *Alexander the Great and the Logistics of the Macedonian Army*. Berkeley, CA: University of California Press.

Fox, R. L. (1973). *Alexander the Great*. London, U.K.: Penguin.

Fuller, J. F. C. (1960). *The Generalship of Alexander the Great*. New Brunswick, NJ: Rutgers University Press.

Goffman, E. (1974). *Frame Analysis*. New York: Harper & Row.

Green, P. (1991). *Alexander of Macedon, 356–323 BC*. Berkeley, CA: University of California Press,

Lloyd, L. G. (1981). *Alexander the Great: Selections from Arrian*. Cambridge, U.K.: Cambridge University Press.

May, E. C., Stadler, G. P., & Votaw, J. F. (1984). *Ancient and Medieval Warfare*. Wayne, NJ: Avery Publishing Group.

Mead, G. H. (1934). *Mind, Self, and Society*. Chicago, IL: University of Chicago Press.

Meindl, J. R., Ehrlich, S. B., & Dukerich, J. M. (1985). The romance of leadership. *Administrative Science Quarterly, 30*, 78–102.

Meindl, J. R., & Ehrlich, S. B. (1987). The romance of leadership and the evaluation of organizational performance. *Academy of Management Journal, 30*, 91–109.

Meyer, J. W., & Rowan, B. (1978). Institutionalized organizations: Formal structure as myth and ceremony. *American Journal of Sociology, 83*, 340–363.

O'Brian, J. M. (1992). *Alexander the Great*. London, U.K.: Routledge.

Plutarch (1959) [2nd century AD]. *Lives of the Noble Greeks*. New York: Nelson Doubleday.

Pondy, L. R., & Mitroff, I. I. (1979). Beyond open systems models of organizations. In: B. M. Staw (Ed.), *Research in Organizational Behavior* (Vol. 1, pp. 3–39). Greenwich, CT: JAI.

Smircich, L. A., & Stubbart, C. (1985). Strategic management in an enacted world. *Academy of Management Review, 10*, 724–736.

Tarn, W. W. (1948). *Alexander the Great* (Vol. 1). Cambridge, U.K.: Cambridge University Press.

Thomas, J. B., Clark, S. M., & Gioia, D. A. (1993). Strategic sensemaking and organizational performance: Linkages among scanning, interpretation, action and outcomes. *Academy of Management Journal, 36,* 239–270.

Weick, K. E. (1977). Enactment processes in organizations. In: B. M. Staw and G. R. Salancik (Eds.). *New Directions in Organizational Behavior* (pp. 267–300). Chicago, IL: St. Clair Press.

Weick, K. E. (1979). *The Social Psychology of Organizing.* Reading, MA: Addison-Wesley.

Weick, K. E. (1988). Enacted sensemaking in crisis situations. *Journal of Management Studies, 25,* 305–317.

Wilcken, U. (1967). *Alexander the Great.* New York: Norton.

# COPING WITH HYBRID ORGANIZATIONAL IDENTITIES: EVIDENCE FROM CALIFORNIA LEGISLATIVE STAFF

Kimberly D. Elsbach

## ABSTRACT

*This article examines how long-term employees who work for an organization with a hybrid identity (i.e. containing stigmatized and non-stigmatized attributes) are able to develop and proclaim positive professional identities. Findings from a qualitative analysis of interviews, archival data, and self-identification artifacts from long-time California legislative staffers suggests that, despite the internal conflict inherent in their organization's identity, most of these employees maintain and display positive self-identifications based on their connections to the California Legislature. In particular, staffers display what might be called organizational "schizo-identification" (where the term schizo is defined as "a combining form meaning splitting, separating, cleavage" [Reber, 1988: 665]), in which they actively identify with some dimensions of the Legislature's identity and actively disidentify with others. Data indicate that staffers use a number of self-identification cues to affirm and display themselves as one of a few well-known types of "schizo-identifiers" within the Legislature. Staffers' ability to develop and proclaim such schizo-identifications with the organization appear to be aided by the obscurity and ambiguity of their professional identities, as well as by their*

Advances in Qualitative Organization Research, Volume 3, pages 59–90.
2001 by Elsevier Science Ltd.
ISBN: 0-7623-0772-2

*perceptions of the organization's identity and reputation as hybrid. These findings suggest a new cognitive adaptation that employees can use to maintain positive social identifications with organizations that possess internally incongruent organizational identities. In particular, schizo-identification processes appear to reconcile competing demands for self-verification vs. self-enhancement in social identification.*

# INTRODUCTION

*Social identity* is a person's self-concept based on his or her cognitive connections with social groups or organizations (Dutton, Dukerich & Harquail, 1994). *Social identifications* are the positive or negative links people perceive between their identities and the identity of a group or organization. While social identifications are defined as self-perceptions (Ashforth & Mael, 1989), a number of researchers have also suggested that people have an innate need to make others aware of these perceptions (Gollwitzer, 1986). Publicly claiming or displaying one's social identifications (e.g. publicly claiming to be a University of California professor, a Humane Society volunteer, or a Honda motorcycle rider) is referred to as *self-identifying* (Schlenker, 1986). Self-identifications, therefore, communicate to others one's self-perceptions about one's social identity.

Social psychological research suggests that people typically self-identify with social groups in ways that enhance both their private self-concepts and their public images (e.g. they advertise their affiliation with a winning football team by wearing team logos and colors; Cialdini et al., 1976). People also use self-identifications to distance themselves from group attributes or identity dimensions that threaten their private self-concepts and public images (e.g. black students distanced themselves from the black stereotype of "rap-music lover" when they feared that such a stereotype would also lead people to assume other stereotypical traits, such as low IQ; Steele & Aronson, 1995).

Similarly, research at the organizational level suggests that individuals self-identify in ways that either link them to prestigious organizations and/or high-status professions or distance them from negatively-perceived organizations or professions (Elsbach, 1999). For example, researchers have shown that organization members may publicly self-identify by conforming to behavioral norms of a favorably perceived employer (Ashforth & Humphrey, 1993), publicly criticizing the ideals of a negatively perceived organization (Elsbach & Bhattacharya, 1998), or dressing in ways that indicate affiliation with a high-status profession and distance from negative stereotypes of that profession (Pratt & Rafaeli, 1997).

Further, recent research suggests that individuals will act strategically in displaying self-identifications that reflect most positively on themselves. So, persons working for a negatively perceived organization may affirm and display positive social identifications with their professional group rather than with their organization (Kramer, 1993), while those working in obscure or stigmatized professions may affirm and display positive social identifications with their organizations rather than with their profession (Zabusky & Barley, 1997). For example, professional basketball players representing the chronically dismal Sacramento Kings may self-identify by displaying affiliation with the prestigious National Basketball Association rather than affiliation with the Kings, while custodians working for the White House may describe themselves as employees of that esteemed institution rather than as members of their commonly stigmatized profession (Bredar, 1996).

Together, the above findings suggest that, in situations where they have a choice, group or organizational members are likely to display self-identifications that affirm and enhance their private self-concepts and their public images and downplay or de-emphasize social connections that threaten those self-concepts and images. Yet, research has not examined self-identifications in situations where individuals face the dilemma of working for an organization whose identity is at once positive and negative. In particular, researchers have not examined the self-identifications of employees of organizations with *hybrid identities* (i.e. "composed of two or more [identities] that would not normally be expected to go together;" Albert & Whetten, 1985: 270), in which some aspects of the identity are stigmatizing and others are enhancing (e.g. working for a police department that has a good record of crime prevention, but also a history of corruption). Such organizational members may face impediments to developing positive social identifications in relation to their work.

First, employees of an organization that is partially stigmatized may be wary of self-identifying with their organization because of its negative reflection on their personal characters (Mael & Ashforth, 1992). For example, Dutton and Dukerich (1991) found that, following bad press about the organization's treatment of the homeless, formerly proud employees of the New York Port Authority became cautious about identifying themselves to outsiders as organizational members.

Second, many employees working in partially stigmatized organizations may find that external confirmation of their professional status is absent because they also work in stigmatized jobs. For example, Hood (1988) found that custodians often avoided contact with fellow workers as a means of distancing themselves from their profession. When such stigmatized employees work in partially stigmatized organizations, they may not have the option of relying on their professional identity to balance shortcomings in their organizational identities.

Despite these handicaps, employees who continue to work for an organization with a partially negative identity may find it necessary to cognitively justify their employment, especially if they are professionals who would presumably have opportunities to work for less controversial organizations. For example, a chemical engineer working for the conglomerate and tobacco giant, Phillip Morris, may wish to explain her obscure job to friends and family without connecting herself to the stigmatized organization with which she has spent a career. How might such self-identification be carried out? Some insight comes from research on stigmatized groups.

### Identity-Management and Stigmatized Groups

Research on stigmatized groups suggests that some group members may attempt to highlight within-group variation as a means of enhancing their own status relative to the most negatively perceived group members (Doosje, Ellemers & Spears, 1995; Goffman, 1963). As Doosje and Ellemers (1997: 260) contend:

> Stressing intragroup variation in unfavorable intergroup comparative contexts can also be considered a *personal*-identity protection mechanism. To the extent that people hold a favorable self-image, the idea that there is considerable variation within the ingroup offers scope to maintain this self-image, even when their group as a whole is seen as inferior to other groups.

Similarly, Goffman (1963: 107) suggests,

> The stigmatized individual exhibits a tendency to stratify his "own" [i.e. he sub-categorizes members within his ingroup] according to the degree to which their stigma is apparent and obtrusive. He can then take up in regard to those who are more evidently stigmatized than himself the attitudes the normals take to him. Thus do the hard of hearing stoutly see themselves as anything but deaf persons, and those with defective vision, anything but blind. It is in his affiliation with, or separation from, his more evidently stigmatized fellows, that the individual's oscillation of identification is most sharply marked.

In the same vein, work in the area of organizational "labeling processes" suggests that individuals may use a number of self-identification tactics to publicly distance themselves from stigmatizing labels they must privately acknowledge (Ashforth & Humphrey, 1995). Ashforth and Humphrey describe a number of "passing tactics" by which individuals may publicly distance themselves from the negative connotations of labels they wear:

> ... individuals with potentially stigmatizing personal histories (e.g. fired from previous jobs) or attributes (e.g. AIDS) may attempt to keep the stigma secret ... such individuals

may vehemently disparage similarly stigmatized people as a way of affirming their newly claimed identity . . . . Individuals who are stigmatized on the basis of age or occupation may defuse tension by making a self-deprecating joke or remark which tacitly acknowledges the stigma in a humorous light. (Ashforth & Humphrey, 1995: 449).

Together, these social psychological findings suggest that individuals who are known to be group members but wish to distance themselves from negative identities of those groups may use refined social labels, categorizations, and comparisons as means of communicating positive self-identifications. It seems possible, then, that such tactics might also be used by members of stigmatized organizations who wish to develop and display positive self-identifications in connection with their work. Yet, these processes have been rarely examined in organizational contexts, and they have not been examined in cases where professional group identifications are also improbable (i.e. in situations where people would choose not to identify with their profession because it was stigmatized or obscure).

In organizational settings, a member's ability to easily redefine or recategorize him or herself may be constrained by formal structures and rules and by informal norms that define the boundaries of categories to which he or she may belong (Carbaugh, 1996). For example, recent research has shown that members of low-ranking business schools were more likely to attempt to enhance the school's status by using alternate comparisons and categorizations of the school than to disconnect themselves from it (Elsbach & Kramer, 1996). Members' disuse of self-categorizations and self-labels may have been a consequence of the public's knowledge of the members' affiliations with the schools and of informal norms of "collegiality" that discourage status-enhancement through deprecation of one's colleagues. Any recategorizations or redefinitions of self that organization members do attempt may be limited to established categories within the organization (e.g. a professor may recategor-ize herself as a teacher vs. researcher, but not as a non-faculty member of the organization), providing little opportunity for creative redefinition by stigma-tized or obscure professionals (Zabusky & Barley, 1997).

The goal of this study is to determine *if and how organizational members who work for organizations with hybrid identities, containing both positive and negative attributes, are able to maintain positive self-identifications that include connections to their work.* In the following sections, I describe a qualitative field study of long-time California legislative staff I undertook to pursue this goal. Findings show that, despite the apparent contextual difficulties, most staff employees developed and communicated positive self-identifications that linked them to the California Legislature. I discuss these findings in terms of their implications for theories of social identity and self-affirmation (Ashmore & Jussim, 1997).

# METHOD

## Research Setting

I collected primary, qualitative data for this research at the Legislative Branch Offices of the State of California in Sacramento, California, during the spring of 1998. This time period was just prior to the June 2 election of State Legislators and coincided with a few months of intense media scrutiny of the California Legislature and its members. I collected additional archival data during the summer and fall of 1998, and spring of 1999.

At the time of this study, the California Legislature represented the largest state government in the United States and administered a $65 billion annual budget. It employed more than 3000 permanent staff members who served the 80 elected members of the State Assembly and 40 elected members of the State Senate. I chose this research setting because the California Legislature was widely known to the general public of California and had been a national role model in policy formation regarding crime prevention, social welfare, and environmental protection. At the same time, the California Legislature had been involved in several well-publicized events during the past ten years that threatened its reputation as a legitimate and prestigious institution (Decker, 1996). Public opinion polls published yearly by the *Los Angeles Times* revealed that, in response to bribery scandals involving state senators, chronically late state budgets that delayed government paychecks, and petty, partisan squabbling among legislators, public approval of the California Legislature ranged from an all-time low of 22% to a high of only 44% during the past 15 years. In general, in addition to praising their state's progressive programs on crime prevention and environmental protection, voters perceived the Legislature as embodying the worst of government stereotypes, i.e. self-interested contributors to the most inefficient and corrupt bureaucracy in the union (Decker, 1995, 1996).

At the same time, *staff members* who worked for the Legislature were fairly obscure to the general public. In interviews (see below), informants for this study confirmed that their family members were largely unaware of what they did at work and that explaining their jobs to outsiders was difficult due to the obscurity of their job titles (e.g. "policy director for Office of Appropriations"). Staff members consistently referred to their professional reputation as "non-existent," because most people could not identify the duties and status of a legislative staffer. As a result, for these staff members, a positive social identity that came from their work was most likely to be gained through connections to their organization – not their profession. These employees appeared to face a dilemma of needing to identify with an organization that was partially stigmatized.

## Informants

Informants consisted of 27 individuals (9 female, 18 male) who held long-term positions as staff members for the California Legislature. Legislative staff members work for a specific legislator or for the Legislature in general, and are involved in preparing and passing legislation, as well as supporting a legislator's campaign (they do not include housekeeping or secretarial staff). I chose long-term staff members because I believed that, during their 10 or more years of service, these individuals would have dealt with the Legislature's negative reputation and their own lack of a positive professional reputation among the general public. Informants' tenure at the Legislature ranged from 11 to 25 years and averaged 19 years. Informants' ages ranged from 31 to 56 years and averaged 45 years. Fourteen informants worked for the State Assembly and thirteen worked for the State Senate. Informants' job categories were: 7 professional consultants (e.g. tax consultants), 12 policy consultants (e.g. experts on environmental issues or individual member consultants), 3 chief counsels (i.e. lawyers), 3 institutional staff members (e.g. Assistant to the Speaker, Secretary of the Senate), and 2 personal staff members (e.g. individuals serving specific Assembly or Senate members). Informants were told that they were participating in a study of long-term staff members of the California Legislature that was aimed at understanding how they perceived themselves and their jobs, and how these perceptions had changed over time. All staffers who were approached accepted the invitation to participate.

## Qualitative Data Sources

### Informant Interviews
I conducted open-ended interviews lasting 60–90 minutes with each informant. I asked informants a series of open-ended questions designed to elicit their self-definitions as employees of the California Legislature. These questions focused on how staffers defined themselves to audiences both inside and outside the State Capital. I also asked informants about specific behaviors (e.g. open criticisms, self-labeling), displays (e.g. dress, choice of title), and personal

events (e.g. personal stands on important issues) that made salient their social identifications with the Legislature. Twenty-six of the twenty-seven interviews were tape-recorded and transcribed. The remaining interview was hand-transcribed.

### Archival Data

I collected all newspaper stories concerning public opinion of the California Legislature published from 1990–1998 in the *Los Angeles Times* newspapers. A total of 67 stories from these sources reported about the reputation of the California Legislature. Further, the *Los Angeles Times* published public approval ratings of the California Legislature at least once a year during this period.

### Artifacts

I collected business cards from each member and had them explain the choices they made in designing their cards and why they made those choices. Unlike many organizations, the California Legislature allows staffers numerous choices in the design of their personal business cards, including choice of: professional title (within a range of acceptable titles), personal information, inclusion of party affiliation and/or member affiliation, print color(s), plain or gold State seal, printer's stamp (i.e. Union printer's "bug" or nothing), and full-color photo of state capital or none. As a result of these personal choices, business cards provided further evidence of informant's "self-identification" with the California Legislature (Swann, 1987).

### Informant Questionnaire

Immediately following the interview, each informant completed a brief questionnaire designed to examine his or her identification and disidentification with the California Legislature and perceptions of his or her professional reputation and the reputation of the California Legislature among the general public. Two questions tapped perceptions of the California Legislature's reputation, two questions tapped perceptions of the reputation of the informant's job, three questions tapped perceptions of identification with the California Legislature, and three questions tapped perceptions of disidentification with the California Legislature. These questions were based on previous research on organizational identification and disidentification (Elsbach, 1999). This questionnaire was not used as a test of hypotheses but as a confirmation of informants' identification with their institution and perceptions of its reputation. Informants indicated how strongly they agreed or disagreed with statements on a nine-point Likert-type scale.

## Analysis

### Qualitative Data

Analysis followed an iterative approach, moving back and forth between the data and existing theory (Eisenhardt, 1989; Huberman & Miles, 1994). To begin, a research assistant and I searched interview transcripts and archival data for staffer statements about their perceptions of the Legislature's identity (i.e. its "perceived organizational identity;" Dutton, Dukerich & Harquail, 1994). Specifically, we searched for statements in the form: "The Legislature is X type of organization," "I view the Legislature as having X parts, these are . . . ," "The Legislature might be defined as X." These types of statements have been used in previous studies as indicators of organizational identity (Elsbach & Kramer, 1996). We found 102 instances of identity labels from this analysis and had an inter-coder reliability of 0.86 (Cohen, 1960). We also searched for evidence about informants' perceptions of the Legislature's reputation and their perceptions of their own professional reputations (i.e. the perceived external image of the Legislature and staffers; Dutton et al., 1994). In these cases, we searched for statements in the form: "People see the Legislature/staffers as X," "I believe people view the Legislature/staffers as X." We also searched for metaphors that informants used to synthesize these numerous identity dimensions. We found 36 comments about the Legislature's reputation and 27 comments about staffers' reputations, and inter-coder reliability here was 0.90.

In middle iterations, we focused on uncovering evidence of self-identification or disidentification with different dimensions of the Legislature's identity. We searched for "identification cues" (Swann, 1987) and self-affirmational accounts that informants displayed in their public communications, dress, business cards, self-descriptions, and accounts of self-defining moments in their legislative careers. In interview transcripts, we searched for identification claims in the form of: "I identify with X aspect of the Legislature," "I see myself as representing the X part of the Legislature," "I am X part of the Legislature," and "I do X to define myself to others." We also looked for claims of organizational disidentification in the form of: "I am not X," "It's important for me to be seen as distinct from X part of the Legislature," "I would never want to be mistaken as X." We found 78 instances of self-identification and 51 instances of self-disidentification from interview data, with an inter-coder reliability of .80 (for the entire set of data). In addition, 22 of the 27 informants noted identification cues on their business cards.

Finally, in later iterations, we searched for evidence of patterns in informants' identifications and disidentifications. Specifically, we searched for evidence that identifications and disidentifications were combined in strategic ways for staff in particular roles (e.g. those working on policy might have different patterns than those working on campaigns). We also searched for evidence that informants widely recognized these "types" of staffers.

*Questionnaire Data*

Members' mean identification scores, disidentification scores, and organiza-tional reputation ratings were calculated by averaging their responses to the three questions tapping identification and the three questions tapping disidentification. Lower scores indicate high agreement with attitude questions (e.g. high identification, good reputation), while higher scores indicate low agreement. Subjects' identification scores ranged from 2.5 to 7.5, with a mean of 5.45, and a standard deviation of 2.35. Subjects' disidentification scores ranged from 5 to 9, with a mean of 7.83 and a standard deviation of 1.86. These scores indicate a moderate amount of identification and a weak (but noticeable) amount of disidentification with the Legislature. Subjects' organizational reputation ratings (the average of the two organizational reputation questions) ranged from 4 to 6, with a mean of 5.37 and a standard deviation of 1.95, while their ratings of their professional reputations (the average of the two professional reputation questions) ranged from 1.5 to 7.5, with a mean of 4.68 and a standard deviation of 2.15. These scores indicate that subjects viewed the organization as having a neutral to slightly negative reputation, while their profession had a neutral to slightly positive reputation.

# RESULTS

In the following sections, I report the tactics and processes used by legislative staffers to maintain and affirm positive social identities over the course of their careers. I also describe and report the evidence I used to identify these tactics and processes. First, however, I will provide an overview and summary of my main findings.

In general, the results of my analysis suggest that long-term, professional staffers working for the California Legislature could, in fact, maintain positive identifications with their organization. These staffers appeared to simultane- ously self-identify and self-disidentify with components of the Legislature's organizational identity as a means of maintaining positive self-concepts and public images. For example, several staffers claimed both identification with the "policy-making" dimension of the Legislature and disidentification with the "partisan, political maneuvering" dimension of the Legislature. As a result, these staffers displayed what might be called organizational "schizo- identification" with the California Legislature.

Organizational schizo-identification appeared to be an adaptive cognitive response by staffers who found themselves working for an organization whose identity embodied both cherished values and the opposite of those values. Using a strategy similar to that used by members of low-ranking business schools (Elsbach & Kramer, 1996), Legislative staffers redefined their own social identities by highlighting variation *within* the organization's identity and connecting themselves to only the positive dimensions of that identity. What is new about their approach is that they also actively distanced themselves from negative dimensions of the organization's identity. As noted earlier, social psychologists have found that members of inferior groups may use a similar approach to redefining their identities (Doosje et al., 1995; Swann, 1987; Ashforth & Humphrey, 1995).

Such schizo-identifications appeared to be possible because: (1) staffers perceived the organization's identity and its reputation to be comprised of several distinct and occasionally dialectic dimensions (e.g. the Legislature combines conflicting ideals of Democrats and Republicans in the same house; public audiences revere the members they elect but blame the membership as a whole for inefficient government), and (2) staffers perceived their own professional identity to be obscure. Hybrid organizational identities and reputations allowed members to split their public self-identifications with the organization in ways that appeared "normal" to insiders and outsiders, and alleviated constraints on self-definitions that may occur in more congruently defined organizations. Further, members' obscure professional reputations made such self-identifications hard to refute.

In the following sections, I present three types of evidence related to the schizo-identifications claimed by staff members of the California Legislature. First, I present evidence about the perceived identity and reputation of the California Legislature, demonstrating the hybrid nature of staffers' perceptions of the institution. Second, I discuss specific tactics staffers used to publicly affirm such identifications. Finally, I describe four distinct types of "schizo- identifiers" that appeared among the California Legislative staff members based on their self-identifications.

### Perceived Organizational Identity and Reputation of the California Legislature

#### Perceived Organizational Identity

Interview and archival data suggest that staffers perceived the California Legislature's organizational identity to be "hybrid" (Albert & Whetten, 1985: 270), that is, "composed of two or more [identities] that would not normally be expected to go together." Albert and Whetten (1985: 271) suggest that "holographic" hybrid identities exist when "each internal unit exhibits the properties of the organization as a whole" while "ideographic" hybrid identities exist when "each internal unit exhibits only one identity."

In defining the identity of the California Legislature, informants appeared to view the organization as an ideographic type – made up of conflicting but separate identity dimensions. Further, many informants noted that these multiple and often conflicting dimensions were part of the design of representative government set down by the "founding fathers." These staffers used the metaphor of "a reflection of general American society" to describe the Legislature's identity. As one informant put it:

> We are in some ways the greatest reflection of our society, because we bring all of these people from across the state with very differing views about what our future ought to be. So this is the branch of government that should be the most confused and contentious.

Similarly, some staffers referred to the Legislature as a "high school," with well-defined niches of members representing diverse dimensions of human behavior. As one informant summarized, "It's like a high school that no one ever leaves. It has all these cliques of different kinds of people. You know, the policy wonks, the political hacks."

Although informants came from several different parts of the Legislature and used these different metaphors to conceptualize the Legislature's identity, there was consistency among informants about the central and distinctive dimensions that defined the organization: almost all informants identified the same four or five dimensions of the legislature's identity. Specifically, informants identified five distinct processes that were at the core of the Legislature's identity: (1) furthering broad ideals through *policy-making*, (2) promoting individual members through *political status endowment*, (3) creating law through *process expertise*, (4) supporting the tradition of *public service*, and (5) providing an arena for *partisan political sparring*. These five aspects were nicely summarized by a 20 + year veteran of the legislative staff. As he put it:

> There's the *policy side* and I put the committees there; there is the *political side* and I put the personal staff there who are supporting an individual member; there is the *process side*

which would include the legislative counsel staff and tax specialists, there is the *institutional functions* such as those who work for the desk or the Speaker, the Sergeant at Arms, and those who train new staffers and serve as role models; and then kind of in the shadows are the more *overtly political*, overtly partisan aspects . . . where people are doing very closed partisan campaigning and political maneuvering.

Similarly, another staffer explained:

I think that the public has this idea that everybody that works here is some sort of political hack. But there are very distinct divisions between people that are exclusively political – you know, working on partisan campaigns – and the ones that are exclusively policy makers. And there are some that go back and forth because they work as consultants for the entire Senate or because they work on a member's personal staff and have to know about policy issues and political issues. So there's the policies, the politicals, and the ones that go back and forth.

Perceived organizational reputation. Second, informants perceived the Legislature's reputation as split, with negative reactions directed at the "political" aspects of government institutions and positive reactions directed at the work of individual members and staffers who were viewed somewhat as "celebrities" working on important problems. As one informant put it, "I think there's a distinction between "those damn politicians" and "Oh, I'm meeting my assemblyman!" Even for people who despise the system. They often have good things to say about the representative they elected to the Legislature". Another echoed:

My experience has been that people actually think working in the Capital is cool. People say, "Oh, you must know something about politics," or "you must know something about law-making." I understand the general negative impression of the Legislature in the polls, but my personal experience is that people think, on an individual level, "Wow, that's neat."

Finally, one staffer explicitly recognized the split nature of the Legislature's reputation among the general public. As he noted,

The situation that members find themselves in when they're involved in a budget that runs late . . . . You know, you usually don't turn somebody around if they're angry about that because, in my view, the public definitely has a schizophrenic sense of how that problem should be resolved. On the one hand, they want the Legislature just to do their job goddammit. On the other hand, they really want them to stick up for what they believe in and not compromise just to get the thing passed on time.

These comments suggest that Legislature was viewed as having some "good people" but as being generally ineffectual, partisan, and self-serving. A recent editorial in the *San Francisco Examiner* nicely summarized this opinion in its condemnation of the Legislature's ballot initiatives but its praise of the local Senator who initiated one:

Maybe it's a negotiating tactic, but on its face the suggestion by state Senate President Pro Tem John Burton to let voters decide in November how to spend California's budget surplus comes across as simple dereliction of duty . . . . The Legislature's failure to tackle in a timely fashion such issues . . . has created an out-of-control ballot initiative process . . . . It's quite possible Burton's take-it-to-the-voters proposal is just a strategy to put some pressure on Governor Wilson and others pushing the car tax cut to back down . . . . Whatever the reason . . . asking voters to take on more decision-making duties about what should be the regular course of business in the state capital is just another reminder of how ineffectual the Legislature can be (June 12, 1998: A24).

### Schizo Self-Identification Tactics Used by California Legislative Staff

Based on the above evidence, I propose that the complex and dialectic nature of the California Legislature's identity and reputation, along with the obscurity of their individual professional identities, provided staff members with the opportunity to split their organizational identifications and disidentifications in self-enhancing ways. Researchers have shown that individuals who are given an opportunity to maintain a favorable self-image and are confident in their self-views will be proactive in their attempts to selectively verify their affiliations with social groups to themselves and others (Schlenker, 1986). William Swan and his colleagues, for example, defined a number of strategies individuals use to confirm their self-views, including: *interaction strategies* designed to elicit confirmatory feedback or to allow them to refute perceived misperceptions and physical *identity-cues*, such as dress, demeanor, display of material possessions, and titles (e.g. Swann, 1987). Such strategies are presumed to affect not only the displayer's self-views but also the views of audience members. As Pelham and Swann (1994: 355) suggest, "If targets do display such cues in their efforts to verify their identities, perceivers will find it easy to make use of these cues in their judgments."

Based on these findings, I suggest that Legislative staff members who had developed confident self-views over time would be likely to affirm these self-concepts by selectively affirming their connections to identity-enhancing dimensions of the Legislature, as well as their disconnections from identity-threatening aspects of the Legislature. Schlenker (1986: 23) defines such self identification tactics as ". . . the process, means, or result of showing oneself to be a particular type of person, thereby specifying one's identity." Consistent with this definition, I observed four distinct types of self-identification tactics used by California Legislative staff: (1) self-identification claims, (2) self-categorizations, (3) counter-stereotype behavior in the face of identity threats, and (4) artifact displays that affirmed organizational identifications. I define these tactics below.

*Self-Affirmations*

Schlenker (1986) describes a number of self-presentational claims people use to affirm a desired identity image. Some of these are defensive accounts, such as excuses ("it wasn't my fault"), justifications ("it was necessary"), or denials ("it didn't happen"), while others are proactive acclamations, such as enhancements ("it is better than you think") or entitlements ("I deserve more credit than I got"). A combination of self-affirming accounts and acclaims may be used to self-identify oneself through both connections and disconnections to a group or organization. For example, Aronson, Blanton and Cooper (1995) found that individuals who felt their positive self-concepts were threatened after they wrote an essay against services for disabled individuals publicly claimed identifications with positive traits that justified their behavior (e.g. a desire for objectivity) and claimed disidentifications with the standards that such behavior violated (e.g. standards of compassion). As they note:

> Successful self-affirmation might involve more than simply focusing on self-esteem resources. It may require doing so in a selective manner, focusing on those aspects of self that are unrelated to the threat (affirmational resources) and distancing oneself from related ones (behavioral standards) (Aronson et al., 1995: 987).

In this vein, California staffers answered the questions "what do you do?" and "how do you identify yourself?" with claims that affirmed both their organizational identifications (e.g. "I have to do with the policy-making process") and their organizational disidentifications (e.g. "I want to make it clear, you know, I don't have anything to do with the election process").

*Self-categorizations*

Self-categorizations help to define a person's identity by specifying the groups of which he or she is a member or non-member (Turner, 1987). Public self-categorizations as a means of self-identification have been observed in contexts where individuals feel they may be mistakenly included in an undesirable group or when they feel that their group may be unfairly perceived because important intragroup or intergroup distinctions are overlooked (Elsbach & Kramer, 1996; Goffman, 1963). In this manner, Crocker and Major (1989) describe how members of stigmatized groups ward off threats to their self-concepts by making salient category distinctions that most positively reflect on the group. They found that group members may label external critics as "prejudiced" rather than as legitimate evaluators and that they may focus attention on intragroup social comparisons as the only trustworthy referent group. Empirical studies of funeral directors, manual laborers, and juvenile delinquents illustrate these defensive self-categorizations as a means of redefining the stigmatized group as a counterculture (Charmaz, 1980; Collison,

1988; Kaplan & Johnson, 1991). As Ashforth and Humphrey (1995: 450) note:

> Indeed, a counterculture may transform a stigma into a badge of honor, such that the individual becomes motivated to act against the values and norms of the dominant culture. Repudiation of the dominant culture affirms his or her worth in the eyes of counterculture members and reconstituted self.

With respect to the current study, legislative staffers used self-categorizations to make clear distinctions between several commonly confused groups (e.g. "policy wonks" vs. "political hacks," "public officials" vs. "private profession-als") and to enhance the status of their groups by suggesting comparison groups (e.g. "we're part of a dying breed of career staffers who care more about the institution than our own political aspirations").

### Identification stands

Extreme attitude claims and behaviors might be used as public "identification stands" to communicate group or organizational identifications and dis-identifications when such social connections are in question. In this vein, Claude Steele and his colleagues (Spencer & Steele, 1994; Steele, 1988; Steele & Aronson, 1995) have examined the behavior of group members who fear they may confirm a negative stereotype about their group by displaying other ingroup traits ( i.e. members who face a *stereotype threat*). For example, Steele and Aronson (1995) examined the behavior of Black students who faced the threat of confirming a negative stereotype about their intellectual ability (in comparison to White students) in taking a verbal-skills test. The findings showed that Black students who experienced stereotype threat were more likely to distance themselves from other "Black" traits, such as claiming preference for rap music (vs. classical or jazz) and basketball (vs. baseball or boxing). The findings suggest that individuals facing threats to a positive self-concept will engage in "stereotype avoidance" by displaying extreme counter-stereotype behavior or attitudes. In related research on intergroup perceptions, researchers have found that when group identification is salient individuals will respond to self-esteem threats by displaying more extreme attitudes toward the outgroup than if group identification is not salient (Meindl & Lerner, 1984).

   In the current study, I found that staffers who feared that they might confirm negative stereotypes of the Legislature (e.g. "I think the public thinks of us as a combination of demi-god fat cats and inefficient bureaucrats") appeared to distance themselves from this stereotype by engaging in counter-stereotypical behavior and by becoming more extreme in their distancing from the stereotype. For example, long-time staffers often discussed how important it was that they be seen as non-political and not in search of an elected office. As one put it:

> We sort of put them on a pedestal; we bow down to them, and they respond as anybody who's put on a pedestal, they become slightly larger than they really should be, and it's sort of part of the tradition. For example, we have to send things up to a member quietly, through a sergeant. We jealously guard our inability to walk up to the senators on the floor.

## *Self-Identification Markers*

Finally, there are a number of visible and symbolic markers that individuals may display to identify themselves publicly (Dittmar, 1994). For instance, researchers have examined the use of dress (Pratt & Rafaeli, 1997; Rafaeli, Dutton, Harquail & Mackie-Lewis, 1997) and office design (Orstein, 1989) as means of identifying one's social status, values, and roles. In addition, markers such as dress may be used to display identification with one dimension of an organization's identity (e.g. rehabilitation in hospitals) and disidentification with another (e.g. acute care in hospitals). As one informant in Pratt and Rafaeli's (1997: 878) study of nursing dress put it, "The philosophy behind [street clothes] is based on the fact that we want patients to see a distinct difference between the acute care unit and the rehabilitation unit".

Among California legislative staff, business cards often served as an effective identity marker. As indicated previously, staff members had a great deal of flexibility and choice in how their cards were designed. The meaning of such choices was much more apparent to the staff members themselves than to most outsiders. Nevertheless, the markers were important to many staffers as an indication of their organizational identifications. As one staffer put it:

> I chose not to have a state seal or senate seal and in particular chose not to have a gold seal on it. And I think a lot about and talk a lot to my colleagues about the role of staff versus the role of member. And so I don't want to put on airs so I don't want the seal on there. I just don't want to be flashy. I don't want to leave the impression that I'm presuming something.

Together, legislative staffers used the four self-identification tactics described above to publicly display and affirm their schizo-identifications with the California Legislature. Data suggest that these schizo-identifications defined each staffer as one of four widely-known types of "schizo-identifiers." I describe these types next.

### *Types of Schizo-Identifiers Among California Legislative Staff*

Proponents of "Labeling Theory" (Ashforth & Humphrey, 1995) suggest that tactics like those defined above are commonly used in the maintenance of social labels that define, demarcate, and make sense of the social environment. In turn, these social labels may distinguish ingroups from outgroups and may be "used as a foil to help crystallize one's own identity and status" (Ashforth & Humphrey, 1995: 422).

Along these lines, informants routinely (at least once in every interview) labeled themselves and their co-workers as one of four recurring types of "schizo-identifiers" present among California legislative staff. These labels were well-known by all informants and were commonly used to categorize and compare groups of staffers. Based on informants common use of terms, I define these labels as: (1) the policy "wonk", (2) the institutionalist, (3) the "professional" staffer, and (4) the political "hack." All of these labels (or versions of them) were used repeatedly by staffers to identify themselves and their colleagues, and appeared to coincide with the five organizational identity dimensions defined above (i.e. "policy wonks" identified with the policy ideals dimension, "institutionalist" identified with the public service dimension, "professional staffers" identified with the law-making dimension, and "political hacks" identified with both furthering member ideals and political sparring). Illustrations of these types of schizo-identifiers and the tactics used to affirm them are discussed below.

*The Policy "Wonk"*

The most common type of schizo-identifier (representing about half of the informants) was the policy wonk. A policy wonk is a staffer dedicatedto and identified with policy ideals and policy-making in line with personal ideals (e.g. environmental policy) and distanced from and disidentified with political maneuvering among members that often compromises those ideals (e.g. campaign politics and personal deal-making).

In many cases, informants noted that the policy ideals with which they identified were the dimensions of state government that brought them to work in the Capitol in the first place. Thus, their schizo-identifications as policy wonks were a means of maintaining their original "visions" of the organization's identity despite their knowledge of its less idealistic political side. For example, one staffer described his open support for policy that ran in the face of his Republican bosses as merely affirming his "intellectual honesty" in this self-identification claim:

> One of the reasons why I'm working for the Democrats now is I think I really burned bridges. I think at some point you can't keep flipping off the larger Republican common good and not have consequences, so when the Democrats lost the leadership the Republicans just weren't ever going to hire me. But part of bitching about it in such a overt way is that in some ways I thought of it as, well just being intellectually honest.

Similarly, another staffer noted his outspoken ideals about advocacy for the poor in this account of counter-stereotype behavior:

> There is a group of cities in California that are sort of relatively wealthy populations, that are relatively well-funded, and they always get special deals. And I have opposed them and opposed them and opposed them because it's not right. And they beat me up all the time. Mostly when I was working for Senator X and there were times that she would say, "Look, I know you don't like it, but it's not going to make a difference. I know what you're going to say; I know it's bad policy; I'm still going to vote for it." But I still wrote the analysis for the bill that says this is stupid, and it's really stupid, and it's really really really stupid and here are 15 reasons why it's stupid and it's still stupid. And they passed the bill every time. I think it allowed me to feel righteous, which is not anything I'm terribly proud of, but it did make me feel righteous. You've gotta speak up for the communities that are poor – and we have wealthy suburban, mostly White communities, and we have poor rural Latino communities that are just going down the toilet, and nobody's standing up for what's right. At least I will, even if I'm going to get rolled on it.

In addition to affirming their connections to policy ideals, policy wonks also affirmed their disidentifications with partisan politics. As one staffer put it in this self-identification claim:

> I've disassociated with member politics. I stay out of the member business. I don't get into their disputes and their collusions and that whole thing. I completely stay out of it. I call it member land. I stay out of member land. You know, some of the other stuff, which goes on all the time is, you know, petty differences between members; you know, Senator so and so did something to really piss me off, so I'm not going to vote for his bill or you know, okay well when he brings the bill to my committee I'm going to do this and that. And that goes on all the time.

Several staff members noted that this distance from the political side of the Legislature also gave them a kind of freedom to speak the truth that was not always available to elected members. This "straight shooting" was a means of affirming both their distinction from elected members who were involved in politics and their apparent rationality in choosing such an identity. One informant explained this self-categorization:

> There are members that I have been approached to help and I've said no. Either because of a stance that they've taken on something that is contrary to what I believe or their approach is one that would leave a perception that they are on one side of an issue when they are not. And that's the other thing that I think is kind of different about me, is that I am not so afraid to do what I need to do and to push for things that I need to push for that I'm going to hold back because I think it means my job. You know, I can either be recognized for what I do and move across or move down, and so there's always [selling jewelry at] Mervyn's. And so, and it's kind of a wonderful kind of freedom because there are a lot compromises that I'm just not going to make. There is a difference between the things that members have to do politically and the things that I have to do.

Another staffer echoed that theme:

I also think it's extremely important to work for somebody you respect. I've thought that to myself many times, "how can she work for him?" Because he just has a bad reputation and he's not one of the ones you feel like you really can feel proud helping to keep them in office.

Several policy wonks also disidentified with working on issues that were connected to political campaigns or campaign funding for special interest groups. As one staffer recalled in this self-categorization:

You know, there's a certain segment of the policy-making process that's pretty sleazy, pretty questionable. And I do my best to stay away from that. I don't like to work on those bills. Most of the bills that I've worked on are not "juice bills," as that term is used. That is, they don't involve big insurance companies; they don't involve trial lawyers; they don't involve horse racing or gambling or liquor licenses. So people don't get a lot of money for them. The *California Journal* came up with the *juice index*, which is a very clever way of measuring the unmeasurable. They looked at the campaign contributions for each member and then clustered them by committee, and then divided the total by the number of members, and that was your juice index. And at that time, there were 22 policy committees and mine came in at 22 out of 22. And I was proud to point out that I was working for the least juiced committee of that index. At the time, that was one of my defenses to criticisms about excessive campaign contributions: "Hey, no, wait a minute, let me tell you who I work for . . . the guys I work for can't even raise money!"

Finally, one staffer noted that the interference of politics with policy ideals was what led to the "hemorrhage point," where he distanced himself from much of the politics of state government.

I was never cynical about the place. What changed that was as part of the budget solution in '92 or '93, we took money from local government and I was the one who originally proposed that, and from the governor on down said, I said, "You cannot take this much money out of the local government system unless you give some expenditure relief." Because that is sort of an equation that has to get balanced. And everyone, from the Governor on down, said, "You're right, we gotta take care of local government on the expenditure side, but first we have to take the money." And as soon as they got the money, all of them forgot about the local governments, and for me that was the real hemorrhage point. Since then, it has been hard to feel good about a lot of the politics that are a part of this place, when you know your work is gonna get so compromised.

*The Institutionalist*
An "institutionalist" was defined by informants as a staffer who had been with the Legislature an especially long period of time (over 20 years). Informants also noted that institutionalists commonly identified with the traditions of the Capitol and the public service ideals of state government and disidentified with the self-promotion and fame-seeking of what they saw as short-sighted, politically ambitious staffers and members. Institutionalists represented a small number of informants (less than 20%), but were recognized and identified by nearly all the informants.

Several self-described institutionalists noted that they believed they were a valuable asset to the Capitol because of their institutional memory, which was significantly longer than that of most members since term limits were imposed for state legislators. They saw this role of "guardian of traditions" as an important part of their identities. One staffer noted",Some of the stereotypes of government as being an old boys' network are still true. But the thing that keeps me from being crazy is that those of us who bring a social conscience into the institution, so that it's not as bad as it would be". Another staffer recounted, "I relate myself more as a teacher than I do a staff person. My goal would be to encourage as many new young faces to come in here regardless of party and kind of keep the traditions of this place alive". Finally, one staffer recalled a counter-stereotype behavior that she enacted as a means of promoting traditions of professionalism and decorum in the Capitol:

> On a day-to-day basis I would say I try to be more considerate, more thoughtful, and more professional in relaying communications than the way something was put to me. A member might say "tell them to take a flying leap." And I would go back and say, "We really appreciate your offer, but so-and-so really doesn't feel that it fits with this bill." Quite frankly, there isn't a high stake put on that anymore around the Legislature.

In other cases, staffers noted that contributing to public service was important to their self-esteem, and they often reminded others and themselves of this with their self-presentations. For example, one staffer discussed the significance of social markers on his business cards:

> Although I work for him, I choose not to have the committee chair's name on my card. I want to be identified as working for The Committee. So I'm an institutionalist and I don't want people to think that I'm here because of Senator Campbell or Senator Bergeson or Senator Schear or Senator Lee or Senator Craven. Although that is certainly true. But I don't want to portray the image that I work only for the Senator, but instead, that I work for the committee, for the Senate. It gives me a sense of my identity. That my loyalty is to The House and the state it serves. I just told someone else today that I'm an old-fashioned committee consultant. And proud of it.

An important aspect of being an institutionalist was to distance oneself from staff and elected members who appeared to have a single-minded desire for fame and celebrity at the cost of tradition and the ideals of public service. For instance, several institutionalists distinguished themselves from politically ambitious and immodest staffers. As one self-categorized:

> There is staff and there is staff. I mean, a lot of staff, like many of the members, are here because being in politics is kind of neat. You get to go to events with important people. You know, they are immodest people with much to be modest about, let me assure you. That's the worst kind

Similarly, another staffer discussed his choice of business card as a social marker that distanced him from immodest, "Johnny-come-lately" staff.

Having a plain business card for me is kind of like what the British soldiers in the Great War called "reverse snobbery." So as I understand it, guys would enlist who had pedigrees, hereditary titles, and would enlist as privates even though they could have gone in as officers or something because it was reverse snobbery. And so it's a form of inverted arrogance if you will.

### The Professional Staffer

Professional staffers described themselves as individuals who played an important role in the process of law-making, without being tied to any particular political ideals or member platforms. Similar to policy wonks, professional staffers were common, representing about a third of all informants. Professional staffers identified with the mechanics of law-making and disidentified with member politics and self-promotion.

More than any other type of schizo-identifier, professional staffers identified with being a critical part of the process of law-making that was the primary business of the Legislature. In particular, they thought of themselves as indispensable to both parties and to both the Senate and Assembly because of their expertise in "working the system." This expertise and its connection to moving bills through the Legislature was the thing they most often noted in self-identifications. As one staffer put it:

I enjoy and identify with process of just how it is that we go about making the law. And that has its own dance, as you know. And because there are so few people here like Chris and I, who have been involved in this process more than ten years, I think that in some ways that makes our jobs even more enjoyable because we recognize we are part of the dwindling group who actually have a lot of knowledge about how this place "ticks" as a matter of process in getting things done.

Similarly, another self-identified:

It is our job to find a way of telling the truth about the bullshit that goes on around here. And that's one of the things that we do our best to do without being offensive . . . but we're generally into saying what a bill does in our analyses. We're able to be fairly direct, and once in a while, we get a little bit rowdy. But, you can do that as a staff member, and a Senator could never do something like that.

Finally, a third staffer explained that he was overtly non-partisan and non-political in providing advice. As he noted in this counter-stereotype action:

When I'm meeting a senator who works for the opposite party of my direct boss, I go in and say "I'll tell you, if you wanted to vote for this bill, three things you could say in committee, but I bet you're going to vote against it, and here are three things you could say to justify that position." And he'd laugh and we'd laugh at each other. And he came to appreciate that. I know, because I've talked with him and his staff about that. He appreciates it. So he knows I'm going to give him a pretty straight shot on the bill and if there's something there that affects him, or might affect him, we're going to tell him that.

Because professional staffers identified with being fair and non-partisan in their work, they disconnected themselves from the partisan political activities of the Legislature. As one noted in this self-identification claim:

> One of the worst things that can happen is that some member stands up and says, "See this right here? This is not objective. This is political." That has never happened to me, you know, where I've been shredded for something that I wrote.

Similarly, another staffer claimed", I don't bullshit with them and I don't lie and I don't have an agenda. I don't care for my personal views to become reality. My personal views are unimportant totally. My job is to help them do what they want".

In addition to disidentifying with partisan politics, professional staffers strongly disidentified with being in the limelight. That is, they disidentified with the celebrity-seeking members and legislators. This disidentification is nicely illustrated by the following self-categorization by one staffer:

> A big difference between members and committee staff is that the trappings of power and prestige and money and so on aren't things that motivate legislative staff. They are people that are essentially idealistic. They like the idea of sharing in decision-making and get satisfaction out of reading in the paper about something that they worked on, but it's not important that their name is on it.

Another staff member echoed this identification:

> I do try to avoid the limelight and I'm somebody who is horrified if my name is ever mentioned in the paper. I think most people here do take pride in what they do. There are some, I don't know what the percentage is, who feel that self-promotion, self-recognition, is what they're really here to accomplish. From time to time, there's a staffer who rises apart . . . who . . . sort of appears to be self important and is referred to as the 41st senator, something like that, and it's not a compliment.

Finally, one staffer recalled an important and difficult decision that, she suggested, affirmed her disconnection from the fame-seekers at the Capital. As she remembered this counter-stereotype behavior:

> A while back the *California Journal* was doing a story on "movers and shakers" among legislative staff, and they wanted to take a picture of these staff members on the floor of the Senate. My boss wanted me to be in the picture. I would have been the only woman in the picture, which would have served as a role model for other women staffers, and it would have been good exposure for my boss. But I knew if I was on the cover I would be seen as someone who has political ambitions and wants to be in the limelight, and that wasn't me. So, against great pressure, I refused.

The political "hack." Finally, a few long-term staffers defined themselves as "political hacks." Political hacks appeared to be rare among long-time staffers because they were usually linked to a specific member, who, with the advent of term limits, would eventually leave office. Similarly, informants identified only a few political hacks among their co-workers. Political hacks identified with member politics, especially forwarding the policy ideals of their member or their party. At the same time, they disidentified with the mundaneness of the mechanics of law-making – referring to such a job as "being like the furniture."

Staff members who self-identified as political hacks saw member politics as an important part of moving forward the ideals of that member and his or her party. To these staff, then, member politics was a more proactive means of pushing policy ideals than merely consulting on bills or, worse yet, working as a professional staff member who provided technical advice. As one idealistic staffer noted:

> It's all about gamesmanship. The Democrats want to make the Republicans look bad and the Republicans want to make the Democrats look bad, and you know, unquestionably there's political maneuvering going on. But a lot of the time it stems from the fact that the Republicans want to solve the problem this way, and Democrats want to solve the problem this way. It's just that it's two fundamentally different ways of approaching it.

Another staffer found it important to self-identify with a political party or individual member as a means of status-enhancement. For example, one staffer described his self-identification through social markers on his business card:

> When the Republicans took over the majority and I took over as chief consultant of the X Committee, I made a point of having the gold seal on our business cards. We pay $35 out of our own pocket for that. And it was important for totemic reasons. The Republicans had not had the majority in 25 years. We needed to establish a perception that this wasn't an aberrant activity. We needed to show that from day one, the day we took over formal control of the committees. So I was very punctilious about that on letterhead, on business cards, on everything where we let it be known far and wide that, you know, this was not an aberration . . . . I also don't have a union "bug" on my card. The union bug is sort of a sign of a democratic staffer, and I'm not.

To political hacks, being part of the political process was also an obligation of a staff member. To ignore politics and political considerations was to pretend that they weren't important to one's member, who was, after all, one's boss. Thus, many political staffers publicly disidentified with professional or policy staffers who appeared "above politics" in their self-identification. As one personal staff member argued:

> But there are, in terms of staff people, you also have your committee consultant types, who just think that they're in an ivory tower, policy-wise. They are very reluctant to step into the political realm in any way and I am once again very critical of that. You need to understand the consequences of being able to say, "If you vote this way, you're going to lose your next election." And there are some people who say . . . they swear off of that . . . they say, "I wash my hands of that" "I'm not involved" and I think they do a disservice to their members, and I'm very outspoken about that. I think that's just wrong.

Finally, there are personal staffers whose identification with the personal political ideals of the member they work for helps them to distinguish and distance themselves from staffers who worked for less revered members. For example, one policy wonk disidentified with the political hacks, referring to them as "crazy members." As she put it:

> We all kind of refer to ourselves as Team [Member X]. So, when things happen that aren't so good, that's not really who you are. You're Team [Member X], you're not involved with the crazy members. I mean, a lot of staff seem like the furniture. They're going to stay and a new member will walk through the door and they will just adopt their point of view. I'm not like that. I just don't really feel like I could just take on the political views of any member.

# DISCUSSION

The data presented in this study suggest that obscure professionals in chronically stigmatized organizations can and will claim organizational schizo-identifications as a means of protecting and affirming a positive self-concept, especially if the organization's identity and public reputation are also perceived as hybrid. Legislative staffers appeared to use a number of self-identification tactics to display and publicly affirm both their identifications and disidentifications with the Legislature's organizational identity. The particular combination of identification and disidentification displays helped to categorize them into one of several widely-known types of schizo-identifiers who mimicked the hybrid nature of the organization's identity and reputation in their own self-identifications.

While early theories of social identity allow for "weak" group or organizational identifications (Mael & Ashforth, 1992), as well as the possibility of identification with specific aspects of an organization's identity (Albert & Whetten, 1985), these models did not allow for simultaneous identifications and disidentifications with a single organization. That is, they did not allow for what might be called organizational *schizo-identification*. The results of the present study provide some of the first empirical evidence that such schizo-identification may exist and may be used to cope with internally incongruent organizational identities. The existence of simultaneous cognitions of oneness and separateness between an organization's and a person's identity presents a new explanation for several social psychological processes, especially the adaptive and strategic uses of social categorization.

*Theoretical Implications of Organizational Schizo-Identification*

The present study may help to expand understanding of individuals as flexible and strategic cognitive adapters who can creatively self-enhance and self-verify their identities even when these goals appear improbable or in conflict. In particular, it may add to our understanding of how individuals deal with: (1) competing goals in self-definition, (2) stereotype threats, and (3) self-presentational dissonance.

*Competing Goals of Self-Verification and Self-Enhancement*
Recent research suggests that the processes of self-verification and self-enhancement operate separately, with the former motivated by needs for predictability and control and the latter motivated by needs for self-esteem maintenance (Swann, Stein-Seroussi & Giesler, 1992). In support of this notion, a number of studies have replicated the finding that people with negative self-concepts seek out unfavorable evaluations and interaction partners, while people with positive self-concepts seek out positive evaluations and interaction partners (Swann, Pelham & Krull, 1989; Swann & Read, 1981; Swann et al., 1992). Apparently, individuals with negative self-concepts have little need for self-esteem maintenance (i.e. because their self-esteem is low) but maintain needs for predictability and control. For these individuals, accurate and self-verifying appraisals are more important than positive appraisals (Swan et al., 1992). In contrast, individuals with positive self-concepts desire both, and choose evaluations that are both positive and verifying (Swann, 1987).

With respect to the current study, these findings suggest that obscure professionals working in stigmatized organizations but who nevertheless perceive themselves positively (i.e. as in the case of legislative staffers) will seek to affirm these positive self-concepts and verify their particular self-views. The present findings suggest that staffers may have attempted to do this through schizo-identification with the Legislature. First, by retaining an identification with the "positive part" of the Legislature's identity, staffers were likely to encounter self-verifying views of themselves from other similarly identified staffers. Second, by retaining a disidentification with the "negative part" of the Legislature's identity, staffers were likely to encounter self-enhancements from outside audiences. If staffers only cared about their self-esteem, one might predict that they would distance themselves from the organization as a whole, ensuring that they were not mistakenly attributed the organization's stigma. Similarly, if staffers only cared about self-verification, they might not worry about distancing themselves (i.e. disidentifying) from negative aspects of the organization's identity and merely focus on their identifications. Thus, the use of schizo-identification by members of stigmatized organizations appears to provide further evidence that individuals with positive self-concepts will seek out both self-enhancements and self-verifications in their self-concept maintenance. Further, it expands these models by suggesting a new mechanism through which individuals facing the threat of stigma can maintain consistency and verifiability in their self-concepts while also enhancing self-esteem.

*Stereotype Threats*
Claude Steele's work on stereotype threat suggests that individuals who feel they may confirm a negative group stereotype on one dimension may attempt to counter such a threat by distancing themselves from other dimensions of the stereotyped group, even if those dimensions are positive (Steele & Aronson, 1995). Stereotype threats may be especially salient to organizational members, such as Legislative staffers, whose professional identity is unknown or vague and whose organization members are subject to a well-known stereotype. In these situations, categorization research suggests that observers may use an automatic categorization process in which they match the person to a stereotype of an organization member (Fiske & Neuberg, 1990). Researchers have shown that observers will only categorize items in comparison to an actual exemplar of a category (i.e. an actual organization member) if they have seen one recently and do not have a well-established category prototype in mind (Elsbach & Simon, 1992).

Yet, the current findings provide an alternative response to distancing oneself from an entire organization in an attempt to counter a stereotype threat. Schizo-identification may be used by individuals to selectively distance themselves from the negative dimensions of the stereotype while maintaining a connection to the more positive dimensions. As noted earlier, such a response may depend on an individual's perception of the organization's identity and reputation as multi-faceted or "split" in nature. Thus, the stereotype of an organization member may also be hybrid in nature.

*Dissonance in Self-Presentation*
Recent research has examined how individuals cope with self-presentations that are counter to their known selves (Banjai & Prentice, 1994). Interestingly, this research suggests that individuals can display disidentification cues at the same time they are engaging in identifying behavior. For example, Fleming and Rudman (1993) found that individuals reading a counter attitudinal speech against affirmative action in the presence of an African-American audience displayed both verbal and non-verbal cues (e.g. disclaimers, body-language)

that communicated their discomfort and distance from the espoused views. This behavior was found to reduce the speakers' dissonance about the speech and reduce attitude changes in favor of the speech. Similarly, Goffman (1963: 109) describes the codes of conduct engaged in by stigmatized individuals, which include a "desirable pattern of revealing and concealing." As he notes:

> The stigmatized individual is asked to act so as to imply neither that his burden is heavy nor that bearing it has made him different from us; at the same time he must keep himself at that remove from us which ensures our painlessly being able to confirm this [stigmatized] belief about him (Goffman, 1963: 122).

In the same manner, the present study identifies a number of schizo-identification cues that legislative staffers displayed to make clear both their identifications and disidentifications with the identity of the California Legislature. Thus, taking a stand against having one's name published on news releases and passing out plain, unpretentious business cards may be used as cues by staffers to other organization members and outsiders that they are not a part of the celebrity-seeking, political aspects of the Legislature, even though they work there. In fact, many staffers noted that the identity stands they took "allowed them to sleep at night" even though they may have caused them hassles at work.

### Practical Implications of Organizational Schizo-Identification

Because organizational schizo-identification allows individuals to manage their cognitive connections to organizations with internally contradictory identities, they provide an adaptive solution to individuals in identity predicaments. In particular, schizo-identifications may be adaptive to individuals who work in organizations with hybrid identities that provide both identity enhancements and identity threats.

A large amount of psychological research suggests that group distinctiveness is an important aspect of a group's identity and its attractiveness to potential members (Brewer, 1991; Turner, 1987). That is, being recognized as a member of a unique group is self-enhancing and desirable. In response, individuals who want to preserve the perceived distinctiveness of their social identities by linking themselves to a highly distinctive group have been shown to "accentuate their prototypicality as group members in order to reassert their common identity as members of a distinct group" (Doosje & Ellemers, 1997: 267).

Yet, many organizations possess multiple identity dimensions on which they claim to be distinct. That is, many organizations are defined by hybrid identities (Albert & Whetten, 1985). While hybrid identities may provide members with flexibility in how they define their connections to an organization (Aronson, Blanton & Cooper, 1995), they may also provide dilemmas for members who wish to actively separate themselves from dimensions of the organization. Members of such organizations may feel considerable ambivalence about linking themselves to the organization as a whole.

One can imagine a number of groups whose members are ambivalent about group identification. For example, cancer survivors may be torn between identifying as "survivors" and disidentifying as "cancer patients." This may explain, in part, why cancer patients take great pains to differentiate themselves from the most severe cases, thus, distancing themselves from the most negative implications of being a cancer survivor (Taylor, Lichtman & Wood, 1984; Wood, Taylor & Lichtman, 1985). Similarly, minority students attending universities with affirmative action admissions policies may feel ambivalence toward identifying as a minority-group student. On one hand, they may wish to identify with other minority students because the group is viewed as successfully overcoming obstacles toward admission and providing role models to other group members. On the other hand, they may wish to disidentify with the group because it reminds people of the "special circumstances" under which they gained admission (Steele, 1992).

The current findings suggest that both group and organizational members can adaptively self-identify themselves in ways that help them cope with their ambivalence about linking themselves to hybrid identities. By claiming and displaying one's schizo-identification with an organization, a person selectively connects himself or herself to distinctive identity dimensions that he or she values (e.g. policy-making) and selectively emphasizes positive social comparisons between organization members (e.g. idealistic policy wonks vs. partisan political hacks). At the same time, schizo-identification allows members to distance themselves from the negative aspects of a hybrid organizational identity without appearing irrational or internally incongruent themselves.

# CONCLUSION

Recent research on social identity in organizations suggests that, rather than being constrained by the formal role requirements and organizational norms dictated by the organization, organizational members consistently act in cognitively adaptive and creative ways to develop and maintain positive and consistent self-concepts (Dutton & Dukerich, 1991; Elsbach & Kramer, 1996; Zabusky & Barley, 1997). The present study confirms and extends this notion by providing evidence that individuals in highly stigmatizing contexts can, nevertheless, adaptively create and display social identifications that help them to maintain a positive self-concept.

# REFERENCES

Albert, S., & Whetten, D. A. (1985). Organizational Identity. In: L. L. Cummings, and B. M. Staw (Eds.), *Research in Organizational Behavior* Vol. 7, (pp. 263–295). Greenwich, CT: JAI Press.

Aronson, J., Blanton, H., & Cooper, J. (1995). From dissonance to disidentification: Selectivity in the self-affirmation process. *Journal of Personality and Social Psychology, 68*, 986–996.

Ashforth, B. E., & Humphrey, R. H. (1995). Labeling processes in the organization: Constructing the individual. In: L. L. Cummings & B. M. Staw (Eds), *Research in Organizational Behavior* Vol. 17, (pp. 413–461).

Ashforth, B. E., & Humphrey, R. H. (1993). Emotional labor in service roles: The influence of identity. *Academy of Management Review, 18*, 88–115.

Ashforth, B. E., & Mael, F. (1989). Social identity theory and the organization. *Academy of Management Review, 14*, 20–39.

Ashmore, R. D., & Jussim, L. (1997). *Self and Identity*. New York: Oxford University Press.

Banjai, M. R., & Prentice, D. A. (1994). The self in social contexts. *Annual Review of Psychology, 45*, 297–332.

Bredar, J. B. (1996). *Inside the White House*. National Geographic Television Production.

Brewer, M. B. (1991). The social self: On being the same and different at the same time. *Personality and Social Psychology Bulletin, 17*, 475–482.

Carbaugh, D. (1996). *Situating selves. The Communication of Social Identities in American Scenes*. Albany, NY: State University of New York Press.

Charmaz, K. (1980). *The Social Reality of Death: Death in Contemporary America*. Reading, MA: Addison-Wesley.

Cialdini, R. B., Borden, R. J., Thorne, A. Walker, M. R., Freeman, S., & Sloan, L. R. (1976). Basking in reflective glory: Three (football) field studies. *Journal of Personality and Social Psychology, 34*, 463–476.

Cohen, J. (1960). A coefficient of agreement for nominal scales. *Educational and Psychological Measurement, 20*, 37–46.

Collison, D. L. (1988). "Engineering humor": Masculinity, joking and conflict in shop-floor relations. *Organization Studies, 9*, 181–199.

Crocker, J., & Major, B. (1989). Social stigma and self-esteem: The self-protective properties of stigma. *Psychological Review, 96*, 608–630.

Decker, C. (1995). The Times Poll: Voters growing angry, cynical about legislature. *Los Angeles Times*, September 13: A1.

Decker, C. (1996). The Times Poll; Confidence is up, but politician's popularity is not. *Los Angeles Times*, March 22: A1.

Dittmar. H. (1994). Material possessions as stereotypes: Material images of different socio-economic groups. *Journal of Economic Psychology, 15*, 561–585.

Doosje, B., & Ellemers, N. (1997). Stereotyping under threat: The role of group identification. In: R. Spears, P. J. Oakes, N. Ellemers & S. A. Haslam (Eds), *The Social Psychology of Stereotyping and Group Life* (pp. 257–272). Oxford: Blackwell.

Doosje, B., Ellemers, N., & Spears, R. (1995). Perceived intragroup variability as a function of group status and identification. *Journal of Experimental Social Psychology, 31*, 410–436.

Dutton, J. E., & Dukerich, J. M. (1991). Keeping an eye on the mirror: Image and identity in organizational adaptation. *Academy of Management Review, 34*, 517–554.

Dutton, J. E., Dukerich, J. M., & Harquail, C. V. (1994). Organizational images and member identification. *Administrative Science Quarterly, 39*, 239–263.

Eisenhardt, K. M. (1989). Building theory from case study research. *Academy of Management Review, 14*, 532–550.

Elsbach, K. D. (1999). An expanded model of organizational identification. In: B. M. Staw & R. I. Sutton (Eds), *Research in Organizational Behavior* Vol. 21, (pp. 163–200).

Elsbach, K. D., & Bhattacharya, C. (1998). *Organizational disidentification*. Paper presented at the Annual Meetings of the Academy of Management, Boston: MA.

Elsbach, K. D., & Kramer, R. M. (1996). Members' responses to organizational identity threats: Encountering and countering the *Business Week* rankings. *Administrative Science Quarterly, 41*, 442–476.

Elsbach, K. D., & Simon, J. R. (1992). The effects of training stimuli and feedback on the categorization of welding defects: A test of classification models. *International Journal of Human Factors in Manufacturing, 2*(2), 139–153.

Fiske, S. T., & Neuberg, S. L. (1990). A continuum of impression formation, from category-based to individuating processes: Influences of information and motivation on attention and interpretation. In: M. P. Zanna (Ed.), *Advances in Experimental Social Psychology* Vol. 23, (pp. 1–74). San Diego, CA: Academic Press.

Fleming, J. H., & Rudman, L. A. (1993). Between a rock and a hard place: Self concept regulating and communicative behaviors. *Journal of Personality and Social Psychology, 64*, 44–59.

Goffman, E. (1963). *Stigma: Notes on the Management of Spoiled Identity*. New York: Simon & Schuster.

Gollwitzer, P. M. (1986). Striving for specific identities: The social reality of self-symbolizing. In: R. F. Baumeister (Ed.), *Public Self and Private Self* (pp. 143–160). New York: Springer-Verlag.

Hood, J. C. (1988). From night to day: Timing and the management of custodial work. *Journal of Contemporary Ethnography, 17*, 96–116.

Huberman, A. M., & Miles, M. B. (1994). Data management and analysis methods. In: N. K. Denzin and Y. S. Lincoln (Eds), *Handbook of Qualitative Research* (pp. 428–444). Thousand Oaks, CA: Sage Publications.

Kaplan, H. B., & Johnson, R. J. (1991). Negative social sanctions and juvenile delinquency: Effects of labeling in a model of deviant behavior. *Social Science Quarterly, 72*, 98–122.

Kramer, R. M. (1993. Cooperation and organizational identification. In: J. K. Murnighan (Ed.), *Social Psychology in Organizations* (pp. 244–268). Englewood Cliffs, NJ: Prentice Hall.

Mael, F., & Ashforth, B. E. (1992). Alumni and their alma mater: A partial test of the reformulated model of organizational identification. *Journal of Organizational Behavior, 13*, 103–123.

Meindl, J. R., & Lerner, M. J. (1984). Exacerbation of extreme responses to an out-group. *Journal of Personality and Social Psychology, 47*, 71–84.

Orstein, S. (1989). Impression management through office design. In: R. A. Giacaloneand P. Rosenfeld (Eds), *Impression Management in the Organization* (pp. 411–426). Hillsdale, NJ: Lawrence Erlbaum.

Pelham, B. W., & Swann, W. B. Jr. (1994). The juncture of intrapersonal and interpersonal knowledge: Self-certainty and interpersonal congruence. *Personality and Social Psychology Bulletin, 20*, 349–357.

Pratt, M. G., & Rafaeli, A. (1997). Organizational dress as a symbol of multilayered social identities. *Academy of Management Journal, 40*, 862–898.

Rafaeli, A., Dutton, J. Harquail, C. V., & Mackie-Lewis, S. (1997). Navigating by attire: The use of dress by female administrative employees. *Academy of Management Journal, 40,* 9–45.

Reber, A. S. (1988). *Dictionary of Psychology.* London: Penguin Books.

*San Francisco Examiner* (1998). Editorial. June 12: A24.

Schlenker, B. R. (1986). Self-identification : Toward an integration of the private and public self. In: R. F. Baumister (Ed.), *Public Self and Private Self* (pp. 21–62). New York: Springer-Verlag.

Spencer, S. J., & Steele, C. M. (1994). *Under suspicion of inability: Stereotype vulnerability and women's math performance.* Unpublished manuscript, State University of New York at Buffalo.

Steele, C. M. (1988). The psychology of self-affirmation: Sustaining the integrity of the self. *Advances in Social Psychology* Vol. 21, (pp. 261–302). New York: Academic Press.

Steele, C. M. (1992). Race and the schooling of black Americans. *The Atlantic Monthly* April, (pp. 23–32).

Steele, C. M., & Aronson, J. (1995). Stereotype threat and the intellectual testperformance of African Americans. *Journal of Personality and Social Psychology, 69,* 797–811.

Swann, W. B. Jr. (1987). Identity negotiation: Where two roads meet. *Journal of Personality and Social Psychology, 53,* 1038–1051.

Swann, W. B. Jr., Pelham, B. W., & Krull, D. S. (1989). Agreeable fancy or disagreeable truth? Reconciling self-enhancement and self-verification. *Journal of Personality and Social Psychology, 57,* 782–791.

Swann, W. B. Jr., & Read, S. J. (1981). Self-verification processes: How we sustain our self-conceptions. *Journal of Experimental Social Psychology, 17,* 351–372.

Swann, W. B. Jr., Stein-Seroussi, A., & Giesler, R. B. (1992). Why people self-verify. *Journal of Personality and Social Psychology, 62,* 392–401.

Taylor, S. E., Lichtman, R. R., & Wood, J. V. (1984). Attributions, beliefs about control, and adjustment to breast cancer. *Journal of Personality and Social Psychology, 46,* 489–502.

Turner, J. C. (1987). *Rediscovering the Social Group: A Self-Categorization Theory.* New York: Blackwell.

Wood, J. V., Taylor, S. E., & Lichtman, R. R. (1985). Social comparison in adjustment to breast cancer. *Journal of Personality and Social Psychology, 49,* 1169–1183.

Zabusky, S. E., & Barley, S. R. (1997). "You can't be a stone if you're cement:" Reevaluating the emic identities of scientists in organizations. In: L. L. Cummings & B. M. Staw (Eds), *Research in Organizational Behavior* Vol. 19, (pp. 361–404).

# FADS/*FADDISME*: COMPARING BUSINESS ENTHUSIASMS IN THE UNITED STATES AND FRANCE

Margaret Brindle and Peter N. Stearns

## ABSTRACT

*The purpose of this article is to probe the sources and meanings of business faddism. We draw on deeper historical roots to lay out significant patterns of comparison between U.S. management fads and the French management experience. Our comparative case analysis illustrates why the French developed an ambivalence toward managerial enthusiasms that originated in the United States, and by analyzing what the French did and did not adopt sheds explanatory light on the U.S. experience with faddism.*

## INTRODUCTION

The rise of organizational fads, gurus, and elaborate consulting facilities constitutes one of the most interesting features of contemporary business. The phenomenon has been examined from several angles in an attempt to explain the nature and extent of change and to assess the means of distinguishing solid content from promotional hyperbole. It is generally agreed that the succession of fads stems from some combination of a rather new and immature discipline of management study – indeed, from tensions between management as an academic field and management as a demonstration of best practices – with an accelerating sense of novelty and crisis that makes confident panaceas

Advances in Qualitative Organization Research, Volume 3, pages 91–128.
2001 by Elsevier Science Ltd.
ISBN: 0-7623-0772-2

particularly appealing. We still lack convincing explanations for the popularity of often simplistic formulas, for the rapidity of particular organizational fashions, for the frequent directional zigzags (Keiser, 1994; Micklethwait & Wooldridge, 1996).

Comparative analysis can further an understanding of what contemporary faddism entails. Most 20th-century business fads have been American in origin, reflecting the size and power of the nation's corporate economy and the unusual proliferation of research universities and business schools. Nevertheless, although American example has drawn wide attention, responses even within the United States have hardly been uniform. Examining different susceptibilities to faddism is important in its own right – in promoting an understanding of current business contexts – and will also extend an understanding of the causation involved in generating or downplaying organizational fashions.

France offers a revealing comparative example in this context. The nation and its business leaders have various historic and contemporary ties with the United States. Yet, there is also a distinctive organizational tradition, combined with frequent, vociferous objection to American cultural hegemony. Given some traditional parochialism, the willingness of French business to accept new levels of American influence is striking in recent history, but so is the selectivity involved. Exploring what has caught on and what has largely fizzled illuminates additional aspects of faddism, not only in France but in the United States as well. Explaining comparative differences and similarities advances the analysis of faddism's causation in each national case--an area where existing accounts, despite some promising indications, have tended to fall short.

While historians have examined French Americanization, the management story has yet to be laid out, and at the same time a rich tradition of business history has not extended to the latter 20th century (Kuisel, 1993; *Revue française de gestion*, 1988). The comparative approach to business fads and gurus is also untapped. There is, to be sure, an available comparative framework, but it tends toward simplification. Analysis of contemporary French (and other non-American) business tends to pull between two poles. Many studies, and even more proclamations, particularly from the management and organizations arena, have assumed that national distinctions count for little where organizational imperatives are concerned. Context can essentially be ignored. If a country like France is not yet like the United States in corporate fashions, it should be. American gurus and consulting firms have been performing in Paris for many decades, with an exponential increase since the 1970s, often confidently proclaiming the applicability of American innovations. For most of the major fads, an imitative French chorus has echoed this theme: there is a single business truth (whatever it is at any particular moment), it is most likely to be American, and France should fall in line as quickly as possible. Even consulting firms that are sensitive to French distinctiveness still tend to take an American (or at least Anglo-Saxon) along for show.

There is also, however, an important body of comparative work, dealing with France, the United States and other industrial countries, that tends to insist on the striking and durable differences among national organizational cultures (Hofstede, 1980; Naulleau & Harper, 1993). Countries like France do have some distinctive organizational traditions which unquestionably mark their reactions to American business fashions. Yet, some of the comparative work verges on stereotype – German bureaucracies, for example, as uniformly rule-bound. In addition, the genre tends to imply both considerable uniformity and considerable changelessness in national traditions. This case can be strongly put, but it often relies on confirming impressions rather than systematic study. A cute example can seem compelling: the French branch of a Swedish company bent on informality, in which management personnel at all levels carefully call each other by first names and the familiar pronoun "tu" while at work, only to revert to the formal "vous" and titles like Monsieur le directeur général when encountering each other off the job. Or a revealing joke, in this case aimed at France's famed enthusiasm for rational generalizations: "This may work in practice, but I doubt it will work in theory" as a reason to reject a particular organizational innovation (Barsoux & Lawrence, 1991).

Obviously, the two dominant approaches – the borderless management wisdom and the distinct and lasting national cultures – cannot both be right, yet there have been few attempts to work out their relationship. Tracing French reactions to American fads offers an obvious opportunity for intermediate analysis, in which undeniably distinctive impulses combine with powerful spurs to innovation – producing significant change, even convergence, which however fall short of full Americanization. Explaining why change occurred, but also why it diverged from the full range of American patterns, in turn contributes to the understanding of French management and faddism alike, the twin goals of this analysis.

## THE FRENCH CONTEXT

New levels of American influence, and with it contemporary business faddism, hit France in the 1970s. The changes inevitably operated within some well-established patterns of management activity, including the fruits of previous American example. Characteristic styles help explain why innovations would not lead to complete Americanization, but they also highlight the extent of change that might be involved – the complementary features of French faddism that must ultimately be explained.

French corporations have long emphasized a more centralized, authoritarian management style than has been characteristic of the United States. It is important not to stretch the stereotypes too far: hierarchical firms may offer some informal touches, while middle management, often described as passive, may take pragmatic initiatives when formal arrangements seem to be breaking down. But the dominant comparative generalization has basis in fact. French managers are much more concerned with having precise answers to questions posed by subordinates than are their American counterparts, as a means of maintaining appropriate hierarchy. They maintain this impulse even when working for international companies that stress a different culture. Thus, employed by an American corporation with an open door policy, French managers diligently leave their doors open without changing their ideas about managerial authority (Laurent, 1986). As in other Latin countries, middle managers seek far more direction from superiors than do Americans (or North Europeans). Thus, the first French reaction to a business problem is to check with a higher-up, in contrast to the German impulse to seek clearer bureaucratic rules or the English tendency to cite inadequate group communication and a need for retraining (McFralin, Sweeney & Cotta, 1992). French business meetings, similarly, tend to involve more stress on information exchange, to provide a context in which managers can later make their own decisions, than the American-style action-oriented meeting expected to generate an action plan directly (*Expansion*, 1997).

Distinctive French characteristics owe much to the historic inspiration of government and military hierarchies. French industrialization, though active from the 1820s onward, was limited by constraints in natural resources and other problems, and lagged organizationally behind a highly centralized state. Top personnel long preferred government service to private employment, which both reflected and perpetuated this imbalance. The great French heroes were kings and chief ministers who furthered centralization and hierarchy – Richelieu, Louis XIV, and Napoleon (Barsoux & Lawrence, 1991; Laurent, 1983; Sparrow & Hiltrop, 1994). One venturesome comparativist even argues that the French pattern goes back to the hierarchical gap between lord and peasant, with managerial lords still expecting servility in response (d'Iribarne, 1989). Hierarchical proclivities were compounded by the rise of technocrats and planners after World War II. Companies taken over by the state thus rarely saw much change in management approach. France lacked the more flexible organizational experiments that marked the World War II experience in the United States, which in turn set a basis for early interests in structural change.

A number of comparative studies emphasize the French proclivity to see organizations as pyramidal structures, and to view business problems as issues for rational solution than as invitations for interpersonal maneuvering (Lawrence, 1993). Emphasis on hierarchy is also held responsible for a French managerial preference for communication in writing (in grammatically correct, elegant language if possible) rather than oral exchange. French managers employed in American companies often find it difficult to adapt to the informal if superficial friendship style that seems to override hierarchy. French professional friendships, in contrast, take years to form (*Expansion*, 1985). Finally, French hierarchical emphasis is combined with a strong impulse toward secrecy, revealed for example in the very limited information provided to shareholders. Both features tend to emphasize the decisive authority of the chief executive.

## Early French Managerial Models

French strength, relatedly, lies more in science and technology than in organizational innovations outside the hierarchical standard. French critics of their own management tradition have sometimes claimed that the nation has "no exportable management model." This is not strictly true. One of the leading authorities on management before World War II was Henri Fayol. Perhaps better known in the United States than in France, Fayol nevertheless summarized a French organizational style. Trained as an engineer who rose through the ranks in the Commentry coal mining company, Fayol regarded himself as the organizational counterpart to Taylor, doing for management hierarchy what Taylor had done for scientific structures on the production side. Writing in 1916, Fayol stressed the comparability of government and business hierarchies. The key to successful administration (management was not yet a French term) were division of labor, authority, discipline, unity of command and direction, subordination of individual to the general interest – in short, centralization and a clear chain of command. Only one superior can oversee the whole operation, and he must be able to discipline subordinates: "centralization belongs to the natural order." Fayol praised Taylor's emphasis on efficiency and careful planning, but faulted him, revealingly, for his tendency to divide command (Fayol, 1949).

Not surprisingly, in this context, French firms had eagerly imported industrial engineering innovations from the United States, beginning in the first decade of the 20th century and extending through the 1950s. "Taylorisation" was a French term by 1910. From Taylor, French manufacturing operations extended the authority of foremen and supervisors over ordinary workers –

enhancing hierarchy, while using time-and-motion studies to speed up the work itself. Again revealingly, other American innovations that built on or modified Taylor's recommendations, particularly by paying greater attention to workers' attitudes, were not widely picked up or even commented upon in France. Elton Mayo's work, for example, had little impact, and there was no flowering of personnel operations in France before World War II, in contrast to the United States. Some observers claimed that undiluted Taylorism not only suited needs in French manufacturing, but resonated favorably with the positivist tradition in the French national culture (Chanlet, 1994).

Unquestionably, then, something of a French management model existed before the rise of contemporary American business faddism and a more comprehensive interest in imitation. The model was distilled and furthered by observers like Fayol. However, lest we fall into the eternal differentiation trap characteristic of some comparative study, two qualifications are essential. First, American management was itself very hierarchical in this period. Choosing between American and French arbitrariness toward labor, including an unwillingness to share power or spontaneously negotiate, would in fact be very difficult. (Labor union weakness is in fact a shared characteristic, despite French labor's political clout, and the similarity has facilitated some common recent management trends. Both countries have rich 20th-century histories of clashes over collective bargaining and other union demands; Chapman, 1981, 1999.) As capitalist, industrial countries, France and the United States, with considerable prior contact, overlapped in management features. This explains the potential for recent imitation. Distinctive emphases in the French patterns, particularly after World War II, were not immune to change, and in some ways provided a clearer target for reevaluation that did slightly blurrier American counterparts. American students of management themselves seized on Fayol, whose influence in the actual organization of firms in the 1930s was probably greater in the United States than in France. A French-American distinction in management impulses after World War II may emerge more clearly, but it does not derive from a mists-of-time contrast.

Second, the French management model was not the only contributor to the context in which the rise of faddism would be received. After all, development or rejection of fads is a product of numerous components. A number of other components must be noted, some pointing to a greater hierarchalism in contradistinction to the United States, but others more complex. Below, we address the critical roles played by the state, business cycles, intellectual trends, and the larger social context. For example, particularly into the 1950s and to an extent since, a larger percentage of French firms were small, even familial, than was true in the United States. This might confirm an authoritarian impulse in one sense, as the powers of father figure and employer merged, but it also meant a great deal of decentralization in practice. This, in turn, might make some of the needs American fads addressed, in attacking centralization, less salient (Fridenson & Straus, 1987; Sparrow & Hiltrop, 1994).

### The Role of the French Government

French government played and plays a greater role in business than is true in the United States. Planning directives, from agencies like the *Office du Plan*, are more elaborate. More administrative procedures apply in the human resources area. It is more difficult, for example, to fire for incompetence. This political context might again confirm French managers' insistence on their own authority where possible, given resentment at state interference, but it also might mute the need for certain fads designed to protect employees against arbitrary initiatives. The advent of a socialist administration in the 1980s, at a peak period of faddism, in some ways confirmed in French employers a reluctance to change unnecessarily (*Nouvel économiste*, 1983). The 1982 Arnoux law required that works councils be consulted over technical issues, and while little actually happened the result might have reduced an interest in participatory management fads. Yet, government measures might also promote an interest in new styles. Another socialist measure, requiring that 7% of the salary budget be devoted to retraining, helped stimulate an unusually strong French interest in the movement toward human resource operations (Chapman, 1999).

### The Role of Business Cycles

Business cycles have not operated exactly the same ways in the two countries. Many French managers argued, into the 1990s, that their economy was more stable (at least since the 1950s) than the transatlantic counterpart, and this reality, or perception, might again cushion the interest in fads. France unquestionably enjoyed higher economic growth rates from the 1950s to the late 1980s, and against an older stereotype, French businessmen eagerly sacrificed security for growth. With a few exceptions, we will see that French managers often professed a lower sense of crisis than their American colleagues in the decades in which faddism emerged. France also historically faced a slightly less diverse labor force, though high rates of immigration, from the 1930s onward, produced effects not dissimilar to those in the United States (Cross, 1983). Certainly, however, perception of diversity as an issue emerged more slowly in France, which again qualified the national response to some of the fads and consulting initiatives that originated across the Atlantic.

### The Role of Academic or Intellectual Trends

There was also an important difference in intellectual trends. French intellectuals and academics after World War II were far more left-leaning than their American counterparts (Hughes, 1968). They had little interest in or sympathy for business management issues. Their approach to sociology in general was not only more Marxist but also more theoretical than that characteristic in the United States – and it was also specifically anti-American. What empirical organizational study there was more often aimed at unions or political groups than at business. American work was seen as too utilitarian and reductionist, with perspectives that lacked an adequate historical sense. The implications here, too, were diverse. On the one hand, France simply did not spontaneously generate the kind of management study that originated in the United States. This might make American models more salient, for lack of native alternatives. On the other hand, the larger intellectual hostility might limit responsiveness to the models, for lack of academic support – even amid businessmen hostile to the left but proud of their intellectual respectability. The first postwar French management researcher to gain international attention, Michel Crozier, illustrates both potentials. He strongly imitated (and added to) American research styles, as his Center for the Sociology of Organizations, founded in Paris in 1962, looked at specific cases of organizational change and urged a "modernization" of French patterns. But he encountered a great deal of Marxist intellectual criticism for what was seen as a pro-management, un-French stance. This climate shifted, to be sure, in the 1980s, with the international failure of Marxism, but it did not disappear (Chanlet, 1994; Crozier & Friedberg, 1977).

### The Larger Social Context

Finally, larger considerations color the comparative context, for faddism responds to broad social forces, and not just business exigencies. Business faddism is hardly the first kind of faddism to emerge in modern societies. Consumerism, urging faddish successions of products and leisure interests, and popularized psychological and medical expertise, both launched faddish commitments in industrial societies by the end of the 19th century if not before. Business managers, later committing to fad processions, were in part reflecting the tenor of the larger society that surrounded them.

But while faddism is part of industrial modernity, it is not invariable. France developed less generalized faddism, and later, than did the United States. To be sure, the nation led in clothing fashions, producing successions of styles from the mid-19th century onward. But the commitment to faddism in other product lines was slower to emerge. Nor was childrearing expertise as volatile as it became in the United States, with generational oscillations between strictness and permissiveness from the 1890s onward (Stearns, 1997). The United States moved into advanced consumerism earlier and more fully than did France: the French actually resisted this aspect of American marketing in the 1930s. The United States also generated more popularized experts, eager to build an audience by arguing that the previous decade's advice was dangerously off the mark. French childrearing advice, for example, depending more fully on medical doctors, was more consistent. The same held true in arenas such as dieting. While Americans grew accustomed to routine about-faces – such as the sudden discovery that after a decade of urging people to eat meat, for protein, rather than pasta, the formula was entirely wrong, and that the reverse was true – French popularizations were more stable (Furlough, 1993; Stearns, 1997).

The self-help impulse, producing a vital component in American business faddism, was and is also less strongly developed in France. Bookstores lack the vast shelves their American counterparts devote to the latest wisdom on how to make oneself rich or successful. The difference is one of degree, not of kind, but it has proved significant. Businessmen in the two countries operate with different expectations about the durability of expertise and the likelihood of obsolescence in expert prescriptions, because they have grown up in somewhat distinctive consumerist contexts.

## The Role of Educational Structure

Completing the overall context, striking and longstanding differences in the educational backgrounds of businessmen in the two countries figure prominently in management styles and potential reactions to most fads. Education both caused and reflected traditions in business and in relevant aspects of intellectual life. France's system of higher education was fixed before industrialization, and industrial needs have been shoehorned in, whereas the reverse has been true in the United States. French managers' position depends far more closely on educational background than is true in the United States. A disproportionate percentage of top managers – over 80% – come from the select Grandes Ecoles, in contrast to the wider range of educational settings that generate American business leaders.

French educational emphasis, particularly in the Grandes Ecoles, has several further effects. First, training is highly quantitative and theoretical. This might incline its recipients to be less interested in fluctuations in management styles, particularly when these derive from pragmatism or popular psychology without much reference to more elegant, abstract models. Second, an unusually large proportion of French managers has been trained as engineers, headed by graduates of the great Ecole polytechnique. Engineers, in turn, tend to focus on issues of production and science, not human relations. Third, the gap between top executives, issuing from the Grandes Ecoles, and middle management, whose members come from other educational backgrounds including regular universities and business schools, is unusually large. This automatically reinforces hierarchy, and it also raises issues of motivation from the middle management group – called *cadres* – for whom promotion opportunities are typically limited, whatever the success in introducing organizational innovations, because of the distinctions in educational origins. Finally, it has been argued that the rigor of the educational levels that generate top management, and the clear superiority of the great schools, combine to generate an unusual degree of self-confidence (or autocratic arrogance) in French business leaders. While elitism in education operates in the United States, it is not exceptional for graduates of lower-reputed schools to run companies and advance to the top. This point, like the earlier suggestion about differences in anxiety levels to which it relates, must be fleshed out in terms of actual reactions to potential business fads (Frommer & McCormick, 1989; Locke & Leuteau, 1988; *Nouvel économiste*, 1995).

In the United States, business fads have been closely though incompletely related to the rise of business schools, particularly since World War II. By 1990, 650 American business schools were generating 67,000 MBAs per year. In France, where only a handful of business schools had attained Grandes Ecoles status by 1990 and where management tracks in units like the *Institut d'Etudes politiques* were seen as inferior to the training for government positions, a few dozen schools generated about 6,000 MBAs annually. Their training and aspirations were not markedly different from those of their American counterparts, not surprising since 80% of French management professors had spent time studying in the United States (Gurviez, 1987). But the differences with the United States were obvious despite this overlap, for French management graduates were far less numerous, even allowing for differences in population size, and their prospects, particularly in French rather than international firms, were much less bright. They would have less impact, collectively, on national business life (*Expansion,*1985).

When educational differences are added to the overall mix, it is obvious that the French climate for business fads was not the same as the American. Education, management tradition, and the wider culture intertwined. But differences in context were not the whole story, partly because they were usually matters of degree rather than stark contrasts. Context, further, was not unchanging, as French business faced many of the same inducements to faddism as did American, with the added pressure of the overwhelming presence of the American models themselves.

## CAUSES OF CHANGE

Insistence on significant differences in tradition and context lead logically to emphasis on belated and incomplete encounters with contemporary management ideas. This story would not be entirely untrue – some French observers, touting or lamenting the national bureaucratic impulses, have sketched similar contours – but it would be seriously misleading. A number of factors, cresting in the 1960s and 1970s, prompted change. A tally of causes must account both for the new receptivity to ideas from the United States and for the particular slant that French imitation took.

Two major currents coalesced: new patterns of contact, that emphasized American superiority and the reality of American economic outreach, and significant new needs. French openness to imitating successful foreign models began with industrialization itself, when the main target was technology and the main source was Great Britain. We have seen that interest in American contributions also began early. The enthusiasm for Taylorisation reflected the acknowledged power of American organization, at a point when French factory industry was eager to borrow to advance. Active imitation of industrial engineering and assembly line procedures continued, with the advance of French industry itself, through the 1950s. French delight in Taylorism was enhanced by reliance on large numbers of immigrant workers, in the 1930s and again from the 1950s onward. The immigrant factor, powerful in United States regimentation early in the 20th century, reverberated longer in France (Chapman, 1981; Cross, 1983; Ogden & White, 1989). Immigrant workers from Poland, Italy, and North Africa gained increasing roles in factory centers even before World War II. On another front, American retail procedures, such as chain stores, had won attention in the 1930s, and though the French on balance insisted on some distinctive bows to quality rather than mass-produced goods, some very similar operations resulted. Segments of French business were, then, conditioned to look abroad, and particularly across the Atlantic, well before World War II (Bounfour, 1992; Kuisel, 1993).

The power of American example increased with the painful economic gap that prevailed from the end of World War II into the 1950s, when at some points it was doubted that Europe could ever recover a competitive position. Marshall Plan aid to France brought additional economic contact. The new *Commissariat de la productivité*, in the late 1940s, urged attention to American organizational models, and sent a number of missions to the United States (Pateyron, 1998). Peter Drucker's major book on organization, urging suppleness and attention to employee contributions, was translated in 1957 (Drucker, 1957). It was at the end of the 1950s that the France began to replicate American-style business schools, with the formation of INSEAD in Fontainebleau in 1959, complete with case methods and a steady stream of American faculty which continues today. (One French business journal, friendly to imitation, persists in regularly describing INSEAD as a "Harvard clone" at the end of the 1990s.) The Gaullist prime minister Michel Debré, during the 1960s, supported the further development of business schools in various French cities. It was at this point also that Michel Crozier became the first French scholar to join his American counterparts in management-oriented research and pleas for more participatory management styles. His own research center was paralleled by the formation of management research units in several existing schools, including engineering schools like the *Ecole polytechnique* (Crozier & Friedberg, 1977; Pateyron, 1998).

### The 1960s: Imitation and Protest

The 1967 publication of Jean-Jacques Servan-Schreiber's *Le Défi américain* (*The American Challenge*) marked a further move toward acknowledging the superiority of American organizational models, a move both symbolic and real. It occurred, obviously, in a context already favorable to imitation, so its impact should not be exaggerated, but it unquestionably contributed to a new surge in the later 1960s. Various members of the Servan-Schreiber clan joined in attacking French management traditions, for their excessive hierarchy and commitment to routine, in the 1960s and 1970s. It was from this group that a new business journal, *L'Expansion*, would emanate, eager for innovation and imitation, though other, existing journals very nearly matched this newcomer in the attention offered to American management examples and expertise. But Servan-Schreiber's book, actively pushed via the latest American-style publishers' marketing methods, really propelled attention to a new plane. The book sold extremely well – better than any French publication in the 1960s, with 400,000 sales in 1967 alone. And its message was not just the superiority of American industry, and the need for France and Europe to wake up to its power, but the location of superiority not in technology but in organization. American structural flexibility and the decentralization of business decisions were contrasted with French rigidity: Taylorism must be attacked through democratization and a liberation of initiative. "Do we or do we not have confidence in the maturity and intelligence of the majority" (Servan-Schreiber, 1968: 32)?

Servan-Schreiber's exordium was supported by the massive student and labor risings that began in May, 1968, though the near-revolution reduced attention to the book itself. The need for change seemed obvious, in business and education alike, and reduction of central authority was a common theme. Jean-Louis Servan-Schreiber, editor of the American-friendly *Expansion*, assumed that fundamental change was imminent, and urged wider participation in management decisions. The example of organizational change elsewhere in Europe, as in Volvo, was also cited. It was at this point also that American purchases of French firms accelerated (this indeed was one of spurs to the publication of the *American Challenge* and to its eager reception). Finally, American consulting firms began their inexorable march into European markets; the late 1960s and the 1970s were crucial here. The first French consulting firm, Bossard, had actually been launched in 1946, but the invasion of Boston Consulting, Anderson, and others easily eclipsed home-grown models. (By 1995 there would be 550 firms in France, both domestic and foreign but with American branches dominating the top ten.) Management seminars became common, and their prestige varied directly with the number of American experts present. In 1969, leading French firms formed a new association, *Entreprise et Progrès*, designed to humanize management if not to unseat Taylorism directly (Servan-Schreiber, 1973; Stern & Tutoy, 1995).

Concurrent changes in French political and economic conditions explain not just how but why new patterns of imitation occurred, gaining eager attention as serious responses to new problems. The American superiority that Servan-Schreiber touted would have counted for little had a perception of new needs not emerged at the same time.

The 1968 uprising cut deeper than its American counterpart, if only because the focus was fiercely domestic and because the protest assumed more revolutionary proportions, with temporary seizure of parts of Paris and worker occupation of many factories. The message pointed in two related directions. First, protesters attacked excessive hierarchy and organization directly, in universities such as the Sorbonne and also in society more generally. Second, the movement led to a new round of labor agitation (similar to the briefer American crest in the late 1960s) that raised demands about work quality and decision making, rather than the more familiar instrumental issues. Formal protest was enhanced by what employers perceived as new and unacceptable levels of turnover and absenteeism. This led directly to employer interest in new management approaches that would respond to, or, even better, preempt collective and individual unrest. The more diffuse anti-bureaucratic protest helped stimulate a vigorous research current, pointing toward greater worker autonomy and more enriching work assignments. Speculations about post-industrial society contained more focus on work issues than did comparable American research (Delanotte, 1972; Touraine, 1969). The Gaullist government, never an unmitigated friend of private enterprise, got into the act, sponsoring several of the labor studies and then, in the mid-1970s, a major inquiry (the Sudreau report) directed toward making corporations more responsive to shareholders and employees alike (Sudreau, 1975). Even without American reference points, based on the French dynamic alone, the common wisdom now held that workers should become clients, not just brute resources, that decentralization and the use of small groups were essential to promote the human dimensions of business – that Taylorism, still fine for focused decisions about specialization or efficiency measurements, must be abandoned as an overall orientation. Groups like the *Fondation nationale pour l'enseignement de la gestion des enteprises*, founded in 1968, specifically responded to the perceived need for change. Even the hallowed position of engineering training was called into question by the Sudreau commission amid appeals for less technocracy and more pragmatism (Gelinier, 1976).

With this, a number of other, related trends coalesced. The interest in change coincided with increasing shifts from manufacturing to white collar emphasis – as in the United States a bit earlier. The literature on innovation in the early 1970s frequently referred to the need to acknowledge a more educated labor force, again in the fruit of developments since World War II – particularly the expansion of secondary and university enrollments – that occurred a bit later than in the United States, but with similar force. While French materials paid less attention to racial diversity in the labor force as a spur to change, the advent of larger numbers of women workers (here, with timing similar to that in the United States) also promoted management adjustments designed at least to acknowledge women's presence. The perceived need for innovation also owed much to a growing realization of global economic forces – more than in the United States, long-sheltered French business would use fad and imitation, to some extent regardless of specific content, as a means of connecting with international trends (Stoffaës, 1980). Finally, the 1970s brought a slowing of economic growth, punctuated by the oil crises. French businessmen felt the change more keenly than their American counterparts because it interrupted over two decades of substantial progress and profit.

A combination of changes, then, caused the need for change in response. Several of them – particularly, the spillover from the 1968 rebellions – also suggested the appropriate directions, by emphasizing major adjustments in management style. These in turn coalesced with the growing adulation of

American innovation, and set up a period of unprecedented openness to imitation. Against all expectations, in a country fiercely proud of its cultural independence, American example took command.

## The Importation of American Fads

It was during the 1960s and 1970s that English words began to pepper French management vocabulary, a development all the more striking given official national resistance to foreign intrusions and faddish neologisms. "Le management" began to replace the perfectly good word "gestion", though there was some discussion about whether "manage" had French roots. Articles could begin to refer routinely to "problem-solving" (untranslated as "la procédure bottom-up"). And the fascination persisted. By the 1990s one could talk of "downsizing," with the French verb "downsizer," or "benchmarking," with the verb "benchmarquer," "outplacement" (and "outplacer"), "learning organizations," "empowriser," and so on. While French managers' facility with English was mixed (67% were not fluent), their enthusiasm for the bastard franglais burned bright. Study trips to the United States became common – a California visit by 15 top executives in 1980 had wide resonance – and a growing number of aspirant managers attended American business schools (Barsoux & Lawrence, 1991; Savall, 1975; Sérieyx, 1983).

A passion for translation began to seize French publishing in the management category, and with it much of the same apparatus of promotions, lectures and best-seller hyperbole that characterized the emergence of gurus in the United States. This had been presaged by the earlier translation of Drucker's work, and the resultant interest in management by objectives (*direction par objectifs*, or DPO), which gained further momentum in the 1970s. Frederick Herzberg's ideas about employee self-realization and task enrichment, as alternatives to the hierarchical French version of Taylorism, gained ground, seen as responsive to the pressures that had bubbled up in 1968 (Herzberg, 1971). Peters and Waterman's work on excellence (*Prix de l'excellence*) became a quick best-seller, and visits by gurus like Peters drew wide attention (Peters & Waterman, 1983). American companies like Hewlett Packard and General Electric were referred to frequently, as beacons of innovation (Boston Consulting, 1990; Demming, 1988; Kotler, 1991; *Nouvel économiste*, 1992; Sérieyx, 1983; Weiss, 1978).

Translations and citations were routinely supplemented by derivative, but enthusiastic French work, sometimes backed by a promotional association. Movements for strategic planning and for quality thus found active French advocates in Godet, Archier and Sérieyx, and Sicard, some of whom had academic connections but many of whom, like some American counterparts, were consultants. France produced no real gurus – Pierre Vernimmen, in finance, came closest – but it developed, among promoters, a similar mix of educators, freelancers, and businessmen-turned-advocates. Groups like the *Institut de l'entreprise* or the European Foundation for Quality Management supported their efforts. The main message was clear, as it echoed key themes in the American Challenge: too many French executives operated without clear direction, with undue rigidity, and with insufficient attention to the initiatives their employees might contribute (Godet, 1986; Moulin, 1986; Page, Turcq, Bailly & Foldes, 1988; Sicard, 1987).

### The 1980s: Quality and Other Impulses

Another surge in the interest in organizational change and foreign models occurred in the early to mid-1980s, as the failure of communism brightened the luster of American capitalism. Previous oil crises, the rise of international competitive levels, and the surge of Japan opened the way for innovation – just as in the United States. French commentators took some nationalist delight in pointing out how Japan seemed to be outdoing the United States, and informational visits to Japan became popular. But in the main, organizational responses came through the medium of American recommendations. There was also a distinctive French ingredient: organizational innovation appealed to businessmen appalled at the new socialist regime of François Mitterand. Discussions of decentralization and spreading initiative could be used against the threat of excessive government control and planning.

In this context, the French showed particular enthusiasm for quality circles, seen as a crucial means of unlocking the creativity of subordinates, increasing flexibility and attacking Taylorism and undue centralization. To be sure, quality circles might also emphasize new efficiency and control: they could be touted as means for checking product deficiencies, which might enhance the role of supervisors. (This aspect of the quality movement touched base with longstanding French interest in measuring standards, reflected in the *Associa-tion française de la normalisation*, 1926, and the *Association française du controle industriel de la qualité*, 1957, backed by government-sponsored labeling.) This ambiguity (again, as in the United States) may well have promoted the appeal of quality circles. But the movement was not just more of the same, as it emphasized structural change and attention to qualitative, rather than the previously dominant quantitative, measurements and attacked the overemphasis on technical analysis preached by the Grandes Ecoles. Emphasis on the circles' capacity to allow "direct expression" was seen as a blow to

Taylorism and socialist heavy-handedness alike. Companies like Solmer (steel), the Raffinerie de Provence (petroleum), the Saint Nazaire shipyards, Peugeot, hotel chains and many others employed substantial numbers of consultants to set up circles, to the extent that one business journal noted the "guruization" of French corporations (*Nouvel économiste*, 1983).

The *Association française pour les cercles de qualité* was set up in 1981, mixing academics and managers, and over one hundred firms had circles in operation. By 1983, 500 companies were maintaining 3000 circles, with the complex task of improving product control, seeking means to economize (one company, Pechinez, claimed 300,000fr. savings through the suggestions emanating from quality circles), and giving employees new voice. Interest persisted: Syntec, a professional organization of 50 consulting firms, was still working on forming "quality clubs" and the processes necessary for quality assurance in the 1990s. And managers were teaching quality seminars in secondary schools (DeClerck, Debourse & Navarre, 1983; *Expansion*, 1989; Lemaitre, 1983; Raveleau, 1983; Sérieyx, 1983).

During the 1980s also, many French companies and consultants worked to introduce some of the principles of "excellence" (many of which dovetailed with quality circles). Attention to personnel measures and the formation of human resources departments also increased. Personnel functions, once an afterthought often assigned to a former military officer, now took on new significance (Frommer & McCormick, 1989). Use of psychological tests in hiring increased, a belated (but explicit) imitation of the American movement than had begun almost half a century earlier (Votier, 1993). Professional organizations formed, like the *Forum de la gestion des ressources humaines*, and research in the area advanced rapidly. One observer cited an "explosion" of human resources activities in the 1970s (Citeau, 1997). Strategic management had its votaries, as did the "intelligent workplace". By the 1990s one Lyons firm (the *Institut de socio-économie des entreprises et des organisations*) reported over two decades of devotion to strategic management, designed simultaneously to cut costs and enhance the loyalty of personnel.

Business schools shifted curricula accordingly, claiming they were following the lead of curricular changes at places like Harvard (Les Professeurs du Groupe HEC, 1994). A business journal noted the popularity of teaching strategy still in 1994, but warned that its faddish quality might doom it to rapid decline. And several books and associations began to tout Total Quality Management by the end of the 1980s. By the mid-1990s, one study cited 50 companies with TQM programs, with 12,000 employees (Sicard, 1987). None of the developments later in the decade matched the earlier and ongoing enthusiasm for quality circles, but seminars, publications and consulting operations clearly reflected interest (Hamalion, 1997; Kotler, 1991; Les Professeurs du Groupe HEC, 1994; Sérieyx, 1986; Stora, 1986).

Imports continued in the 1990s. It was at this point that the idea of benchmarking caught wide notice, from tentative origins in the mid 1980s, as against earlier corporate impulses for secrecy. An American company, Data Edge, was employed to help pharmaceutical firms exchange information. While several accounts argued that the practice was not really new – and that there used to be a perfectly good French term for it, competitive analysis (*analyse concurrentiel*) – consulting firms urged wider usage. In 1994 the consultant Colba-Mid organized the first benchmarking seminar in Europe, dealing with administration and customer satisfaction. By 1994, 54% of the larger French companies used benchmarking (*Nouvel économiste*, 1994). Translation of American works on reengineering prompted attention to this approach as well, though as we will see the French response was both hesitant and belated. INSEAD put reengineering into its curriculum in 1993. One 1996 article, in best faddist fashion, claimed however that reengineering was beginning to fade because it was so widely known. Companies wanted something new, as reengineering had "fallen into the public domain, like a generic medicine" (*Expansion*, 1996: 50). Frederick Reichhold's work on employee loyalty and participation, echoing old quality circle concerns, caught attention in this context (Reichheld, 1996). An interest in motivational "coaching" also spread from the United States. By 1996, the inevitable *Société française de coaching* had 136 members ("Avec le coaching," 1998).

American-inspired fads dominated the business scene in France at least from the 1960s onward. To the extent that fads were current at all – and there was lots of resistance and continuity alike – U.S. origin was a common denominator. French experts might claim some distinctive twists. An early 1990s interest in "enterprise projects" and values seemed to have no particular American referent. Overall, however, organizational innovation, or faddism, largely meant some degree of Americanization. An editor at *Expansion* put it succinctly, in 1994: "If we have become one of the countries with the highest standard of living in the world, we owe this to the management models learned in the business schools and in the American books" (*Expansion*, 1994: 79). The magazine worried that not all French managers had mastered the lessons yet, but it did not hesitate to pinpoint their source.

# CHANGE

Imitation of American business enthusiasms obviously qualifies some of the crudest cultural approaches to national management styles. France had its own tradition, but it was capable of developing an eager audience for selective alternatives. How it chose, adapted and ignored cannot of course be discerned from a sketch of faddism itself, for the sketch might misleadingly suggest that the French blindly followed the American lead, differing only by a slight lag in time. But before turning to this essential analysis, it is important to note how the patterns of imitation, including the procession of different specific enthusiasms, fit into a pattern of genuine, measurable change. Even if, as we will see, some initiatives proved hollow (as was true in the United States as well), even if strong and distinctive continuities persisted, French management patterns proved open to significant adjustment.

Education provided a crucial test, in reflecting and furthering adjustments. Already in the 1970s, key engineering schools set up management research and training groups, like the *Centre de recherche de gestion* (interestingly, "gestion," not management) at the prestigious *Ecole polytechnique*. By the 1980s observers noted that management training was altering the outlook of engineering graduates, as they became less riveted on technological solutions, indeed less arrogant. Business school curricula shifted, particularly toward the area of human resources and communication (obligatory, for example, in the third and fourth years of the chain school, Institut Supérieur Européen de Gestion). Business schools (which *Expansion* claimed "owed everything" to American example) also gained ground in their own right, by the 1980s. By 1989 thirteen management schools were accredited by the *Conférence de grandes écoles*, a marked advance from the list of four in 1980, and the number of graduates of business schools in general was rising rapidly. Also in 1989, the business track at the *Institut d'Etudes politiques* surpassed the government track for the first time (Frommer & McCormick, 1989; "Hit-Parade des écoles de commerce," 1987; Usunier, 1990).

Change affected business itself. By the 1980s, foremen were being retrained, "detaylorized", in a pattern similar to that in the United States a few decades earlier. They were increasingly placed as facilitators in production teams, and by 1987 their number had declined by 20%. Many corporations were also abandoning functional divisions in favor of more horizontal structures based on market categories (*Nouvel économiste*, 1987). By 1990, over 50% of all corporations had human relations divisions, and France actually had emerged as the European leader in renaming personnel activities, expanding operations, and placing the division head on the board of directors (Sparrow & Hiltrop, 1994). Training programs for middle managers (encouraged by the government expenditure requirement) also expanded rapidly by the later 1980s. Some managers were actually joining to share experience with other firms, as in the

Simarks group established for part-time training and evaluations commitments (*Nouvel économiste*, 1987).

Individual companies changed. L'Oréal became known for its anti-bureaucratic approach. Renault set up semi-autonomous work groups in 1973. Carrefour, a retail chain, deliberately hired business school graduates not from the Grandes Ecoles, because it found them more flexible and easier to motivate. A major Marseilles bank hired an academic consultant in 1983 to reduce problems of absenteeism. The result was a radical new organizational structure involving more frequent group meetings, for decisions rather than information exchange, and a great deal more internal cooperation. BSN-Gervais Danone experimented with new teams from 1972 onward, while the state railway agency (SNCF) used decentralized participatory techniques as part of a major systems change in the 1980s, under the banner "One can no longer reform companies in a technocratic fashion." The Bull computer firm, using consultants, by the early 1990s worked for a "non-pyramidal" structure and team collaboration. Aérospatiale, a large and "arrogant" company, restructured in the 1980s, spurred in part by the new government requirements for worker voice. It first reserved nine work hours a year, per employee, for meetings. In 1985 it introduced psychological training for all managers, focused on delegating authority and running participatory meetings. Quality circles, ultimately numbering thirty, dealt with technical and work issues, with the leaders urged to facilitate, not dictate. Trips and inhouse journal articles rewarded workers who contributed good ideas (though the company, like most in Europe, opposed extra pay for this purpose). Reengineering had its adepts also, in the 1990s. In 1995 Moulinex downsized, as part of a reengineering process, and like its American predecessors immediately saw its stock values soar by 21% (Dumont, 1996; Frère, 1991; Micklethwait & Wooldridge, 1996; Savall, 1975; Touraine, 1966). Clearly, as more general figures on the introduction of quality circles or benchmarking suggest, the interest in new management measures was not mere window dressing. By the 1980s France had far more quality circles than any other European country.

Revealing also was the increasing capacity of French consultants to take on something of a leadership posture, complete with slogans and acronyms. Michel Godet suggests a case in point, as he advocated a "future scenarios" method by the 1980s that smacked of the (widely translated) work of American futurologists and strategic planners, applied to specific companies. His method had been worked out in the latter 1970s with the Department of Futures Studies in the SEMA Metra Consulting group. His approach helped the Elf group anticipate vulnerabilities in Algeria. In the early 1980s he applied his method to the Renault car companies, setting up "strategic prospective workshops" that used a "tree of relevance" method to decide what projects were contributing to company objectives (Godet, 1986: 40). Godet-led seminars with middle managers considered structural issues, in Operation IESC (Industrial, Economic and Social Change), which led to some downsizing. Another Godet application helped the Lafarge cement company project a decline in demand for their product with resultant plans for diversification. Methods employed in these projects included software programs like MICMAC, for seeking key variables, and MACTOR, for analyzing actor strategies. Elaborate charts allowed the weighing of factors and options, while the a model dubbed POPOLE identified components of decision making (Godet, 1994). More generally, consulting in France, while ranging widely from accounting to law to information systems, focused heavily on issues of strategy, organizational structure, and human resources (Bounfour, 1992).

Change, imitation, and the rise of disproportionately American or American-style consultants and various gurus were all in play, from the 1970s onward. In 1997 *Expansion*, ever optimistic, cited one manager's view of the future: "In the years to come, hierarchical links will give way to a work relationship based on autonomy" (*Expansion*, 1997: 94). The forecast echoed sentiments expressed, often around themes of Americanization, for the previous thirty years. They may have been overconfident, but they did accurately convey a theme of change that had come to inform a number of key components of French business organizations and training. While France did not develop international leaders in management change, as Britain and Scandinavia did by the 1990s, it actually, and by national business traditions quite surprisingly, topped the charts in several key implementation areas.

## THE FRENCH STYLE

Imitative faddism, French traditions, and the nation's new business needs inevitably merged, producing a French approach to management changes that differed from its American counterpart despite obvious overlaps. Three points loom large. First, many fads were explored rhetorically, with few or no adjustments in fact. Second, particularly by the 1980s, a number of fads were critiqued and renamed – which did not deprive them of substance, but suggested a need to adapt. Third and most important, available models were used selectively, and the full range of American faddism was not carried through. Amid extensive imitation and real change, a distinctive set of French interests emerged that would dampen sheer faddism and guide the process of innovation itself.

*Ambivalence*

The tension between enthusiasm for new management models in principle and reluctance in practice was hardly distinctively French, since it operated widely in the United States as well. However, frustrated reform-minded observers sometimes claimed that their nation was unusually laggard, bedeviled by the traditions of elitist company directors and autocratic style and structure. From the 1970s to the 1990s, recurrent laments focused on the merely rhetorical commitment to new structures such as quality circles, or on the routine-mindedness of managers who feared to change despite knowing what they should do. Many quality circles, *Expansion* reported in 1987, applied to only a minority of workers, involved in technical innovation, while assembly-line procedures continued to command the majority. Other firms picked up the product control and efficiency side of the circles, which simply enhanced Taylorism, while ignoring their expressive potential. Correspondingly, the *Ministère des affaires sociales* ruled that the presence of circles did not fulfill legal requirements for employee voice. Other half-measures were noted. Peugeot had genuinely decentralized by the early 1990s, but top management continued to pride itself on special cleverness, intervening even in the choices of model colors. A 1987 article put the case directly: French executives, while claiming interest in employee participation, continued to look for decisive authority as the key to success. The chief executive was alone responsible for innovation ("Métier du patron," 1987; Moulin, 1986). But other reports located the key implementation problem elsewhere, commending top executives and claiming that it was middle management that dragged its feet. And it is important to remember that tensions between the need for leadership in introducing participation, and participation itself, surfaced in the United States as well, as the French noted in evaluating Jack Welch's work at General Electric (Barsoux & Lawrence, 1991; Doblin & Ardouin, 1989; *Expansion*, 1984, 1987; "Métier du patron," 1987; *Nouvel économiste*, 1983).

Not surprisingly, early commentary, as the imitation process began to move into high gear, was particularly gloomy about the pace of change. A number of assessments noted widespread failure to adopt management by objectives in the 1970s. Managers feared face-to-face conflict if they moved in this direction. The lower cadres, accustomed to passivity, sought to protect themselves from the further interaction with higher authorities that performance evaluation might entail, while the latter refused to acknowledge that subordinates might have valid ideas. Both management groups tried to protect autonomy: "I know my job, if I am controlled, this means they have no confidence in me" ("Benchmarking," 1994: 56). So, performance appraisals, when introduced, differed from American patterns, particularly through greater imprecision and with less impact on inequalities within management. But performance assessments increased in the 1980s, as innovation became more familiar and the pressures of international competition increased (d'Iribarne, 1989; Sparrow & Hiltrop, 1994).

The French also pursued a distinctive course in the human resources area. One evaluation (which again noted that French companies had elevated human resources operations more than most European enterprises) argued that France and the United States were about the same in wishing to promote empowerment, but that France sought to combine the approach with far more emphasis on vertical hierarchy and centralization, less interest in flexible work practices (Sparrow & Hiltrop, 1994). The French also moved slowly in their adoption of assessment centers for selecting new managers and evaluating current ones either for competence or for retraining. Only 19% of French companies, all quite large, had moved to this method by 1995. The reasons were twofold: reliance on educational results and contacts continued to seem valid, combined with a traditionalist belief that a good manager had a certain unmeasurable quality, a "je ne sais quoi," that could only be discerned in repeated interviews. But second, surprising preferences for quantitative tests long established in French practice, notably handwriting analysis, continued to compete with American-style assessments. (Graphology ranked just behind interviews in company preferences, into the mid-1990s, as the French continued to believe that handwriting revealed traits not apparent in other data.) While assessment centers were copied from the United States as early as the 1970s, the French argued that they promoted an unpleasant feeling of "being judged." But again, there was gradual change toward American-style norms and practice. Competitive pressure and alterations in personnel functions prompted companies, like many banks or the international Novotel chain, to adopt assessment procedures by the 1980s (though sometimes, to remove judgmental implications, they were renamed *Centres d'appréciation des compétences en situation*). The new law that required expenditure on retraining contributed to this trend. Other traditions yielded. By the late 1990s, only 10% of all personnel advertisements were requiring handwriting samples, as even this remnant of cherished 19th-century positivism waned (Balicco, 1994; Bolton, 1995; Shackleton & Newell, 1993).

Even as adaptations cut into initial resistance, claims of hollowness persisted. Management styles, responsiveness, and use of consultants were all indicted. In 1988, Jacques Volle, a quality consultant since 1958, argued that quality circles had ceased to be effective, because authoritarianism undermined them. Top managers persisted in responding to suggestions defensively, citing personal achievements to justify sticking to current policies. Volle noted, to be sure, that the same thing had happened in the United States a bit earlier, and that only the Japanese had really applied quality circles to the whole personnel. And he admitted that individual French companies had really redefined themselves, focusing on management from the top down in the name of quality and mutual participation and spending substantial sums on retraining. But he argued that, overall, the need to restructure must precede any specific innovation, for change to have any chance (*Nouvel économiste*, 1988).

On another front, despite verbal enthusiasm for Total Quality Management in the 1980s and 1990s, French companies were indicted for paying only lipservice to customer data. Only 9% of all concerns studied customers closely, and whereas 70% measured client satisfaction and 89% did market studies, only 35% used the results. The majority had a complaint office, but only 1% forwarded complaints to relevant divisions. A mere 6% of French companies had adopted the American practice of sending fake customers to test service. Only a few companies – Renault, Club Med – had really moved to innovate. "Customer orientation is only in its beginning stages in France" (*Expansion*, 1995: 60).

Relations with consultants were often ambivalent. In other areas, too, French companies often seemed to employ consultants and then systematically ignore their advice. A number, for example, regularly ordered reports from the McKinsey group, but ignored the reports once received (*Guide du consulting*, 1992; Zarka & Jarrosson, 1995). In response, consulting firms eased up a bit in their insistence on American best practices. Arthur Anderson, in 1995, insisted that its agents were not "fanatics for every conceivable American model," though it was true that "many best practices [a phrase left in English] come from American groups, for they are often the best performers in the world" (*Expansion*, 1999: 24). And one report, in the mid-1990s, argued that French firms were rebelling against consulting, in the name of returning traditional decision-making power to top managers (*Guide du consulting*, 1992; Zarka & Jarrosson, 1995). Yet, despite the apparent ambivalence, U.S. consulting firms continued to expand efforts in France with firms such as Arthur Anderson opening on the Champs Elysées.

Most industrial countries, including the United States, displayed a gap between profession and practice when it came to faddish innovation. Given evidence of substantial change, even leadership in certain categories, there is no reason to believe that levels of French recalcitrance were unusually high. Some shortfalls reflected the ambitions involved: a bank director rejected a *projet d'entreprise*, because there was insufficient prior community of interests, while vowing to continue better-prepared decentralization efforts (Fichter, 1988). The only clear comparative difference involves not levels of French resistance, but distinctive reasons for it, reflecting the more hierarchical tradition and greater managerial self-confidence. Thus benchmarking, though widely noted, was less widely practiced than in the United States – reflecting customs of fiercely-guarded privacy. An early-1990s poll suggested that 49% of all managers judged themselves competent enough to do without external advice – a pattern noticeably different from the consulting-crazed United States (Bounfour, 1992).

## Insistent Frenchness

Along with gaps between apparent interest and real practice came a frequent desire, in commentary, to cushion against any impression that France was responding to every American whim. Some of this was bombast, like the articles around 1980 that trumpeted the rise of Japan and American discomforture (though it quickly became apparent that Japanese models were more difficult or less relevant than adaptations in the United States, with imitative recommendations once again on the rise; Stoffaës, 1980). Some reflected leftist disgruntlement that actually confirmed some successful importations, because they fell short of larger ideals and at the same time impeded protest. Thus Jean-Pierre LeGoff condemned manipulative efforts, writing of a steady decline in the workplace "from the failure of May 1968 to the gentle barbarism of [contemporary] management" (LeGoff, 1992, 1996: 112). But three more pervasive and substantive differentiations emerged, that really did suggest a distinctive selectivity amid the enthusiasm for innovation.

Struggles to assert some measure of independence abounded. In 1989, for example, the *Association internationale (francophone) du management stratégique* was formed (based in Quebec) to respond to the dominance of the American Academy of Management. Wit might be used to soften the impact of imitation on national pride: "No managerial theory can long resist gallic humor." Jean-Paul Sallenave, writing on "antimanagement" from his experience as a Frenchman working for Boston Consulting in the United States, suggested a new, French set of rules: "It is better to give orders than to receive them." "It is better to avoid problems, for we're rarely capable of resolving them." His sharpest barbs were reserved for the sanctimony of the Total Quality Management movement (Chanlet, 1994: 32–33; Sallenave, 1993).

Jokes aside, the French worried considerably (as did some American observers to be sure), about faddishness, preferring a sense of consistency and logical sequence. Thus an article anxiously assessed reengineering as "innovation or fad?" Michel Godet, though in some sense an ardent if undeclared faddist as consultant, delighted in poking holes at American claims of innovation. Strategic management was "silly," for all management consists of deciding on strategic directions. The excellence fad easily became excessive, as Godet noted that many of the American companies devoted to excellence were in trouble by the mid-1980s. "Carried away by their 'passion for excellence', they turn it into a religion and their book [Peters and Waterman] becomes a catechism where company heads are transformed into mythical heroes playing the role of apostles." Peters' later book on chaos, urging tremendous flexibility and abandonment of mass production, was "delirium," for coordinated planning is essential. And again, the caution about faddism: "Good ideas and new ideas, unfortunately, are not the same thing." Often, specific American suggestions were valid, like quality circles and some decentralization, though even then the innovation claims were usually ridiculous ("as if this were a historic discovery in the annals of management"). "Do we need to pay $12,000 for each conference devoted to the articulation of these holy principles?" "I am convinced that most best sellers in the field of management are the equivalent of American TV serials." "If the recipes presented by American business schools and management best sellers are as useful as claimed, American businessmen would be performing better and United States industry less sick" (Godet, 1986: 68).

Godet and Sallenave, to be sure, were only individual observers, and Godet's comments, as an eager-to-be-hired French consultant, were self-serving. There were plenty of imitate-at-all costs promoters as well, as we have seen. But even reform outlets disliked presenting one innovation after another in terms of dramatic novelty. They did see in American faddism not only foreignness, but symptoms of American extremism that might link with televangelism and religious excess. They disliked the guru approach. Again, without denying diverse responses, there was something of a French style in the way American fads were received, similar to responses to oscillating American-inspired enthusiasms in other areas. Even when American superiority was granted (and Godet pointed to excellent performance models in the French backyard), aspects of hyperbole and sudden about-faces, the hallmarks of the faddish aspect of American management styles since the 1970s were not appreciated. The *Nouvel économiste* suggested the main point, in 1995: fads should not be accepted blindly, either because they are American or because they are new. Rather, they should be assessed by results and executives should cut through the faddism to seek valid continuities among them (*Expansion*, 1992).

With some exceptions, then, French businessmen and observers did not resonate to the thirst for constant novelty that seems to describe American faddism – where according to one assessment the best predictor of a new fad is simply the lapse of time since the last one (Abrahamson, 1996). While publicists echoed American fluctuations, serious interest did not follow up. Rather, assurances that an innovation was not brand new, certainly not transient, assured wider attention. Relatedly, French commentators explicitly shied away from the religious intensity, the quest for a holy grail, that so often surrounded American presentations, as in the Total Quality Management movement. Constant warnings were directed against hyperbole, even in movements that were being recommended. Good ideas could be "killed" by pushing too far, too fast, and American extremism was a real danger here. Quality circles thus were great, but people must be warned against "quality in excess", which stemmed from a pseudo-science that risked imposing arbitrary controls from outside the company (d'Iribarne, 1989: 60). Excess here could vitiate the very goals of change, by imposing new regimentation in place of the old. A number of observers commented on a "very emotional religiosity" that permeated American business fads, that would have no place in France (d'Iribarne, 1989; Landier, 1988; *Nouvel économiste*, 1994). Finally, the third substantive distinction, along with dislike of movement for its own sake and rejection of undue intensity, the plea for moderation carried with it explicit recommendations of flexibility and lack of dogmatism (Les Professeurs du Groupe HEC, 1994). French managers, according to a number of consulting firms (including some American branches) are more comfortable with ambiguity than their American counterparts, less keen on standardized templates. In sum, French business accepted innovation, even some fads, within a distinctive cultural context, that reshaped the movement considerably from its American prototypes. Here was one possible explanation for the absence of real national gurus: it was hard to muster up the dogmatic enthusiasms of which faddish leadership was made.

## *Selectivity*

From the origins of the new interests in the 1960s and 1970s, French innovators – commentators and executives alike – sought a consistent basic goal, and tended to downplay or reject American imports that could not be turned to that goal. In the process, sometimes unwittingly, they used but also departed from the American models. The essential focus served as a litmus with which successive American fads were tested.

From the start, the goal was an alternative to hierarchy and "Taylorism", a vivid focus that accepted American techniques, but also transformed them.

American and French innovators often shared a desire for decentralization, new attention to human resources, and movements for wider employee participation, but the French alone applied these specifics to a single past model – the Taylor model – and discarded many fads that did not seem to further the basic transformation from a bad or outmoded past to a brighter present and future. While virtually every American fad had its advocates and groupies, as we have seen, in fact the real thrust of imitation was surprisingly consistent.

Examples abound, from the early 1970s to the late 1990s. Articles on quality circles might be entitled "Good-bye mister Taylor", blasting the "old certitudes of the Taylor era." In contrast, the new goal, the alternative to Taylorism, was "to mobilize the women and men of the company around their activities and their projects." The thrust was to "detaylorize and humanize," with "detaylorization" fulfilled in "the company that mobilizes everyone's intelligence." The goal, again, was not a series of fads, but a consistent effort to replace an outdated model with a new one. "All the skills, all levels of hierarchy must meet" (Archier & Sérieyx, 1986; Peyrefitte, 1986; Raveleau, 1983; Sérieyx, 1983).

The early enthusiasm for quality circles was a key result of this interest, as they were immediately cast into a "detaylorizing," participatory mode considerably different from the American prototypes, that were more focused on measuring performance and output (Doucet, 1986; Gagne, 1997). Circles would cut costs – Sérieyx claimed that existing efforts cost only 20% of what they saved – but through regular meetings of small groups of employees, not the statistical measurements associated with the movement in the United States. Hence, early on, a claim that the circles, though imported, were being implemented "a la française" (Bemeer, 1986; Sérieyx, 1986). The quality circle movement seemed to offer a response to international competition, given its apparent success not only in the United States but also Japan. It answered earlier pleas, as in Servan-Schreiber's *American Challenge*, to address basic culture and structure, beginning with the penchant for centralization and hierarchy. It suited the moment, around 1980, when global pressures were mounting and when business sought alternatives to socialist pressure. It allowed French companies, haltingly and incompletely to be sure, to address their own rather authoritarian heritage, which was the key point. And the interest persisted, still under discussion in the latter 1980s. Other fads, widely trumpeted in the United States, might thus be folded into to the existing French trajectory. In this vein, French advocates presented elements of Total Quality Management in terms of improving and extending the effort to modify taylorist organization. Here was another chance to reduce central direction in favor of releasing initiative throughout the company. It was not, supporters like Sérieyx suggested, a fad at all, but rather an integration of valid portions of a number of specific theories plus a large dollop of common sense. While the reminder of familiar truths was welcome, response did not require a host of expensive conferences (Archier & Sérieyx, 1984; Sérieyx, 1986).

Finally, it was the basic interest in a participatory alternative to "Taylorism" and hierarchy that defined key responses to later American fads. Enthusiasms that seemed to gain a separate life in the United States, like Total Quality Management, received relatively little play. Key books were translated but not widely reviewed, and the crusading American tone was largely absent. Supportive associations formed, to be sure. But the zealousness of TQM advocates already ran afoul of the French style, and the merits of the movement largely fit into the decentralization, anti-Taylorist efforts already underway. TQM did, to be sure, add a salutary interest in the customer, which French observers, even in the Ministry of Industry, acknowledged and praised, but this was an accretion, not a separate initiative. And in practice, most specific TQM ideas were divided into separate categories, not given the worshipful attention that the movement gained in some American quarters (Noye, 1997). Business school curricula did not in the main add Total Quality courses, as their American counterparts did so eagerly. Previous adjustments, as in the addition of human resources components, largely sufficed (Cohen, 1995; Sérieyx, 1986).

In the same context, a number of other American enthusiasms received at best passing attention. Strategic management did not catch on too widely, arguably because most interested French companies thought they were doing it already. Consulting firms offered help, but without quite as much priority as in the United States, where it typically headed the list of services in management consulting firms (Bounfour, 1992). The variety of leadership movements, addressed to individual self-improvement, were also at best modestly popular. French managers assumed, as we have seen, that they had the necessary attributes (or perhaps, if not graduates of the best schools, would not benefit from additional training). American oscillations between recommendations of decentralization and then a return to centralization were simply not echoed in France. "Pendulum swings" cited in American business literature from the 1950s onward do not crop up in French materials – save in observations about the United States. There was a French debate, to be sure, between the centralizing tradition and the new reform impulse, but managers were more interested in taking a stance within the debate than in zigzagging from one pole to the other.

Hesitations about faddism that diverged from the core French concern about authoritarianism versus participation showed clearly in the belated and skeptical response to the American reengineering movement of the early 1990s. Translations of the initial work came quickly, to be sure. But most French managers and commentators seemed to find the approach contradictory to the attention to a more participatory management style. Rather, it was a new incarnation of Taylorism, a "neo-Taylorism" that should be rejected. Some also criticized it as a technique without clear goal. But the main comment focused on reengineering's scorn for "human capital," precisely the entity that earlier reforms had highlighted. French observers focused on the downsizing aspect, which they professed to find socially irresponsible (particularly when combined with the widely-noted "indecency" of American chief executive salaries and the social costs of excessive deregulation). Thus, companies picked up reengineering late, again with some individual exceptions. The movement was termed in decline almost immediately, again because of its social liabilities and potential abuse. The French publisher of the original reengineering book actually refused to translate Hammer's new book *Beyond Reengineering*, citing lack of interest – a rare explicit move. American programs that succeeded reengineering, notably Reichhold's fidelity movement, won more approving attention, precisely because they rejoined the reform current that most interested French managers (*Certification, Qualité et emploi*, 1997; Chartier, 1996).

It is important not to oversimplify. There was faddism in France, based particularly on repeated enthusiasms for (almost) all things American where business was concerned. The central innovation interest, in using new, often imitative techniques to modify key management traditions, was not uniformly triumphant, precisely because it did attack well-established beliefs and practices. But the basic debate that resulted was somewhat more consistent, somewhat less faddish and more guru-resistant, than the business climate on the other side of the Atlantic. From 1989 onward, *Expansion* began to talk recurrently of a more confident new managerial generation in France, less interested in importing foreign styles and eager to "forge their own model, better integrated with the French temperament" (AFCET-AFPLANE, 1990: 100–102). French business schools, correspondingly, were posed to break away from the unduly specialized and technical American models. The verbiage was vague, for the French alternative was not clearly presented. It reflected no small amount of national wishful thinking, at a point when American business was poised for new dynamism. But a French adaptation had occurred to a degree, and a partial distancing from faddish enthusiasms was part of the process.

# FACTORS IN MANAGEMENT INNOVATION AND FADDISM

Examination of changes and continuity in French management styles contributes to the explanation of business faddism, as the important parallels as well as the differences play out in juxtaposition to American patterns. Both cases, for example, reveal the lack of correlation between surges of enthusiasm and current economic conditions. Faddism can accelerate during prosperity, as in the American turn to strategic planning and reengineering during the 1990s or the growing French interest in imitation in the late 1960s. It can recede in initial response to a downturn, as in France during 1992–1994. What matters is business perception of possible future problems – again, France in the 1960s is a clear case in point – and above all a somewhat freefloating anticipation of major changes to come.

For faddism most clearly responds, if sometimes rather obliquely, to a desire to prepare for the unknown, for a future that will differ fundamentally from the recent past. In this sense, it differs from earlier developments, like Taylorism, that focused on clearly defined workplace problems. Fads reflect a growing sense of uncontrolled chaos and unpredictability. Anticipated uses of new technology, for example in changing the nature of communication, can play a role here. Obviously, the transition from a largely manufacturing base to service and information functions (with related changes in the composition and educational background of the labor forces) figures very prominently, as in the French identification of a need to jettison what they (perhaps unfairly) call Taylorism in favor of a more open-ended model. Specific business fads can seem unfocused, even superficial, but they are designed in hopes that innovation will improve capacities to deal with issues that cannot be precisely defined save as differing substantially from what has been familiar. French and American business has shared this general impulse during the past three decades, and the French zeal for imitation of prior American anticipations reveals the common context.

At the same time, of course, specific definitions of the past and projections of future needs vary, in part according to prior traditions. The French have been clearer in their focus on hierarchy and the dominance of engineering models as the framework to be modified. American targets are less explicit, more open to fluctuation despite or perhaps because of a more wholehearted devotion to the idea of change. French fads, furthermore, have more overt political content, in reacting to an interventionist state, than is true in the United States. France has also used imitative faddism, almost regardless of precise contours, as a means of dealing with prior parochialism, of joining an international mainstream. While references to globalization pepper American faddism, along with a desire to react to the unexpected success of foreign competition, the sense of an isolation to overcome is less well developed. Precisely because faddism is intended to deal with diffuse problems and projections, its purposes reflect different national needs.

But faddism reflects more than statements of problems, however indirect. It also mirrors elements in cultural traditions and educational structures, and some of these run surprisingly deep. American consumer culture, including promotional opportunities in publishing and conferencing, is more fully adapted to faddism and guruism than is the French culture. Expectations about fads and about the need for popularized expertise in other aspects of life differ, and this conditions business reactions. Americans are more other-directed than the French, and so more open to signals from popularizations (Riesman, 1981; Stearns, 1999). The role of popular psychology differs in the two cultures, and this shows up for example in human resources commentary and the differing numbers of self-help management books. The relationship between business and academe is more tense in the United States than in France, and the result encourages individual entrepreneurs to go one up on academics by citing their practical experience while encouraging venturesome academics to out-guru (and outearn) the promotional entrepreneurs. French academics, though interested in applied work, are more comfortable with their own domain. Greater French caution about fads in part reflects a greater hesitation to defy academic respectability or to bend academics to whimsical winds. French business commentators, and perhaps managers themselves, display a greater historical sense than their American counterparts, reflecting possible cultural differences but also different degrees of mobility from one organization to the next. While French executives are also told to worry about faulty organizational memory (Bon & Ourset, 1988), discussions of fads are guided by a clearer sense of a prior historical model (Taylorism) and by more frequent injunctions to recognize that a fad, while new, actually contains elements already in practice, perhaps as a result of a previous fad. The greater continuity, in France, between quality circles and TQM is a case in point.

The role of business schools is vital. American business schools have been cited for their emphasis on constant innovation (O'Shea & Madigan, 1997). The rapid expansion of MBAs has not been accompanied by a movement for professionalization – which would involve greater standardization (in part around established knowledge), testing and the like. The quest for innovation and frequent curriculum changes in this sense substitutes for profession-alization, providing a sense of special knowledge without the rigidity (and potential bargaining power) that professionalization brings. The Academy of Management meeting in 1999 thus featured 150–200 new titles from each top publisher, claiming – through remarkably similar-sounding titles – access to the latest fads. These factors are present in France as well, as imitation and faddism have been part of a struggle to establish business schools and their graduates in an educational system far more fully dominated by engineering. But the business school role, while growing, remains smaller, and the competition requires greater curricular circumspection in business school ranks. Manage-ment training provides a clear target for French reformers, and real changes have occurred as a consequence, but the context inhibits the freewheeling atmosphere that sees many American business schools straining to keep pace with the latest business fashions.

Finally, differential faddism reflects distinctions in managerial self-con-fidence. Adoption of recurrent fads helps American managers build a sense of leadership and woo their subordinates, as some TQM adepts noted, this function can be independent of the precise content of a given fad. Fads also respond to a pervasive sense of worry and insecurity in American managerial ranks. French managers are more self-assured. Their reactions, whether justifiable or not, stem from greater postwar economic success plus the more secure rankings provided by the educational system. The hierarchical tradition assures a loyalty that fads need not buy. The result is not, overall, a total resistance to change, but a clearly selective approach to innovation and imitation (Micklethwait & Wooldridge, 1996).

# CONCLUSION

French reactions to American business trends since World War I follow a classic cultural-imitation model. The power of foreign example is granted, and a variety of contacts expand awareness of what this example entails, in this case, including the procession of American management styles. Resistance includes outright attack and cynicism, a reluctance really to change much even when apparent imitation occurs, and a desire to shake off tutelage in favor of one's own defined style. Important elements of the pre-contact management culture persist. But there is change as well, based not on wholesale importation but on selectivity and blending with existing patterns. The result is hard to define, for it is neither traditional (classically French) nor entirely convergent

(Americanized). But it has its own flavor, in this case including a somewhat distinctive reaction to faddish swings. Above all, the central problem is not for the most part portrayed as catching up to a superior model, but using elements of this model to deal with a set of issues that are domestic and domestically defined.

Has the French approach worked better than the American? It is certainly tempting to emphasize its greater consistency, but also possible, as some French observers themselves have noted, to belabor undue timidity and selectivity. Further comparative analysis is clearly warranted, and it is also possible to conclude, precisely because of the importance of traditional and structural factors in the development of contemporary faddism, that no single optimum can be identified in any event. It is difficult to decide if fads have been useful even within the United States. Some analysis inclines to the affirmative, while noting however the legion of companies cited one year for their innovative leadership that have gone down the tubes three years later (Micklethwait & Wooldridge, 1996). French economic results, overall, since the 1960s advent of faddism, compare very favorably to those in the United States. One account, even in the 1990s where the balance seems to incline toward recent American advantage, notes a 12% French lead in productivity per worker (*Nouvel économiste*, 1996). Certainly, it is possible to suggest a somewhat different mix of problems and strengths with regard to faddism. Greater American willingness to innovate relates to frequent changes in signals, as in the shift from participatory TQM to hierarchical downsizing with reengineering. French business, though not unwilling to change, may nevertheless hesitate unduly, while at the same time serving up less confusion to the labor force.

The French experience, however difficult to evaluate comparatively, offers one other important lesson. American observers, including businessmen, frequently belabor the French hierarchical and elitist proclivities (*Nouvel économiste*, 1995). How much the comments reflect stereotypes and how much they result from ongoing experience is not always easy to sort out. Recent management history shows clearly that there are distinctive French ingredients in the contemporary business equation but also that significant change and adaptation are significant parts of the story. It is vital to keep the diversity and responsiveness of French business in mind, and imitative faddism has a significant role in the comparative story. Ultimately, the most interesting prospect may be the hesitant emergence of a newer assertion of differentiation, based not primarily on tradition but on a distinctive definition of the kinds of changes to be sought in contemporary management.

## ACKNOWLEDGMENT

Research for this article was generously supported by a grant from the Carnegie Bosch Institute.

*Author contact*: Meg Brindle, Department of Public and International Affairs, George Mason University, Fairfax, VA 22030.

## REFERENCES

Abrahamson, E. (1996). Management fashion. *Academy of Management Review, 21*, 254–285.

AFCET-AFPLANE (1990). *Vers une école européene du management stratégique* [Toward a European school of strategic management]. Paris: AFCET.

Archier, G., & Sérieyx, H. (1986). *Pilotes du troisième type* [Guidelines of the Third Type]. Paris: Seuil.

Archier, G., & Sérieyz. H. (1984). *L'Entreprise du troisième type* [The company of the third type]. Paris: Seuil.

Balicco, C. (1994). *Methodes d'évaluation des ressources humaines: la fin des marchands de certitude* [Methods of evaluating human resources]. Paris: Ed. d'Organisation.

Barsoux, J. L., & Lawrence, P. (1991). The making of a french manager. *Harvard Business Review, 69*, 58–67.

Bemeer, L. (1986). French quality circles multiply, but with a difference. *International Management, 44*, 12–23.

Bolton, M. (1995). *Assessment and Development in Europe: Adding Value to Industries and Organizations*. London: McGraw-Hill.

Bon, J., & Ourset, R. (1988). L'Entreprise amnésiaque [The forgetful firm]. *Revue Française de Gestion, 69*, 178–183.

Boston Consulting (1990). *Les mécanismes fondamentaux de la compétitivité* [The basic mechanisms of competitiveness]. Paris: Hommes et Techniques.

Bounfour, A. (1992). *Chers consultants: Enjeux et règles de relations enterprises-consultants* [Dear consultants: Processes and rules for business-consultant relationships]. Paris: Dunod.

*Certification, qualité et emploi* [Certification, quality and employment] (1997). Paris: Economica.

Chanlet, J. (1994). Francophone organizational analysis (1950–1990): An overview. *Organization Studies, 15*, 47–79.

Chapman, H. (19810. *State Radicalism in the French Aircraft Industry.* Berkeley, CA: University of California Press.

Chapman, H. (1999). *A Century of Organized Labor in France.* New York: St. Martin's Press.

Chartier, E. (1996). *Le re-engineering du système d'information de l'entreprise* [Re-engineering the information system of a firm]. Paris: Economica.

Citeau, J. P. (1997). *Gestion de ressources humaines* [Management of human resources]. Paris: Armand Colin.

Cohen, A. (1995). *MBA management: Synthèse des meilleurs cours des grandes business schools* [Synthesis of the best courses of the great business schools]. Paris: Maxima.

Cross, G. (1983). *Immigrant Workers in Industrial France.* Philadelphia: Temple University Press.

126 MARGARET BRINDLE AND PETER N. STEARNS

Crozier, M., & Friedberg, E. (1977). *L'Acteur et le système* [The actor and the system]. Paris: Seuil.

d'Iribarne, P. (1989). *La logique de l'honneur: Gestion des enterprises et traditions nationales* [The Logic of Honor: Business management and national traditions]. Paris: Editions du Seuil.

Declerck, R., Debourse, J. P., & Navarre, C. (1983). *Méthode de direction générale: Le management stratégique* [General Management Method: Strategic Management]. Paris: Hommes et Techniques.

Delanotte, Y. (1972). *Recherches en vue d'une organisation plus humaine du travail industriel* [Research Toward a More Humane Organization of Industrial Work]. Paris: La documentation française.

Demming, W. E. (1988). *Quality: Le rêve du management* [Quality: The Dream of Management]. Paris: Economica.

Doblin, S., & Ardouin, J. L. (1989). *Du rouge au noir ou les profits retrouvés* [From Red to Black, or Rediscovering Profit]. Paris: Publi-union.

Dominique, M. (1994). Benchmarking, ou le droit de copier [Benchmarking, or the right of copy]. *Nouvel économiste, 929*, 59.

Doucet, C. (1986). *La Maitrise de la qualite* [Mastering Quality]. Paris: ESF.

Drucker, P. (1957). *La Pratique de la direction des entreprises* [The Practice of Management]. Paris: Ed. d'Organisation.

Dumont, G. (1996). *Innovation organisationelle et résistance au changement* [Organizational Innovation and Resistance to Change]. Paris: Université Panthéon.

*Expansion* 1980–1999 (Vol. 218–576).

Fayol, H. (1949). *General and Industrial Management* (trans. C. Storrs). London: Pitman.

Fichter, J. L. (1988). Non au project d'entreprise [Rejecting the Business Project]. *Revue Française de Gestion, 68*, 85–88.

Frère, M. (1991). Participative management at Aérosptaiale. *European Participation Monitor P +, 2*, 15–18.

Fridenson, P., & Straus, A. (1987). *Le Capitalisme français, 19e–20e siècles: blocages et dynamismes d'une croissance* [French Capitalism, 19th-20th Centuries: Spurs and impediments to growth]. Paris: Fayard.

Frommer, J., & McCormick, J. (1989). *Transformations in French Business: Political, Economic and Cultural Changes from 1981 to 1987*. New York: Quorum Books.

Furlough, E. (1993). Selling the American Way in Interwar France: Prix Uniques and the Salons des Arts Menagers. *Journal of Social History, 26*, 491–519.

Gagne, J. M. (1997). *Le paradigme de la qualite* [The Quality Paradigm]. Paris: Economica.

Gelinier, O. (1976). *Politique sociale de l'entreprise* [Social Policies of the Firm]. Paris: Hommes et Techniques.

Godet, M. (1986). *Perspective et planification stratégique* [Strategic Perspective and Planning]. Paris: Economica.

Godet, M. (1994). *From anticipation to action: A handbook of strategic perspective*. Paris: UNESCO.

*Guide du consulting* (1990–1998).

Gurviez, J. J. (1987). Hit-Parade des écoles de commerce [Hit Parade of Business Schools]. *Expansion, 304*, 46–47.

Hamalion, E. (1997). *Objectif qualité totale: Des enterprises français temoignent* [Objective Total Quality: French Firms Testify]. Paris: Economica.

Herzberg, F. (1971). *Le Travail et le nature de l'homme* [Work and the Nature of Man]. Paris: Enterprise moderne d'édition.
Hofstede, G. (1980). *Culture's consequences: International Differences in Work-Related Values.* Beverly Hills, CA: Sage.
Hughes, H. S. (1968). *The Obstructed Path: French Social Thought in the Years of Desperation, 1930–1960.* New York: Harper & Row.
Kieser, A. (1994). Why organization theory needs historical analyses. *Organization Science, 5,* 608–620.
Kotler, P. (1991). *Vers l'entreprise intelligente* [Toward the Intelligent Workplace]. Paris.
Kuisel, R. (1993). *Seducing the French: The Dilemma of Americanization.* Berkeley, CA: University of California Press.
Landier, H. (1988). *Vers l'entreprise intelligente* [Toward the Intelligent Firm]. Paris: Calmann-Lévy.
Laurent, A. (1983). The cultural diversity of western conceptions of management. *International Studies of Management and Organization, 13,* 5–96.
Laurent, A. (1986). The cross-cultural puzzle of international human resource management. *Human Resource Management, 25,* 91–102.
Lawrence, P. (1993). Management development in Europe: A study in cultural contrast. *Human Resources Management Journal, 3,* 11–23.
Le Goff, J. P. (1992). *Le Mythe de l'entreprise* [The Myth of Enterprise]. Paris: EditionsLa Découverte.
Le Goff, J. P. (1996). *Illusions du management* [Illusions of Management]. Paris: Découverte.
Lemaitre, P. (1983). *Methologie appliquée au "problem-solving"* [Problem-solving as applied methodology]. Paris: Chotard.
Les Professeurs du Groupe HEC (1994). *L'ecole des managers de demain* [The School for Tomorrow's Managers]. Paris: Economica.
Locke, R., & Leuteau, M. (1988). Formation à la gestion en France et en Allemagne [Management Training in France and Germany]. *Revue Française de Gestion, 70,* 186–202.
McFralin, D., Sweeney, P., & Cotta, J. (1992). Attitudes toward employee participation in decision-making: A compendium of European and American managers in a United States multinational company. *Human Resource Management, 31,* 363–384.
Métier du patron [The Boss's Profession] (1987). *Nouvel économiste, 27,* 39.
Micklethwait, J., & Wooldridge, A. (1996). *The witch doctors: Making sense of management gurus.* New York: Times Business.
Moulin, G. (1986). *Monsieur le président directeur général* [Mr. CEO]. Paris: Ballard.
Naulleau, G., & Harper, J. (1993). A comparison of British and French management cultures. *Management Education and Development, 24,* 14–25.
*Nouvel économiste* (1983, 407); (1985, 471); (1986, 552–560).
Noye, D. (1997). *L'Amélioration participative des processus* [Improving Process through Participation]. Paris: Ministère de l'industrie.
Odgen, P. E., & White, P. D. (1989). *Migrants in Modern France: Population Mobility in the Late Nineteenth and Twentieth Centuries.* London: Unwin Hyman.
O'Shea, J., & Madigan, C. (1997). *Dangerous Company: The Consulting Powerhouses and the Businesses They Save and Ruin.* London: Nicholas Brealey
Page, J. P., Turcq, D., Bailly. M., & Foldes, G. (1988). *La recherche de l'excellence en France* [The Quest for Excellence in France]. Paris: Dunod.
Pateyron, E. (1998). *La veille stratégique* [The Strategy Watch]. Paris: Economica.

Peters, T., & Waterman R. (1983). *Prix de l'excellence* [In search of excellence]. Paris: InterEditions.

Peyrefitte, A. (1986). *Le mal français* [The French Problem]. Paris: Fayard.

Raveleau, G. (1983). *Les cercles de qualité français* [French Quality Circles]. Paris: Entreprise moderne.

Reichheld, F. (1996). *L'effet loyauté* [The Loyalty Effect]. Paris: Dunod.

*Revue française de gestion* (1975–1999).

Riesman, D. (1981). *The Lonely Crowd: A Study of the Changing American Character*. New Haven, NJ: Yale University Press.

Sallenave, J. P. (1993). *De l'antimanagement* [On Antimanagement]. Paris: Ed. d'Organisation.

Savall, H. (1975). *Enrichir le travail humain: l'Évolution économique* [Enriching Human Work: Economic Evolution]. Paris: Dunod.

Sérieyx, H. (1983). *Mobiliser l'intelligence de l'entreprise: Cercles de qualité et cercles de pilotage* [Mobilizing intelligence in the firm: quality circles and guidance circles]. Paris: Entreprise moderne.

Sérieyx, H. (1986). Management in, management out. *Expansion, 11*, 21–35.

Servan-Schreiber, J. L. (1973). *L'Entreprise à visage humain* [Business with a Human Face]. Paris: R. Laffont.

Servan-Schreiber, J. J. (1968). *The American challenge*. New York: Atheneum.

Shackleton, V., & Newell, S. (1993). How companies in Europe select their managers. *Selection and Development Review, 9*, 62–65.

Sicard, C. (1987). *Pratique de la stratégie d'entreprise* [The Practice of Business Strategy]. Paris: Editions Hommes et Techniques.

Sparrow, P., & Hiltrop, J. M. (1994). *European Human Resource Management in Transition*. Englewood Cliffs, NJ: Prentice Hall.

Stearns, P. (1997). *Fat history: Bodies and Beauty in the Modern West*. New York: New York University Press.

Stearns, P. (1999). *Battleground of desire: The Struggle for Self-Control in America*. New York: New York University Press.

Stern, P., & Tutoy, P. (1995). *Le métier du consultant* [The Consultant's Profession]. Paris: Ed. d'Organisation.

Stoffaës, C. (1980). La fin du modèle industriel américain [The End of the American Industrial Model]. *Revue Française de Gestion, 26*, 39–49.

Stora, G. (1986). *La qualité totale dans l'entreprise* [Total Quality in the Firm]. Paris: Ed. d'Organisation.

Sudreau, P. (1975). *Rapport du comité d'étude pour la reforme de l'entreprise* [Report of the Study Committee on Business Reform]. Paris: Documentation française.

Touraine, A. (1966). *L'evolution du travail ouvrier aux usines Renault* [The Evolution of Work in the Renault Factories]. Paris: A. Colin.

Touraine, A. (1969). *La société post-industrielle* [Postindustrial Society]. Paris: Denoil.

Usunier, J. C. (1990). French international business education: A pessimistic view. *European Management Journal, 8*, 388–393.

Verret, A. (1998). Avec le coaching, l'entreprise retrouve l'esprit [With Coaching, The Firm Gains Morale]. *Nouvel Économiste, 11118*, 69–79.

Weiss, D. (1978). *Le démocratie industrielle: Cogestion ou controle ouvrier* [Industrial democracy: Co-management or worker control]. Paris: Ed. d'Organisation.

Zarka, M., & Jarrosson, B. (1995). *Le stratégie réinventée* [Reinventing Strategy]. Paris: Dunod.

# BANKING ON EACH OTHER: THE SITUATIONAL LOGIC OF ROTATING SAVINGS AND CREDIT ASSOCIATIONS

Nicole Woolsey Biggart

## ABSTRACT

*Poverty stems from many causes and has multiple expressions around the world. Nonetheless, in recent years international development agencies and governments have focused above all on one strategy for poverty alleviation: microlending programs that provide credit to groups of poor people, usually women, for small business activities. While microlending programs such as those developed by the Grameen Bank in Bangladesh are politically and morally attractive, in fact there is little understanding of the social conditions under which these programs are likely to succeed or fail. Using an interpretive comparative case methodology, I analyze a globally widespread and naturally occurring type of group financing organization, the rotating savings and credit association, to identify those social structural characteristics associated with successful peer group lending arrangements. I demonstrate the utility of an economic sociology approach – seeing economic organizations as rooted in social structure – to understanding an important credit institution.*

## INTRODUCTION

In February, 1997 an extraordinary gathering of 2000 officials and dignitaries from 137 countries declared a commitment to end poverty through the

Advances in Qualitative Organization Research, Volume 3, pages 129–153.
2001 by Elsevier Science Ltd.
ISBN: 0-7623-0772-2

extension of credit to 100 million of the world's poorest families by the year 2005. The Microcredit Summit, held in Washington, D.C. attracted five heads of state and four first ladies, including Hillary Rodham Clinton. Numerous parliamentarians and ministers, including U.S. Secretary of the Treasury Robert Rubin, joined activists from the United Nations, international aid agencies, philanthropic foundations, and religious leaders at the meeting. Members of the international banking community, including World Bank President James Wolfensohn, and executives from Citicorp, Wells Fargo Bank, Monsanto Corporation, and many other large financial and commercial institutions participated.

This unprecedented assemblage of governmental, philanthropic, religious and business elites from around the world convened to lend political and financial support to a single solution to the problem of poverty: microcredit. Microcredit is the loan of tiny amounts of money for entrepreneurial business activities to poor women organized in solidarity groups. The groups, typically of 15–20 participants, are organized by paid employees of non-governmental organizations (NGOs). The NGOs lend money to members who must repay the funds on time in order to get further loans. Successful repayment of small loans may lead to more substantial loans. The money in the fund, initially supplied by the NGO, "belongs" to the group and if there are defaults there is less money available to everyone.

An estimated 1.3 billion people live in poverty today, and it is arguably the largest and most intractable social problem in the world. The microcredit movement has gained force as a solution to this problem for at least three reasons. First, microcredit targets women and therefore serves the interests of children who represent many of the world's population of poor people. Second, microcredit promises to be a cost-effective solution that puts most resources directly in the hands of the poor, not development bureaucracies or corrupt governments. Third, the microcredit idea brings together groups that histor-ically have not been allies. Advocates for the poor have found new support from business elites attracted to the concept of self-sufficient enterprise as a tool for poverty reduction, especially since microcredit relies primarily on loans and not grants.

Microcredit joins ideas about financial responsibility and business acumen with beliefs about the effectiveness of peer pressure and assistance to help participants make good business decisions and to repay loans on time. Established microcredit programs, such as the Grameen Bank in Bangladesh, give credibility to the idea of peer group lending as an effective tool for poverty alleviation. However, the rapidity with which microcredit is being spread globally to very different settings suggests that a dispassionate analysis of the conditions under which microcredit works, or fails to work, is crucial. To date, there has been no such analysis and at least a few researchers suggest that microcredit programs can be difficult to sustain (Bouman, 1994; Taub, 1998).

I believe that an existing type of indigenous peer lending arrangement, the Rotating Savings and Credit Association or "rosca," offers an important opportunity to understand the conditions under which microcredit programs might flourish. Roscas are a globally widespread type of informal organization that brings together social familiars for purposes of saving and lending. While microcredit programs and roscas vary in particulars, they both organize groups of people for the purposes of enforced saving and extension of collateral-free loans, and they both rely on social pressures to make periodic payments. Microcredit is targeted primarily at women (an estimated 80% of participants), and while roscas involve men in some settings, they too are primarily used by women in many locations. The comparability of the two forms has not gone unnoticed and microcredit proponents sometimes refer to the success of "naturally occurring" roscas as evidence that "induced" microcredit arrangements can be efficacious. In this study I use available data on roscas to identify conditions that seem common to successful roscas in a variety of settings, and by extension, to suggest those factors that may be crucial to the success of microcredit arrangements organized by development agencies.

Secondarily, this study substantiates the utility of an interpretive economic sociology perspective to understand the economic logic of a widespread, socially embedded credit institution. Economic theory has long accepted that credit granting is a matter of converting the uncertainty of repayment into a calculable risk (Knight, [1921] 1964, [1935] 1976). The presumption is that the most efficient way to allocate credit is to match large numbers of savers with large numbers of borrowers through the brokerage of intermediary institutions that assess the credit worthiness of applicants – the "efficient market" hypothesis. Institutions such as banks perform ex-ante screening of borrowers for their ability and willingness to repay by assessing past debt repayment, the likely future income stream, and the value of assets that may be used for collateral should a borrower fail to repay. Intermediaries exercise post-ante sanctions in the case of default, for example the seizure of assets, garnishing of wages, and reporting default to credit information agencies. Banks and other intermediaries that do not have rich information about borrowing strangers, whom they match with depositors, spread risk over large numbers of transactions. Trust in individual borrowers is made irrelevant; it is only necessary that the class of borrowers as a whole return a sufficient spread between the costs of paying interest to savers and the costs of lending.

Roscas do not utilize unknown intermediaries, do not involve large numbers of borrowers and lenders, and do not demand collateral. However, the structure of roscas has a clear economic logic that employs both ex ante screening and the threat of post ante sanctions. As will be shown below, they have an economic logic rooted in social structure and social relations.

## ROTATING SAVINGS AND CREDIT ASSOCIATIONS

Roscas have a number of variations but typically are "an association formed upon a core of participants who agree to make regular contributions to a fund which is given, in whole or part, to each contributor in rotation" (Ardener, 1964: 201). For example, eleven acquaintances might agree to contribute $10 to a fund once each month for eleven months. Once during that period each contributor would take the monthly $100 "pot" of contributions. This arrangement allows people who find it difficult to raise money to periodically have access to relatively substantial amounts of capital useful for business purposes, consumption or income smoothing. Roscas often involve very small amounts of money, but can be rolled over to buy more substantial purchases such as real estate and business inventories. In some locations people will belong to more than one rosca.

Roscas are important in many developing countries in Africa, South America, and Asia, and have been researched extensively by anthropologists, sociologists and economists (e.g. Bouman, 1979, 1990; Castells & Portes, 1989; Cubitt, 1995; DeLancey, 1977; Freidrich, 1965; Kerry, 1976). Researchers have noted rosca use among Jamaican migrants to British cities (Sterling, 1995), Japanese villagers (Embree, 1939), Bolivian office-workers (Adams & Canavesi, 1989), Nigerian farmers (Nwabughuogu, 1984), rural Indians (Anderson, 1966), and diasporic Chinese (Wu, 1974). For the most part, research on roscas consists of case studies that examine the operation of rosca arrangements in neighborhoods, or communities. These studies provide detailed understanding of the economic and social role roscas play in local settings and offer important insight into the interplay of economic and social relations.

Recently, development scholars have attempted to move beyond localized case analyses and create more general understanding of roscas. For example, Bouman (1995) extrapolated features from known roscas in various settings to discuss two important savings and lending forms and hybrid variations. Development economists have often attempted to apply neoclassical principles to informal economic activity generally (cf. Feige, 1990; Hoff & Stiglitz, 1990) and have even created econometric models of the financial conditions under which roscas are economically rational and sustainable (Besley, Coate & Loury 1993, 1994). Economic studies of roscas have also tended to focus on the role of informal credit markets in regional economic development, often in comparison with regulated markets (e.g. Chu, 1995; van den Brink & Chavas, 1997).

I believe that the voluminous material on roscas also offers the opportunity to do a comparative analysis of the social conditions under which peer lending arrangements are successful. Thus, in the present study I analyze a large cross-section of case studies of roscas in Sub-Saharan Africa, Latin America, the Indian subcontinent, East Asia, and diasporic communities in North America and Europe to deduce the conditions under which diverse peoples use peer lending arrangements. My analysis seeks to answer the question, "Under what social circumstances will people pool their money successfully for personal or mutual gain?"

## FIVE COMMON CIRCUMSTANCES

Roscas are widespread and are found in very different types of societies. They appear in patrilineal and caste-based social orders, in cities (Adams & Canavesi, 1989) and in rural settings (Bouman, 1984). They are used for purposes of consumption (Mayoux & Anand, 1995), commerce (Little, 1972), and income-smoothing (Sethi, 1995). They exist among Hindus (Sethi, 1995), Christians (Mayoux & Anand, 1995), Moslems (Bouman & Moll, 1992; Srinivasan, 1995), and Confucians (Wu, 1974). There is no clear set of structural, occupational, geographic, cultural, or religious factors that are associated with roscas, and there is no evidence that this financial form diffused from one society to another. They do not, however, exist everywhere. I argue instead that roscas exist under a set of conditions where they satisfy a *situational logic*.

Situational logics are constellations of factors that together lead actors to view certain courses of action as efficacious and sensible. For example, Hobsbawm (1981) analyzed the conditions under which banditry, found in societies as diverse as China, Peru, Sicily, the Ukraine and Indonesia, occurs. Banditry is "one of the most universal social phenomena known to history, and one of the most amazingly uniform," but its "uniformity is not the consequence of cultural diffusion, but the reflection of similar situations" (1981: 18). Hobsbawm's interpretive analysis of diverse case materials demonstrated that banditry occurs as a form of retributive justice in societies transitioning between monarchic kinship and market societies, forming what Walton calls a "universal case" (1992: 128).

Methodologically similar to Hobsbawm's approach, my interpretation of the position of diverse actors allows me to reconstruct the situational logic of rotating savings and credit associations. A reading of a wide variety of cases of roscas around the world shows that amazingly similar sets of circumstances are common to most, if not all, and represent the "universal case" of a situational logic. While not all roscas in all places and times share exactly the same features and conditions, the differences are very much variations on a discernible theme, as indicated in Table 1.

Indeed, at least five common social conditions are associated with roscas in the cases I examined. These conditions are not clearly separable in practice – in fact, they are overlapping and mutually reinforcing. However, I separate them for analytical purposes in order to isolate the role each plays in contributing to a situational logic in which pooling money with others makes sense.

Roscas, as informal and unregulated financial institutions, cannot rely on legal and state controls to assure enforcement of payment agreements made by participants. Roscas seldom maintain written records, much less formal contracts, and do not have collateral agreements to materially mitigate against default. Moreover, every member in the rosca rotation except the last, who is simply getting back contributions already made, has an opportunistic financial incentive to take the pot and not continue to pay into the fund. Nonetheless, roscas are widely reported to have very low default rates (e.g. Angel, deGoede & Sevilla, 1978; Bonnett, 1981; Burman & Lambete, 1995; Kennedy, 1973; Wu, 1974). Both the character of the social setting and attributes of the participants involved help explain the presence and sustainability of roscas. Case analyses indicate that five of the most basic of these are: (1) a communally-based social order, (2) obligations that are held to be collective in nature, (3) social and economic stability, (4) social and economic isolation, and (5) similarity among rosca members in social status.

### Communally-Based Social Order

Although roscas are found in many differently organized societies, they only exist where social structure is built on strong communal ties. Roscas are found in societies organized by kinship networks, clan membership, and common identification with a native place or place of cohabitation (Roberts, 1994). In communal social orders, the group is both a social and financial resource and a powerful socializing and coercive agent. When actors perceive that social or economic advancement is defined and controlled by the group, subordination to group practice makes sense as independent action cannot lead to success.

Table 1. Regional and Social Structural Comparison of Rotating Savings and Credit Associations.

| | AFRICA & WEST INDIES | EAST ASIA & PACIFIC RIM | MEXICO & LATIN AMERICA | INDIA & CENTRAL ASIA |
|---|---|---|---|---|
| **Communally Based Social Order** | The historical emphasis on tribal and familial obligations remains crucial in urban and rural settings. Tribal members in both settings are expected to assist one another socially and economically, and failure to do so is seen as placing both the family reputation and the tribe's future at risk. Nwabughuogu, 1984; Soan & DeCamaramond, 1972. | Kinship ties and tribal or clan affiliations, especially among certain groups of Pacific Islanders, remain central components of social organization. Extended family members and clansmen are expected to assist members in need, and failure to do so results in social ostracism. Geertz, 1962; Kulp, 1925; Light, 1972; Miyanaga, 1995. | Urbanization and industrialization have not significantly decreased the communal basis of social organization and similar attitudes within the community increase membership homogeneity. Cope & Kurtz, 1980; Keefe, Padilla & Carlos, 1979; Keefe & Padilla 1987; Lewis, 1959; Lomnitz, 1977; Véléz-Ibañez, 1983. | Social ties between individuals with similar class (caste) and religious backgrounds, as well as a strong emphasis on kinship ties, continue to fortify social cohesion and mutual responsibility. Ahuja, 1993; Beteille, 1995; Desai, 1982; Faneslow, 1995; Mayer, 1960. |

*Table 1.* Continued.

| | AFRICA & WEST INDIES | EAST ASIA & PACIFIC RIM | MEXICO & LATIN AMERICA | INDIA & CENTRAL ASIA |
|---|---|---|---|---|
| **Social/Geographic Isolation** | Both poor rural and urban dwellers are excluded from formal banking institutions. Migrants to cities duplicate traditional village structures and create informal banking systems based around tribal and familial structures. In immigrant and migrant communities, social ties serve as a resource for capital accumulation.<br><br>Bortei-Doku & Aryeetey, 1995; Burman & Lambete, 1995; Bouman & Harteveld, 1975; Soan & DeCamaramond, 1972. | Poor rural residents are almost entirely excluded from formal banking institutions, as are poor urban dwellers and recent urban migrants. Kin and clan groups in rural areas create their own informal finance systems which are then duplicated by migrants to cities. For many recent urban migrants, ROSCA participation is an important way of becoming integrated into urbancommunities<br><br>Skeldon, 1980 Chhetri, 1995; Hospes, 1995; Morton, 1978; Sexton, 1982; Skeldon, 1980; Wu, 1974. | Kinship support is not significantly damaged by geographic inaccessibility. Among socially marginalized communities, there is a mistrust of formal financial institutions combined with a frequent lack of direct access.<br><br>Carlos & Sellers 1972; Keefe, Padilla & Carlos, 1979; Kurtz, 1973; Lewis, 1959, 1961. | Formal financial institutions primarily address the needs of the wealthy. Socially and economically disadvantaged populations are suspicious of formal banking institutions.<br><br>Chhetri, 1995; Mayoux & Anand, 1995; Nayar, 1973; Sethi, 1995. |

*Table 1.* Continued.

| Collective Obligations | The possession of debt and a commitment to lend to others is a valued characteristic and signify a commitment to the community. While ROSCA members are not necessarily known to each other, ROSCA leaders must earn community respect, and leading or participating in a ROSCA reflects favorably on the individuals involved. Failure to repay debt can result in serious sanctions against not just the individuals involved, but also against whole families. Ajisafe, 1924; Bascom, 1952; Bonnett, 1981; Bortei-Doku & Aryeetey, 1995; Burman & Lambete, 1995; DeLancey, 1978; Nwabughuogu, 1984; Ottenberg, 1968; Rowlands, 1995; Soan & DeCamaramond, 1972. | Mutual aid is a cornerstone of social organization, and timely repayment of debt is paramount to earning and maintaining respect in the community. Those who do not participate in community-oriented activities, including ROSCAs, may face isolation or ostracism. Dishonor follows those whofail to make good on debts, or who fail to participate in community activities. Geertz, 1962; Miyanaga, 1995; Morton, 1978; Sexton, 1982; Skeldon, 1980; Wu, 1974. | A sense of collective obligation deters against the individualism necessary for capital formation, particularly among the poor. Mutual aid is provided by extended family and relations of fictive kinship through the institution of compadrazgo. "Socialcapital is generated by individual members' disciplined compliance with group expectations" (Portes & Sensenbrenner 1993: 1325). Carlos & Sellers, 1972; Keefe, Padilla & Carlos, 1979; Kurtz, 1973; Kurtz & Showman, 1978; Lomnitz, 1977; March & Taqqu, 1986; Portes & Sensenbrenner, 1993; Vélez-Ibañez, 1983. | Attitudes towards ROSCA participation and debt repayment echo long-standing traditions of community participation and sharing within village, class or religious groups. Reputation often hinges on debt repayment and failure to repay desecrates not only the individual'sname, but also the family name. Angel de Goede & Sevilla, 1978; Ardener, 1964; Krishnan, 1959: Mayoux & Anand, 1995; Nayar, 1973; Sethi, 1995; Srinivisan, 1995. |
|---|---|---|---|---|

*Table 1.* Continued.

| | AFRICA & WEST INDIES | EAST ASIA & PACIFIC RIM | MEXICO & LATIN AMERICA | INDIA & CENTRAL ASIA |
|---|---|---|---|---|
| **Social/Economic Stability** | ROSCA leaders are chosen for their stability and trustworthiness. Likewise, members are chosen based on stability within the community, the definition of which varies across regions but generally includes family and occupational stability and position within the community.<br><br>Bortei-Doku & Aryeetey, 1995; Burman & Lambete, 1995; Nwabughuogu, 1984; Ottenberg, 1968. | The stability of ROSCA members is primarily assessed based on familial and financial stability. Those with long-standing ties family ties to the community and steady income are preferred ROSCA leaders and members. In migratory situations, wage laborers are often preferred.<br><br>Miyanga, 1995; Morton, 1978; Skeldon, 1980. | Boundaries are based on patterns of behavior, cultural expectations and the presence of confianza. Uncertainty is reduced by privileging membership qualities that socially anchor the individual in the community (shared language, similarity of values, class, marriage stability).<br><br>Cope & Kurtz, 1980; Lomnitz, 1977; Vélez-Ibañez, 1983. | Organizers and members are expected to have extensive ties to the community, particularly through family obligations. Stability is largely defined by family ties, and, for those who are employed or whose spouses are employed, by job stability. New members are selected largely based on their family's reputation.<br><br>Bouman, 1984; Nayar, 1973; Sethi, 1995. |

*Table 1.* Continued.

| **Similarity of Social Status** | ROSCA members are usually drawn from similar labor fields and share a similar position within theoccupational hierarchy. Gender and ethnicity/tribal affiliation also determine participation in certain ROSCAs. Risk of default is reduced by limiting membership to those who are known in the community and who share certain traits (type and length of employment, family stability, position within the community).<br><br>Bortei-Doku & Aryeetey, 1995; Burman & Lambete, 1995; Brana-Shute, 1976; Nelson, 1995. | Social status is often classified at various levels in the formation of ROSCAs. For example,Hospes' work on Indonesian arisans finds that there are three types of arisans: the arisans of economic peers, of neighborhoods, and of religious groups. The degree of use of these three types varies across regions, and in some areas these elements of stability may also be combined.<br><br>Geertz, 1962; Hospes, 1995; Sexton, 1980. | Cultural patterns and local ideologies of confianza and reciprocal obligation arereproduced within the institutionally variable contexts (family, business, politics). Networks of social relations among people of similar status (class, gender, ethnicity) operates as a vital market and non-market economic resource.<br><br>Adams & Canavesi, 1989; Lommitz & Melnick, 1991; Kurtz & Showman, 1978; Pérez-Lizuar, 1997; Véléz-Ibañez, 1982; Wilson, 1993. | Class (or caste) position is the most significant determinant of ROSCA membership. ROSCAmembers are often drawn from either real or fictive kinship networks and from workplaces. Group homogeneity is further reinforced by comparable income levels, geographic proximity, shared religious and language practices and similar status within the community.<br><br>Bouman, 1984; Mayoux & Anand, 1995; Nayar, 1973; Sethi, 1995. |
|---|---|---|---|---|

Conversely, roscas are not found in societies where individualism is strong, where people are only weakly tied to each other, and where actors believe that financial and occupational mobility can be achieved by personal efforts.

Roscas are widespread in Asian countries and enclaves, including Chinese (Kulp, 1925; Lee, 1990; Weber, 1951; Wu, 1974), Korean (Light & Zhong, 1995), and Indonesian (Hospes, 1995; Partadireja, 1974) societies (and historically in Japan; Izumida, 1992), where the dominant form of social structure is the patrilineal or patrimonial network (Hamilton & Biggart, 1988). In such societies, personal identity is closely bound with family ties, and behaviors that dishonor the family are both strongly sanctioned and self-limiting. In traditional Chinese roscas, known as *hui*, family members were morally obligated to pay off any delinquent debts incurred by the default of a family member (Bonnett, 1981; Geertz, 1962). Some Asian societies, for example Korea and Taiwan, utilize ancestral native places as a basis of social formation; people who trace ancestry to a common locale feel a kinship that may be the basis of trust in rosca formation. To the extent that ties with people back in these locales are still active, they form a type of reputational insurance against default. Light (1972) argues that regional and kinship ties are essential components upon which roscas have operated in both Chinese and Japanese communities.

Roscas are also widely present in Africa (Amogu, 1956; DeLancey, 1992; Little, 1951; Miracle, Miracle & Cohen, 1980; Mrack, 1989; Nadel, 1942) and go by various names including *tontines* in Francophone West Africa (Bouman, 1994), *esusu* in Anglophone West Africa (Bascom, 1952; Bouman, 1994; Maynard, 1996), and *stokvel* in South Africa (Bonnett, 1981; Burman & Lambete, 1995). Among Cameroon women, where access to formal credit institutions is limited, interest rates high and economic confidence weak, the *njangi* is used to pool funds for saving and lending to group members. In at least some cases, a woman is only permitted to join a *njangi* if sponsored by another member (Niger-Thomas, 1995). Among the Bamileke men of southwestern Cameroon, rosca default is rare: not only is it frowned upon socially, but normative sanctions are accompanied by fines imposed on delinquent members. Bouman (1994) has noted that the *tontine* of Senegal, based on traditional village communal relations, also exists among Senegalese urban migrants.

Among Latino families, large networks of extended family have strong reciprocal obligations to other relatives (Carlos, 1973; Lewis, 1965a, b: Nutini, 1976). Mexican-American migrants are likely to live in towns or areas where other family members also live and with whom mutual aid is exchanged

(Keefe, Padilla & Carlos, 1979). Kurtz (1973) suggests that shared impoverishment is an important criterion for rosca participation, where roscas can serve to reduce the uncertainty associated with poverty. Mexican rosca formation depends on reciprocal obligation (Lomnitz, 1977; Véléz-Ibañez, 1983). According to Véléz-Ibañez, "In all informally organized [roscas] the cultural 'glue' of *confianza* is the means by which bonds of mutual trust are maintained" (1983: 2).

The poor in Mexican and Mexican-American communities often distrust formal financial institutions (Kurtz, 1973; Kurtz & Showman, 1978; Véléz-Ibañez, 1983). Because personalism is valued in Mexican culture, the formality and impersonal distance of market relations deters many from using banks. Moreover, the poor generally cannot afford the high interest rates charged by banks. While banks demand material collateral, roscas operate on the social collateral of reputation and network ties which Mexicans view as placing stronger demands than the arms-length obligations represented by bank loans. Indeed, roscas which do not involve profit-making are called "*tandas vivas*" (live tandas) while those organized for self-serving economic purposes are referred to as "*tandas muertas*" (dead tandas). What makes a *tanda* "live" is reciprocal social obligations based on mutual trust. When profit is achieved at the expense of the other members it represents a lack of mutual trust, is devalued, and is closer to market relations where social obligation is not as strong (Véléz-Ibañez, 1983).

Roscas in India go by a variety of names, most notably *chits*, *kametis*, and *kuries* (Nayar, 1973; Radhakrishnan, 1975; Sethi, 1995; Srinivisan, 1995). Some suggest that Indian associations date to ancient times when rice was pooled among village women on a rotational basis (Krishnan, 1959; Nayar, 1973; Radhakrishnan, 1975). The variety of Indian roscas is astounding and their rotational form often complex, but their logic is similar to that of Chinese, Mexican, and African funds.

Today, large commercially organized chit fund companies coexist with small interpersonal roscas in India. Commercial chit fund groups can be very large and composed of strangers. Consequently, rates of default are higher than they are among small roscas (Sethi, 1995). Other evidence suggests that in small Indian roscas, organized mainly by women well known to each other, community pressure and fear of ostracism are deterrents against default (Mayoux & Anand, 1995).

Although both men and women participate in roscas, in societies with strong gender divisions women's communal obligations are often oriented toward other women and center around activities traditionally seen as women's work. Sexton (1982), for example, found that women in Papua were expected to assist each other, whether they were real or fictive kin, during times of need by providing meals, cleaning, and performing child care. Sexton argues that *wok meri*, local roscas, build upon traditional patterns of cooperation while incorporating modern ideas about financial assistance. Similarly, recently divorced women in South Africa help each other with child care and emotional support, but also aid each other financially through roscas (Burman & Lambete, 1995). Market women in Ghana share a strong norm of solidarity and often do not permit men to join their roscas, which are typically used for business capital (Bortei-Doku & Aryeetey, 1995).

## *Obligations are Collective*

Embedding the rosca in existing social networks assures that participants have a common understanding of institutional rules regarding reciprocity, as well as reputational collateral (Vogel & Burkett, 1986a, b). As Granovetter argued, "The widespread preference for transacting with individuals of known reputation implies that few are actually content to rely on either generalized morality *or* institutional arrangements to guard against trouble" (1985: 490).

Granovetter's insight can extend beyond the individual to collectivities, however, as more than individual reputations are often at stake in roscas. In many communally-based social orders, families feel an obligation to pay off a family member's failed debt rather than besmirch the family name. For example, default on a rosca debt in Taiwan is likely to be made up by family members who fear tarnishing the family name. Under such circumstances, obligations tend to be collective. Reputation is an important source of social collateral and all members of a dishonored family are damaged by the default of any one member. In communal settings, then, obligations tend to be diffuse and not limited by contract, either real or implied. Familial reputation, as much as individual reputation, can serve as assurance against malfeasance, although in some settings, the organizer takes on the financial guarantee personally in the event of default (Bascom, 1952), and it is the organizer's responsibility to find members who are "sincere, solvent, and known."

In some parts of Africa, debt is not a vice. Instead, it is believed to be closely related to mutual aid and trust, which in turn are interpreted as being the keys to financial and political success. According to Rowlands, in the Cameroon Grassfields, "Since debts have primordial values, not only can they not be discharged, they must constantly be extended with the transmission of substances of all kinds in exchange (blood, semen, witchcraft, substance, money)" (1995: 117). Even in the *esusu* described by Ajisafe (1924) and Bascom (1952) where the members may not necessarily be well known to each other, there is a shared sense of collective obligation. An "individual's credits and debits in an *esusu* group are inherited as part of his estate" (Bascom, 1952: 66). Thus, even the living have strong collective obligations to the dead that are not easily dismissed. Bonnet notes that roscas are used by detribalized immigrants "as a mechanism to increase their sociability and strengthen the bonds of solidarity now weakened by exposure to an impersonal urban cultural milieu" (1981: 19).

In some areas, women's sense of collective obligation may be stronger than men's because of gender ideologies that stress women's honesty and purity. As moral overseers of households, women's obligations to pay can be stronger than their husbands'. Bortei-Dokhu and Aryeetey (1995) indicate that men had higher rates of default than women; women would go so far as to borrow money rather than face the humiliation of default. According to Burman and Lambete, South African women were "bemused when asked what would happen if someone did not pay her contribution: it was clearly unthinkable" (1995: 38). Among women Asian migrants to an English enclave "The question 'What if someone does not pay?' gets little response, as non-payment is practically unheard of . . ." (Srinivasan, 1995: 203).

In addition to reputational capital and collective obligations, roscas often use structural techniques to mitigate against default until the newcomer is known and integrated into the group. For example, they may place newcomers at the end of the rotation where they are merely getting funds returned to them (Niger-Thomas, 1995). In some instances the organizer takes the first payment as a form of insurance against having to pay a defaulting borrower's turn (Bascom, 1952; Kulp, 1925; Light, 1972). The recruitment process may screen for similar life attitudes, social values, class standing, and a commitment to remaining in the same community, all of which contribute to greater membership homogeneity and presumed bases for solidarity (Cope & Kurtz, 1980). Members know, too, that if they fail to pay, their reputation will be damaged and they may not be invited to participate in the future (Ardener, 1995).

## Social and Economic Stability of Individuals

Even in settings where roscas are common, not all people are allowed to participate. Rosca members, often through the agency of an organizer, exclude people who do not demonstrate social or economic stability. In the close communities in which roscas typically form, participants have rich, direct information both on the economic condition of actors, and on their moral standing. People who are unemployed, who are careless with money, or who have made questionable choices in the past are excluded. Morally suspect actors, however that is locally defined, are also passed over.

Along these lines, Cope and Kurtz analyzed the characteristics of participants in *tandas*, a type of rosca common among Mexicans. Their study demonstrated clearly that people with certain social attributes are disproportionately involved in *tandas*. These characteristics are those associated with "stability or permanence of the individual in the community" (1980: 229). For example, people voluntarily separated or divorced were excluded from tandas, whereas widowed people were participants. "[D]ivorce or separation, as well as not being socially acceptable, also demonstrates one's irresponsibility and also may increase the possibility of one [sic] relocating" (1980: 229).

Other characteristics that people view as indicators of stability, for example having children, were also associated with rosca participation in Mexico. Organizers appear to choose for attributes likely to predispose financial responsibility and maintain information networks about the morality of potential members, their financial situation, and the likelihood of family members stepping in, in the case of default.

### Social and Geographic Isolation

Roscas are commonly found in settings of social or geographical isolation. In some instances, geographic segregation for ethnic and racial reasons serves to coerce responsible financial behavior. Roscas are widely found, for example, in Hispanic, West Indian, and Asian enclaves among immigrant populations in the U.S. (Bonnett, 1981; Laguerre, 1998; Light, 1972; Light, Kwoun & Zhong, 1990, Light & Zhong, 1995; Maynard, 1996). Low rates of geographic mobility make reputational maintenance an important factor – people who perceive no alternative than local residence must sustain their reputation. Anderson, writing about an Indian chit fund describes the situation: "the extensive network of mutual interrelationships weaves such a tight net that no villager can hope to survive in the village if he does not fulfill his obligations" (1966: 338).

In Nepal, indigenous roscas known as the *dhikuri* are prevalent in many urban and rural areas (Chhetri, 1995; Messerschmidt, 1978; Vinding, 1984). Rotation is generally determined by competitive bidding with the deductions of imputed interest divided between members who have not received their turn. Contributions in *dhikuris* can be either monetary or non-monetary, such as grain or livestock. Unlike many roscas, *dhikuri* membership can often span significant distances and ethnic boundaries. However, because of the risk of default and lack of intimate knowledge about the social and economic stability of some other members, the poor and geographically fixed are unlikely to "participate in interregional and inter-community *Dhikuris*. [Rather] they prefer to be involved in *Dhikuri* with smaller shares and fewer members from their own village" (Chhetri, 1995: 450). In the event that a member defaults, the organizer bears the financial responsibility. Consequently, fees are paid to the organizer for bearing the risk and running the *dhikuri*. Membership is based on mutual trust and each member of the association must take turns hosting a dinner for the other members. Because 90% of Nepali people live in rural areas without convenient access to urban banks, which may be days away, roscas serve as a viable alternative for saving money and acquiring loans.

Even in areas where low-income men may have access to some forms of formal banking, women are often excluded. In Ghana, for example, women are rarely able to participate in formal banking institutions, both because of gender discrimination and because women are less likely to engage in formal economic activity or cash crop farming. Likewise, in India, poor women have a harder time obtaining credit than their male counterparts "because of lack of resources, prejudice in the lending agencies, and power relations in the family" (Mayoux & Anand, 1995: 187). Consequently, Indian women are far more likely than men to participate in roscas (Bortei-Doku & Aryeetey, 1995). Likewise, in Papua New Guinea, women have little economic control in the household or beyond; roscas are one of few ways they can generate large sums of money without the interference of their husbands (Sexton, 1982). In Tanzania, where women have traditionally pooled clothing or food, female entrepreneurs now participate in cash roscas so that they do not have to ask their husbands for money (Tripp, 1997).

### Similarity of Social Status

Roscas are seldom formed among people of unequal social status, as a markedly more powerful member would be difficult to control through the informal means available to the other rosca members. The presumption is that a powerful person would be able to extract funds from the other members or renege on promises to social lessers with impunity. However, sometimes a person of higher status who is connected to the group, for example a relatively well-off relative, acts as an informal guarantor in case someone has difficulty making a payment; this person would arrange repayment with the cash-short individual so that the rosca could proceed uninterrupted.

Other forms of informal finance among unequal parties are found alongside roscas, however. For example, there are reports of various informal financing arrangements between landlords and tenants, employers and employees, and vendors and buyers (Mayer, 1960). Roscas, however, appear to only occur among people of like status and often similar and overlapping social attributes. Shipton described the situation in Gambian roscas, known as *osusu*, as "overlaying ties of neighborhood, gender, age, kinship, and ethnicity [which] all seemed to give the groups the capacity for peer-group pressure . . ." (1992: 33).

## ECONOMIC SOCIOLOGY AND THE SITUATIONAL LOGIC OF ROSCAS

The five conditions that I have identified are, of course, part of an experiential whole for participants, a social world of a particular kind. The group is an emotional, social and economic resource. It is a source of identity and affirmation, and it is difficult to conceive of oneself apart from the community. The group defines success, and in any case, access to alternative paths to success is limited if even imaginable. Actors in this world, especially poor ones with little or no access to banks or other regulated financial institutions, come to see roscas as a natural and efficacious strategy for capital accumulation and lending.

Although the group can exert meaningful pressures on actors to participate as promised, the group can also use its intimate knowledge of each other's lives to limit participation to those with the social and moral capital necessary to repay as agreed. If circumstances or miscalculation lead an actor to fail to pay at her turn, or worse, to run off with the pot, then relatives can be pressured to make good on the debt. Failure to meet the kin's obligation can lead to social ostracism or to exclusion from rosca membership, a real hardship where roscas play an important economic and social role in the community. Gender, poverty, and social and geographic isolation make the community the only realistic place in which to construct a life.

The possibility of default, while typically low, is always present. Members know the incentive for appropriation is the greatest for those who receive the hand early in the rotation, when one is a net borrower, diminishing to nothing for the last person who merely receives back contributions, a net lender. Therefore, placing the most unknown, riskiest, and least experienced rosca members near the end of the rotation limits incentives to flee. It also provides an opportunity to socialize and observe new members without much risk. Several researchers who have studied rotating savings and credit associations note that they are frequently accompanied by regular social events, such as feasting at the beginning of the cycle or meeting over lunch during each rotation. These events, which while pleasant, also serve to reinforce solidarity and give an opportunity to gather intimate information (Morton, 1978; Sethi, 1995).

Roscas, unlike formal financial institutions that intermediate between unknown borrowers and lenders, are typically formed among people who know each other well and anticipate knowing each other into some unknown future. The probability of future relations with each other is an important pressure to maintain obligations in any given round. In fact, the pressure is often used by members to discipline *themselves* to save – much like voluntary entry into twelve-step programs, such as Alcoholics Anonymous, or behavioral modification groups such as Weight Watchers. Participants speak of self-imposed social coercion in order to achieve financial objectives. For this reason, development specialists have sometimes argued that the element of social coercion can be an important factor in a successful aid policy (Shipton, 1992).

Roscas do not approach the conditions economists usually assume necessary for an efficient credit market given that they are composed of a small numbers of participants who usually know each other well. They do, however, reveal an economic logic rooted in a belief in the efficacy of social structural factors as both ex ante screen for credit worthiness, and as ex post sanctions in the case of default. Rosca participants around the world, even the impoverished and financially unsophisticated, show keen understandings of the traits likely to yield trustworthy co-borrowers and of the recourses they can initiate in the event of default.

## IMPLICATIONS FOR MICROCREDIT ARRANGEMENTS

Roscas and microcredit lending arrangements have important similarities. They both organize poor people, mostly women, into groups for mutual assistance and particularly for savings and lending. Both involve periodic payment by members into a communal fund, and both depend on peer pressure to sustain participation and prevent default. For this reason, microcredit arrangements are likely to work well in environments that emulate in important ways the situational logic of rosca settings. In social worlds where groups are important organizers of experience and activity, where obligations are collective, and where alternative sources of identity and mobility are absent or constrained, microcredit offers an important tool for poverty alleviation.

Matching these social-setting characteristics is not enough, however. It is equally critical to recruit individuals who are of like social status, who are organized with others with whom they have (or come to have) a social bond and basis of mutual obligation, and who have faith in the practical and moral credibility of fellow peer group members. This poses a difficult challenge to those committed to microcredit. NGO organizers of peer lending groups may not have detailed and nuanced knowledge of participants, even if they employ women organizers from the region or community. Indeed, the research of Taub (1998) on the Good Faith Fund, a microcredit institution in Arkansas modeled after the Grameen Bank in Bangladesh, suggests that the difficulties the Fund has encountered have much to do with the geographic and social integration of participants into a world greater than their community. Nonetheless, microcredit is an important and promising vehicle for poverty alleviation in places as different as Cameroon and Vietnam, but as in roscas, the social bases of economic activity are crucial.

## ACKNOWLEDGMENTS

Earlier versions of this study were presented to the Organization Science Winter Conference 2000, and the August 2000 meetings of the American Sociological Association. I appreciate the research assistance of Paul R. Davis, Katja Guenther, Randy Bonnell, and the economic insights of Richard P. Castanias. This research was supported by grants from the Institute of Governmental Affairs, University of California, Davis.

## REFERENCES

Adams, D. W., & Canavesi, M. L. (1989). Rotating savings and credit associations in Bolivia. *Savings and Development, 13*, 219–236.

Ahuja, R. (1993). *Indian Social System*. New Delhi: Rawat Publications.

Ajisafe, A. K. (1924). *The Laws and Customs of the Yoruba People*. London: G. Routledge & Sons.

Amogu, O. O. (1956). Some notes on the African economy. *Social and Economic Studies, 5*, 202–209.

Anderson, R. T. (1966). Rotating credit associations in India. *Economic Development and Cultural Change, 14*, 334–339.

Angel, G., & Sevilla, D. (1978). Sharing the risk of being poor: Communal saving games in Bangkok. *Journal of Siam Society, 66*, 121–145.

Ardener, S. (1964). The comparative study of rotating credit associations. *Journal of the Royal Anthropological Institute, 94*, 201–229.

Ardener, S., & Burman, S. (1995). *Money-Go-Rounds: The Importance of Rotating Savings and Credit Associations for Women*. Oxford, U.K.: Berg.

Bascom, W. R. (1952). The Esusu: A credit institution of the Yoruba. *Journal of the Royal Anthropological Institute, 82*, 63–69.

Besley, T., Coate, S., & Loury, G. (1993). The economics of rotating savings and credit associations. *The American Economic Review, 83*, 792–810.

Besley, T., Coate, S., & Loury, G. (1994). Rotating savings and credit associations, credit markets, and efficiency. *Review of Economic Studies, 61*, 701–719.

Beteille, A. (1995). Caste in contemporary India. In: C. J. Fuller (Ed.), *Caste Today* (pp. 151–179). New Delhi: Oxford University Press.

Bonnett, A. W. (1981). *Institutional adaptations of West Indian Immigrants to America: An Analysis of Rotating Credit Associations.* Washington, D.C.: University Press of America.

Bortei-Doku, D., & Ernest, A. (1995). Mobilizing cash for business: Women in rotating Susu clubs in Ghana. In: S. Ardener & S. Burman (Eds), *Money-Go-Rounds: The Importance Of Rotating Savings and Credit Associations for Women* (pp. 77–94). Oxford, U.K.: Berg.

Bouman, F. J. A. (1979). The rosca: Financial technology of an informal savings and credit institution in developing economies. *Savings and Development, 4,* 253–276.

Bouman, F. J. A. (1984). Informal saving and credit arrangements in developing countries: Observations from Sri Lanka. In: D. W. Adams, D. H. Graham & J. D. Pischke (Eds), *Undermining Rural Development with Cheap Credit* (pp. 232–247). Boulder, CO: Westview Press.

Bouman, F. J. A. (1990). Informal rural finance. *Sociologia Ruralis, 32,* 157–173.

Bouman, F. J. A. (1994). *Financial Landscapes Reconstructed: The Fine Art of Mapping Development.* Boulder, CO: Westview Press.

Bouman, F. J. A. (1995). Rotating and accumulating savings and credit associations: A development perspective. *World Development, 23,* 371–384.

Bouman, F. J. A., & Harteveld, K. (1975). The Djanggi, A traditional form of saving and credit in West Cameroon. *Journal of Rural Cooperation, 3,* 101–119.

Bouman, F. J. A., & Moll, H. A. J. (1992). Informal finance in Indonesia. In: D. W. Adams & D. A. Fitchett (Eds), *Informal Finance in Low-Income Countries* (pp. 209–223). Boulder: Westview Press.

Brana-Shute, R. (1976). Women, clubs and politics: The case of a lower-class neighborhood in Paramaribo, Suriname. *Urban Anthropology, 5,* 157–185.

Burman, S., & Lembete, N. (1995). Building new realities: Women and ROSCAs in urban South Africa. In: S. Ardener & S. Burman (Eds), *Money-Go-Rounds: The Importance of Rotating Savings and Credit Associations for Women* (pp. 23–48). Oxford, U.K.: Berg.

Carlos, M. L. (1973). Fictive kinship and modernization in Mexico: A comparative analysis. *Anthropological Quarterly, 46*(2), 75–91.

Carlos, M. L., & Sellers, L. (1972). Family, kinship structure and modernization in Latin America. *Latin American Research Review, 7*(2), 95–124.

Castells, M., & Portes, A. (1989). World underneath: The origins, dynamics, and effects of the informal economy. In: A. Portes, M. Castells & L. A. Benton (Eds), *The Informal Economy* (pp. 11–37). Baltimore, MD: Johns Hopkins University Press.

Chhetri, R. B. (1995). Rotating credit associations in Nepal: Dikhuri as capital, credit, saving and investment. *Human Organization, 54,* 449–453.

Chu, J. J. (1995). Taiwan: A new regional centre in the making. In: K. Cao (Ed.), *The Changing Capital Markets of East Asia* (pp. 72–127). New York: Routledge.

Cope, T., & Kurtz, D. V. (1980). Default and the Tanda: A model regarding recruitment for rotating credit associations. *Ethnology, 19,* 213–231.

Cubitt, T. (1995). *Latin American Society.* Essex, U.K.: Longman Scientific and Technical.

DeLancey, M. W. (1977). Credit for the common man. *The Journal of Modern African Studies, 15,* 316–322.

DeLancey, M. W. (1978). Institutions for the accumulation and redistribution of savings among migrants. *Journal of Developing Areas, 12,* 209–224.

DeLancey, V. (1992). Rural finance in Somalia. In: D. W. Adams & D. A. Fitchett (Eds), *Informal Finance in Low-Income Countries* (pp. 57–69). Boulder: Westview Press.

Dotson, F. D. (1953). A note on participation in voluntary associations in a Mexican city. *American Sociological Review, 18*, 380–386.
Embree, J. F. (1939). *Suye Mura: A Japanese village*. Chicago: University of Chicago Press.
Feige, E. L. (1990). Defining and estimating underground and informal economies: The new institutional economies approach. *World Development, 18*, 989–1002.
Friedrich, P. (1965). A Mexican Cacicazgo. *Ethnology, 4*(2), 190–209.
Geertz, C. (1962). The rotating credit association: A "middle rung" in development. *Economic Development and Cultural Change, 10*(3), 241–263.
Granovetter, M. (1985). Economic action and social structure: The problem of embeddedness. *American Journal of Sociology, 91*, 481–501.
Hamilton, G. G., & Biggart, N. W. (1988). Market culture and authority: A comparative analysis of management and organization in the Far East. *American Journal of Sociology, 94*, 52–95.
Hobsbawm, E. J. (1981). *Bandits*. New York: Pantheon Books.
Izumida, Y. (1992. The KOU in Japan: A precursor of modern finance. In: D. W. Adams & D. A. Fitchett (Eds), *Informal Finance in Low-Income Countries* (pp. 165–180). Boulder, CO: Westview Press.
Hoff, K., & Stiglitz, J. E. (1990). Introduction: Imperfect information and rural credit markets – Puzzles and policy perspectives. *World Bank Economic Review, 4*, 235–250.
Keefe, S. E., Padilla, A., & Carlos, M. L. (1979). The Mexican-American extended family as an emotional support system. *Human Organization, 38*, 144–152.
Keefe, S. E., & Padilla, A. (1987). *Chicano ethnicity*. Albuquerque, NM: University of New Mexico Press.
Kennedy, G. F. (1973). *The Korean fiscal kye (rotating credit association)*. Unpublished doctoral dissertation, University of Hawaii.
Kerry, J. N. (1976). Studying voluntary associations as adaptive mechanisms: A review of anthropological perspectives. *Current Anthropology, 17*, 23–47.
Knight, F. [1921] (1964). *Risk, Uncertainty and Profit*. New York: Augustus M. Kelley.
Knight, F. [1935] (1976). *The Ethics of Competition and Other Essays*. Chicago: University of Chicago Press.
Krishnan, V. (1959). *Indigenous Banking in South India*. Bombay, India: The Bombay State Cooperative Union.
Kulp, D. H. (1925). *Country Life in South China, I: Phenix Village, Kwantung, China*. New York: Bureau of Publications, Teachers College, Columbia University.
Kurtz, D. V. (1973). The rotating credit association: An adaptation to poverty. *Human-Organization, 32*, 49–57.
Kurtz, D. V., & Showman, M. (1978). The Tanda: A rotating credit association in Mexico. *Ethnology, 17*, 65–74.
Laguerre, M. S. (1998). Rotating credit associations and the diasporic economy. *Journal of Developmental Entrepreneurship, 3*, 23–34.
Lee, S. Y. (1990). *Money and Finance in the Economic Development of Taiwan*. London: MacMillan.
Lewis, B. C. (1976). The limitations of group action among entrepreneurs: The market women of Abidjan, Ivory Coast. In: N. J. Hafkin & E. B. Bay (Eds), *Women in Africa: Studies in Social and Economic Change* (pp. 124–142). Stanford, CA: Stanford University Press.
Lewis, O. (1959). *Five Families: Mexican Case Studies in the Culture of Poverty*. New York: Basic Books.

Lewis, O. (1961). *The children of Sanchez: Autobiography of a Mexican family.* New York: Random House.

Lewis, O. (1965a). *La Vida: A Puerto Rican Family in the Culture of Poverty – San Juan and New York.* New York: Random House.

Lewis, O. [1952] (1965b). Urbanization without breakdown: A case study. In: D. B. Heath & R. N. Adams (Eds), *Contemporary Cultures and Societies in Latin America* (pp. 424–437). New York: Random House.

Light, I. (1972). *Ethnic Enterprise in America: Business and Welfare Among Chinese, Japanese and Blacks.* Berkeley, CA: University of California Press.

Light, I., & Zhong, D. (1995). Gender differences in Rosca participation within Korean business households in Los Angeles. In: S. Ardener & S. Burman (Eds), *Money-Go-Rounds: The Importance of Rotating Savings and Credit Associations for Women* (pp. 217–240). Oxford, U.K.: Berg.

Light, I., Kwuon, I. J., & Zhong, D. (1990). Korean rotating credit associations in Los Angeles. *Amerasia, 16*(2), 35–54.

Little, K. (1951). The role of voluntary associations in west African urbanization. *American Anthropologist, 59,* 579–596.

Little, K. (1972). Voluntary associations and social mobility among the west African women. *Canadian Journal of African Studies, 6,* 275–288.

Lomnitz, L. A. (1971). Reciprocity of favors in the urban middle class of Chile. In: G. Dalton (Ed.), *Studies in Economic Anthropology* (pp. 93–106). Washington, DC: American Anthropological Association.

Lomnitz, L. A. (1977). *Networks of Marginality: Life in a Mexican Shantytown.* New York: Academic Press.

Lomnitz, L. A., & Melnick, A. (1991). *Chile's Middle Class: A Struggle for Survival in the Face of Neoliberalism.* Boulder, CO: Lynne.

March, K., & Taqqu, R. L. (1986). *Women's Informal Associations in Developing Countries: Catalysts for Change?* Boulder, CO: Westview Press.

Mayer, A. C. (1960). *Caste and Kinship in Central India: A Village and its Region.* Berkeley, CA: University of California Press.

Maynard, E. S. (1996). The translocation of a west African banking system: The Yoruba Esusu rotating credit association in the Anglophone Caribbean. *Dialectical Anthropology, 21,* 99–107.

Mayoux, L., & Anand, S. (1995). Gender inequality, ROSCAs, and sectoral employment strategies: Questions from the South Indian silk industry. In: S. Ardener & S. Burman (Eds), *Money-Go-Rounds: The Importance of Rotating Savings and Credit Associations for Women* (pp. 179–196). Oxford, U.K.: Berg.

Messerschmidt, D. A. (1978). *Dhikuris: Rotating Credit Associations in Nepal.* The Hague: Mouton.

Miracle, M. P., Miracle, D. S., & Cohen, L. (1980). Informal savings mobilization in Africa. *Economic Development and Cultural Change, 28,* 701–724.

Miyanaga, K. (1995). Economic Kou (ROSCAs) in Japan: A review. In: S. Ardener & S. Burman (Eds), *Money-Go-Rounds: The Importance of Rotating Savings and Credit Associations for Women* (pp. 149–162). Oxford, U.K.: Berg.

Morton, K. L. (1978). Mobilizing money in a communal economy: A Tongan example. *Human Organization, 37,* 50–56.

Mrack, M. (1989). Role of the informal financial sector in the mobilization and allocation of household savings: The case of Zambia. *Savings and Development, 1,* 65–85.

Nadel, S. F. (1942). *A Black Byzantium*. Oxford, U.K.: Oxford University Press.

Nayar, C. P. S. (1973). *Chit Finance: An Exploratory Study of Chit Funds*. Bombay, India: Vora & Co. Publishers.

Nelson, N. (1995). The Kiambu group: A successful women's ROSCA in Mathare Valley, Nairobi (1971–1990). In: S. Ardener & S. Burman (Eds), *Money-Go-Rounds: The Importance of Rotating Savings and Credit Associations for Women* (pp. 49–70). Oxford, U.K.: Berg.

Niger-Thomas, M. (1995). Women's access to and control of credit in Cameroon: The Mamfe case. In: S. Ardener & S. Burman (Eds), *Money-Go-Rounds: The Importance of Rotating Savings and Credit Associations for Women* (pp. 95–110). Oxford, U.K.: Berg.

Nutini, H. G. (1976). Introduction. In: H. G. Nutini, P. Carrasco & J. M. Taggart (Eds), *Essays on Mexican Kinship* (pp. 3–27). Pittsburgh, PA: University of Pittsburgh Press.

Nwabughuogu, A. I. (1984). The Isusu: An institution for capital formation among the Ngwa Ibo; Its origin and development to 1951. *Africa*, 54: 46–58.

Ottenberg, S. (1968). The development of credit associations in the changing economy of the Afikpo and Igbo. *Africa*, *38*, 236–252.

Partadireja, A. (1974). Rural credit: The Ijon system. *Bulletin of Indonesian Economic Studies*, *10*, 54–71.

Portes, A., & Sensenbrenner, J. (1993). Embeddedness and immigration: Notes on the social determinants of economic action. *American Journal of Sociology*, *98*, 1320–1350.

Portes, A., & Walton, J. (1981). *Labor, class and the international system*. New York: Academic Press.

Radhakrishnan, S. (1975). Chit funds and finance corporations. In: S. L. N. Simha (Ed.), *Chit Funds and Finance Corporations* (pp. 1–161). Madras, India: Institute for Financial Management and Research.

Roberts, B. (1994). *Informal economy and family strategies*. Oxford, U.K.: Blackwell.

Rowlands, M. (1995). Looking at financial landscapes: A contextual analysis of roscas in Cameroon. In: S. Ardener & S. Burman (Eds), *Money-Go-Rounds: The Importance of Rotating Savings and Credit Associations for Women* (pp. 111–124). Oxford, U.K.: Berg.

Sachs, J. (1999). Helping the world's poorest. *The Economist*, August 14, 17–20.

Sethi, R. M. (1995). Women's roscas in contemporary Indian society. In: S. Ardener & S. Burman (Eds), *Money-Go-Rounds: The Importance of Rotating Savings and Credit Associations for Women* (pp. 163–178). Oxford, U.K.: Berg.

Sexton, L. D. (1982). Wok meri: A women's savings and exchange system in highland Papua New Guinea. *Oceania*, *52*, 167–198.

Shipton, P. (1992). The rope and the box: Group savings in Gambia. In: D. W. Adams & D. A. Finchett (Eds), *Informal Finance in Low-Income Countries* (pp. 45–89). Boulder, CO: Westview Press.

Skeldon, R. (1980). Regional associations among urban migrants in Papua New Guinea. *Oceania*, *50*, 248–272.

Soan, D., & DeComaramond, P. (1972). Savings associations among the Bamileke: Traditional and modern cooperation in southwest Cameroon. *American Anthropologist*, *74*, 1170–79.

Srinivasasn, S. (1995). Roscas among south Asians in Oxford. In: S. Ardener & S. Burman (Eds), *Money-Go-Rounds: The Importance of Rotating Savings and Credit Associations for Women* (pp. (199–208). Oxford, U.K.: Berg.

Sterling, L. (1995). The social organization of rotating savings and credit societies among Excilic Jamaicans. *Sociology*, *29*, 653–667.

Taub, R. P. (1998). Making the adaptation across cultures and societies: A report on an attempt to clone the Grameen Bank in southern Arkansas. *Journal of Developmental Entrepreneurship, 3*, 14–29.

Tripp, A. M. (1997). Deindustrialization and the growth of women's economic associations and networks in urban Tanzania. In: N. Visvanathan, L. Duggan, L. Nisonoff, & N. Wiegersma (Eds), *The Women, Gender and Development Reader* (pp. 238–249). London, U.K.: Zed Books.

van den Brink, R., & Chavas, J. P. (1997). The microeconomics of an indigenous African institution: The rotating savings and credit association. *Economic Development and Cultural Change, 45*, 745–772.

Vélez-Ibañez, C. G. (1982). Social diversity, commercialization, and organizational complexity of urban Mexican/Chicano rotating credit associations: Theoretical and empirical issues of adaptation. *Human Organization, 41*, 107–120.

Vélez-Ibañez, C. G. (1983). *Rituals of marginality: Politics, process, and culture change in urban Central Mexico, 1969–1974.* Berkeley, CA: University of California Press.

Vinding, M. (1984). Making a living in the Nepal Himalayas: The case of the Thakalis of Mustang District. *Contributions to Nepalese Studies, 12*, 51–105.

Vogel, R. C., & Burkett, P. (1986). Deposit mobilization in developing countries: The importance of reciprocity in lending. *The Journal of Developing Areas, 20*, 425–437.

Vogel, R. C., & Burkett, P. (1986). *Mobilizing Small-Scale Savings: Approaches, Costs and Benefits.* New York: World Bank Industry and Finance Series.

Weber, M. (1951). *The Religion of China: Confucianism and Taoism.* New York: Free Press.

Walton, J. (1992. Making the theoretical case. In: C. C. Ragin & H. S. Becker (Eds), *What is a Case? Exploring the Foundations of Social Inquiry* (pp. 121–138). Cambridge, U.K.: Cambridge University Press.

Wu, D. Y. H. (1974). To kill three birds with one stone: The rotating credit associations of the Papua New Guinea Chinese. *American Ethnologist, 1*, 565–584.

# HOW ORGANIZATIONS RESOLVE EMPLOYEE FRAUD: FACTORS THAT HELP AND HINDER SUCCESS

Judith A. Clair and Christine M. Pearson

## ABSTRACT

*How do organizations deal with employee fraud? What factors influence this process, positively and negatively? To investigate these questions, four forms of data – interviews, archival company records of prior fraud incidents, public documents, and interviews with key informants – were analyzed in an inductive study. Analysis culminated in a model of how employee fraud can be successfully resolved.*

## INTRODUCTION

If someone wants to steal from [our organization], they will (interview participant no. 19).

Our product is other peoples' money. Because of that, the object of theft in our company is money. I think it makes us a logical target for people who are looking for an easy way for getting funds or who have "crossed the line" and begun to steal (interview participant no. 01).

Abuse and fraud will never end [in our organization] as long as Medicare is there. It's just like a big bank with an open door (interview participant no. 12).

Five persons pleaded guilty, in federal court . . . to charges they used an insurance company to defraud the government of $350,000 in Medicare payments . . . . According to a U.S. Attorney's spokesperson, the accused submitted phony medical receipts either directly to the insurance company . . . or to the U.S. Department of Health, Education and Welfare (newspaper clipping).

Advances in Qualitative Organization Research, Volume 3, pages 155–188.
Copyright © 2001 by Elsevier Science Ltd.
All rights of reproduction in any form reserved.
ISBN: 0-7623-0772-2

Fraud is the "willful misrepresentation, concealment or nondisclosure of a material fact or misleading conduct that results in some unauthorized benefit such as receiving money" (Stuart, 1995: 29). Estimates of the national costs of fraud range from 10 to 40 billion dollars annually (Bourque, 1995). As many as 90% of fraud cases remain undetected (Sieh, 1993). For the average organization, 6% of total revenue may be lost to fraud (Spencer, 1996). Three-fourths of fraud in organizations is perpetrated by company employees (Anonymous, 1997).

Just as an organization's crisis management practices can strongly influence the degree of damage from organizational crises (Pearson & Clair, 1998), so too might organizational responses to incidents of fraud affect the degree of fraud loss and the likelihood of future fraud attempts. Managers need to understand how to manage incidents of employee fraud to minimize losses. However, despite the existence of a burgeoning practitioner literature on employee fraud, scholars have paid relatively little attention to this topic. Further, while practitioners have provided advice on a variety of issues associated with employee fraud, they have paid little attention to the process of incident response leading to successful resolution of a fraud or to what helps and hinders this process of successful response.

The need for scholarly research and practical insight on these issues led to the present article, which reports the results of an inductive qualitative study. One purpose of this study was to understand the process by which employee fraud is successfully resolved. A second purpose was to understand what helps and hinders this process, making successful resolution of fraud more and less likely. We studied employee-perpetrated fraud incidents occurring over more than ten years in an insurance industry organization that processed Medicare claims for the U.S. government. Our analysis led to the development of a model that maps processes involved in the successful resolution of fraud, and enabled us to identify a series of factors that help and hinder these processes.

## EMPLOYEE FRAUD IN ORGANIZATIONS

Organizations face fraud regularly. Employees, managers, vendors, and customers all attempt to deceive companies for personal gain. Employee fraud involves a situation where employees deceive their company by covertly taking assets, and thus differs from other types of fraud such as investment scam (e.g. fraudulent investments are sold to investors), vendor fraud (e.g. vendors overcharge for goods, ship inferior goods, or fail to ship pre-purchased goods), and customer fraud (e.g. customers fail to pay for goods or manipulate the organization for personal gain) (Albrecht, Wernz & Williams, 1995).

Employee fraud is a type of antisocial behavior, that is, a behavior engaged in by employees that harms, or is meant to harm, an organization or its stakeholders (Giacalone & Greenberg, 1997). Employee fraud is sometimes considered to be equivalent to another type of antisocial behavior, "theft" (e.g. Greenberg, 1997). However, we view it as a distinct concept. An employee commits theft when he or she takes company property for personal use or sale without the authority to do so (Greenberg, 1997). He or she may or may not engage in deception to commit theft. However, deception is considered a critical dimension of fraud (Albrecht et al., 1995; Hooks, Kaplan & Schultz, 1994; Johnson, Grazioli & Jamal, 1993; Loebbecke, Eining & Willingham, 1989). Thus, an employee may steal company property such as office supplies (e.g. paper clips, paper, folders) for personal use without attempting to actively deceive co-workers or managers. However, he or she has committed fraud if, for example, this employee alters records so that it looks like office supplies were sent to particular office locations when in reality they were kept for personal use.

Employees are thought to commit fraud for a variety of reasons. Much of the literature on fraud adopts a "bad apple" perspective (Trevino & Youngblood, 1990) which suggests that employees commit fraud because they are inherently corrupt, unethical, or have other personality traits that increase personal proclivities to commit fraud. Adoption of this perspective is evidenced by employee screening, (to ensure that corrupt individuals are not hired by an organization), which is frequently pursued as a key to fraud prevention (Hays, 1998; Luizzo, Luizzo, Van Nostrand & Luizzo, 1996; Randle, 1995; Stavros, 1998; Security, 1997).

Albrecht and colleagues (1995) identify a number of additional motivators of fraud. First, even good individuals may commit fraud when they are faced with significant pressures such as financial problems. Second, work-related pressures, such as feelings of injustice or inequity may also motivate fraud. Finally, perceived opportunity to commit and conceal fraud may also be a motivator.

Given these motivations to commit fraud, how does an organization control fraud behavior? Albrecht and colleagues (1995) propose that fraud control can be achieved when an organization has a control environment, an accounting system, and control procedures. A control environment is a work atmosphere that lessens the likelihood of employee fraud. It may include modeling of appropriate behavior by top executives and managers, communication by management about appropriate and inappropriate behavior, hiring procedures that screen out prior (or likely) offenders, an organizational structure that ensures individual accountability, and assigned responsibility for security and loss prevention. A system for employee whistleblowing (Hays, 1998) within a context where employees trust that they will not be punished for reporting fraud (Anonymous, 1998) may also contribute to this control environment. A code of ethics is an additional recommended tool (Souter, 1995).

A second method for fraud control is an accounting system that provides an audittrail of written records (Albrecht et al., 1995; Gup, 1995). Investigators may identify symptoms of a fraud when information in these accounting records is missing or seems altered.

Finally, internal controls are a third recommended method for fraud control (Guercio, Rice & Sherman, 1988; Hays, 1998; Johnson, 1996). Albrecht and colleagues (1995) identify five types of control procedures: segregation of duties (i.e. eliminating one employee's complete control over an entire transaction), a system of authorizations, monitoring, checks of an employee's work, and physical safeguards (e.g. safes, fences, locks).

Despite well-developed control systems, employees find new ways to commit fraud. Moreover, organizations experience frequent changes generated by employee turnover, shifts in rules and procedures for how work is done, re-engineering of reporting relationships, and transformation and upgrading of computer systems. All of these changes alter the control environment in the organization. Thus, fraud perpetrators and investigators continually play a game of cat and mouse: perpetrators find new ways to commit fraud as the system changes, and investigators attempt to detect and respond to these fraud attempts (Sparrow, 1996). For these reasons, in addition to having a system for fraud control, an organization must also have methods that ensure successful resolution of employee fraud once such fraud has occurred.

In general, theoretical scholarship on employee fraud within organizations is rare (Sparrow, 1996). One reason for this may be that scholars find it difficult to gain access to study employee fraud because of the sensitivity of data. Another reason may be that scholars have typically viewed employee fraud as a security problem for organizations rather than as a domain for theoretical research and scholarship (Sparrow, 1996). In the literature geared toward practitioners, we found one model (built from the authors' observations as consultants to organizations dealing with fraud) that described how fraud detection and response might occur in organizations (Albrecht et al., 1995). The first stage ensues when a fraud incident occurs. This stage triggers a crisis response within an organization as managers attempt to identify perpetrators, minimize negative impact, and recover losses. In the second stage, investigation ensues as security or audit officials become involved in trying to contain and resolve the fraud. In stage three, the investigation is concluded and action is taken against perpetrators. Stage four marks the end of the pursuit of the fraud case.

Albrecht and colleagues' (1995) model suggests one possible evolution of fraud detection and response in organizations. Their work also suggests some ways in which organizations seeking to control fraud might be made more or less effective. Nonetheless, additional research on the successful resolution of employee fraud is needed, given the paucity of scholarly work on this issue. For this reason, with the present study we aim to make a contribution to scholarship and management practice. Specifically, we attempt to build theory in an area that is lacking theoretical development. We also seek to provide practical insights for organizations that have failed to address employee fraud effectively.

# METHODS

## *Moving from General to Specific Research Goals*

Glaser and Strauss (1967) indicated that a viable approach to inductive research is to start with general research goals and questions, and then, as data collection and analysis unfolds, move to specific, perhaps even radically different research questions. Scholars who allow the focus of their research to evolve may glean desirable outcomes such as more rigorous theory building, greater insight, and more interesting outcomes. The present study was based on such an approach. We started with an initiation (or pilot) phase where very general goals were defined. Specifically, at the outset of our research, we had a general interest in how organizations successfully detect and respond to threats and opportunities such that a crisis is averted. However, as our research progressed, a more specific (and we thought) interesting organizational threat revealed itself: employee fraud. In the following paragraphs, we describe our organizational setting and the issue of employee fraud that prompted our attention, and our methods of data collection and analysis.

## *The Organizational Setting and the Issue of Employee Fraud*

For this study, we used a case approach, which lends itself to theory building in areas that lack rigorous conceptual development and empirical investigation (Yin, 1984). We studied an organization, Medi (organizational names are pseudonyms), that had faced escalating employee fraud. Medi is a West Coast division that represents 25% of parent-company Insurance Corporation's total business. Insurance Corporation operates in the United States and Canada, and has an employee base of almost 4,000, as well as contract relationships with about 16,000 insurance brokers and 2,000 insurance agents. Medi employs 1000 full time equivalent staff members located in its downtown headquarters and in two satellite offices.

Insurance Corporation was a sponsor of a research center (specializing in crisis management) at which we were researchers at the time of this study. At our annual sponsor meeting, representatives of Insurance Corporation discussed with us their interest in improving Insurance Corporation's skills at detecting and responding to issues (threats and opportunities) that could evolve into crises. As researchers at this center, we were asked to conduct a study that would help Insurance Corporation identify areas of strength and weakness in the detection and response to such threats and opportunities.

In a series of pilot interviews (to be discussed in more detail below) in which respondents were asked to identify possible threats to Insurance Corporation, employee fraud at Medi was raised as an important issue. This prompted a subsequent conversation between Insurance Corporation representatives and us where we jointly agreed to refocus our study specifically on employee fraud at Medi. We jointly agreed with our Medi contacts that this study would have two goals. First, it would be designed to have immediate practical value to Medi. Second, it would be conducted in a way intended to contribute rigor to research on employee fraud.

Medi is a medicare carrier for the U.S. government, servicing more than 59,000 physicians and medical suppliers and more than 1.5 million beneficiaries. During the year of our data collection, Medi processed 21 million claims and provided two billion dollars in benefits, at a total administrative cost of 50 million dollars. Medi's mission is to administer Medicare Part B administrative services to medical providers (e.g. doctors, HMOs) and beneficiaries (e.g. senior citizens who receive government reimbursement for personal medical costs) on behalf of Insurance Corporation. Medi's primary activity is the processing of Medicare claims. In addition, Medi processes overpayments (e.g. checks returned to Medi because excessive reimbursement was paid to a beneficiary or a provider).

The U.S. government provides a budget for processing Medicare claims. The more efficiently Medi processes insurance claims, the more of the lump sum Medi retains. Competition for Medicare government contracts is intense, and the U.S. government rates Medi's performance annually. As one of ten criteria for rating their performance, minimization of insurance fraud losses has an important influence on Medi's ability to keep its government contract. Fraud schemes perpetrated by doctors and other medical providers are known to be widespread (Sparrow, 1996), and thus, the focus of government performance measures is on doctor and medical provider (rather than employee) fraud. However, at the time of our investigation in 1993, employee fraud was becoming a problem at Medi. Two major cases of employee fraud had been detected and resolved in the late 1970s and early 1980s, then almost ten years passed before the next employee fraud was detected. Thereafter, within a brief period of time, Medi detected eight additional cases of employee-perpetrated fraud.

These prior incidents indicated that Medi was most vulnerable to fraud in several areas of its operational system. Many pieces of data are entered in this system. Among these data, insurance claims and returned checks that entered Medi through its mailroom created a most important vulnerability to employee fraud. Insurance claims regularly arrived at Medi's mailroom, where employees identified each claim and assigning it a control number. After doing so, the insurance claim was to be sent to claims processing agents, who would then enter the claim into Medi's computer system. Medi also regularly received checks sent by beneficiaries and providers in the mailroom. Sometimes beneficiaries and providers would receive an "overpayment" from Medi – more money than they should have been reimbursed for a claim. By law, the beneficiaries and providers were required to reimburse Medi the difference between what they were owed and received.

Prior fraud cases indicated that Medi was vulnerable to fraud in the mailroom for two reasons. First, mailroom employees could steal checks before the checks were assigned a control number, then hide the theft by denying that the check had ever arrived at Medi. Medi was especially vulnerable to such fraud in cases where payment was made by personal check or where no one outside of the mailroom expected to receive the check. Second, Medi employees could also commit a fraud by creating a false claim using any of several methods. One such method involved the creation of a totally fictional claim by an employee who would then send it to Medi as if it were real. Unsuspecting mailroom employees would assign this claim a control number and send it on for processing as if totally legitimate. Second, mailroom employees could engage in a practice called "tear and flush", using information from a real claim to create a new, false claim. In so doing, the employees made key changes to the claim that benefitted themselves, such as changing the address on a claim so that a check would be sent to them instead of the beneficiary. Then they tore up the original claim and flushed it down a toilet (or disposed of it in another manner) to hide their tracks. Third, employees sometimes also "took work home", meaning that they took real claims home, altered them (i.e. changed names and addresses on the claim so that checks would be cut to them or co-conspirators), and then reinserted them into a batch of valid claims upon returning to work.

Medi was especially vulnerable to such practices because the mailroom lacked security cameras or other methods for monitoring employee activities. However, one auditing feature in Medi's system could possibly determine, after the fact, whether fraudulent mailroom activities had occurred. Specifically, files where overpayment checks had been expected would be "flagged" by the computer system for further review, if they had not been received within an expected timeframe. This would initiate a process of investigation that might uncover fraudulent claims.

After they had been entered into the accounting books in the mailroom, checks and insurance claims were forwarded to other employees who worked in different parts of Medi's operational system and elsewhere in its building. One group of employees "controlled" returned checks (i.e. indicated in the appropriate beneficiary or provider file that Medi had been reimbursed). Other employees, insurance claims agents, received the insurance claims and entered all of the data appearing on them into Medi's computer system. Once data were entered, a check would be "cut" and sent to a beneficiary or provider.

In addition to mailroom vulnerability, records of prior fraud indicated that Medi was also vulnerable to employee fraud at a second point in the operational system. A claims processor could simply enter a claim into the computer system that had never been sent to Medi, thus creating a false claim. Or, a claims processor could alter data in a written claim as he or she entered information into the computer system. For example, a processor might accurately enter all of the data on a written claim except for the address to which a check should be sent (e.g. changing it to his or her own address or to an accomplice's address). In response to prior employee fraud experiences, Medi had created employee passwords for each claims agent in an attempt to avert this type of illicit activity.

Information appearing on each insurance claim was subjected to a series of process controls after claims processors entered it into the computer system, to assess and ensure quality. However, in response to earlier employee fraud incidents, a small number of control measures were developed which could expose fraudulent behaviors. One audit searched for "once in a lifetime procedures" for which a second claim had been submitted. For instance, the same patient could not have more than one gallbladder removed. Claims were audited to ensure that auditors' expectations about how claims data should appear, such as those associated the "once in a lifetime" rule, were not violated. If a claim violated an audit parameter, it was "flagged" and sent to a high-level claims examiner or a manager (as appropriate) for further examination, who determined whether the violation was due to a legitimate mistake in need of correction or due instead to fraud. In the former case, the mistake would be corrected and the claim reprocessed. If examination of the claim triggered suspicions of fraud, the claim was supposed to be sent to the "Program Integrity" area, which dealt with investigations of fraud. A small number of claims that were not flagged at this point could still be subjected to any of several random quality audits before a check was cut. However, since the control measures were oriented toward identification of mistakes or anomalies, such audits were unlikely to reveal fraud if the information in the claim was false but appeared to be accurate.

Checks were cut following the completion of the control process. After being cut, checks were subjected to one more audit to ensure their accuracy. Then they were prepared for mailing to the beneficiary or provider. Before the checks were mailed, Medi was vulnerable to one more type of employee fraud. All checks were printed in one room in Medi's main facility, in order to provide security. Nonetheless, past fraud had occurred when employees gained entrance to the room, stole several checks, then covered their tracks through deception. There were no security cameras or other devices in the room to monitor wrongdoing.

On occasion, Medi has found out about fraud after it has occurred, through feedback from a variety of sources. For instance, Medi has found out about employee-perpetrated fraud incidents when beneficiaries or providers have notified Medi representatives about their failure to receive expected checks. Medi has also found out about stolen checks (either overpayment checks or those newly printed) when a bank teller or other bank official has suspected foul play and contacted the company. In addition, police and law enforcement officials have uncovered suspicious information during investigations into other crimes such as drug dealing, and contacted Medi.

In sum, Medi was vulnerable to fraud throughout its operational system, thus fueling interest in learning more about how the organization had successfully responded to employee fraud in the past, and how it might improve its success in doing so in the future.

## Data Collection

We collected data from four sources for our analysis of Medi's operational processes – in-depth interviews, archival company records, public documents, and an interactive session with a team of key informants. To build a model of how specific instances of fraud were successfully detected and addressed at Medi, we used data from the archival data and public documents as well as interview data that concerned focal incidents. To build insight into factors that help and hinder the general process of detecting and resolving employee fraud at Medi, we used data from all four sources.

## *Interviews*

One person conducted all of the interviews for this study. The sensitive nature of the topics discussed in the interviews necessitated that they be recorded in hand-written notes rather than taped and transcribed. Each of the interviews was roughly one hour in length. The interviews took place in two phases.

A first series of interviews initiated the study in general. In this pilot phase, we interviewed twenty-two senior executives and managers of Insurance Corporation to explore the types of problems and opportunities that Insurance Corporation was currently facing, and perceptions of how these problems and opportunities were being handled. Our goal was to gain insight into Insurance Corporation's general approach to detecting and responding to possible crises.

The same series of questions were asked in the same order in all interviews. First, participants were asked: "Please tell me about your responsibilities and history at Insurance Corporation". This question allowed us to gather information about the participants and also allowed us to establish a bond with participants before moving on to sensitive topics. Next, we sought to identify the types of issues that Insurance Corporation was currently facing and whether, from the perspective of the participant, these issues represented a problem or opportunity (or both) for Insurance Corporation. To do so, participants were asked: "Right now, what issue(s) would you say have the potential to significantly affect Insurance Corporation?" We also wanted to know whether Insurance Corporation was treating these issues as important, and thus, asked: "Which of these issues are given highest priority at Insurance Corporation? Are there other issues that are given high priority?"

We sought to understand how information labeled as a threat or opportunity flowed through Insurance Corporation such that issues of importance were identified. To understand this movement of information we asked: "How do you typically find out about potential threats to Insurance Corporation? Is this different than how you would find out about opportunities? What do you do with information on a possible threat once you have it? What would you do with something that seemed to be a potential opportunity? Who at Insurance Corporation is usually first aware of problems or opportunities which arise from within the organization? Who in Insurance Corporation spreads the word about these issues? Have there been instances where you have not received information soon enough? Why did this happen?"

Finally, we sought to understand whether there were formal procedures or systems at Insurance Corporation that ensured that information on threats and opportunities was relayed to those who could make sense of and respond to it. We asked: "What formal procedures are there in Insurance Corporation for passing on this information? Are there better ways to get information? Would you give some examples? How does management support and/or reward the gathering and sharing of such information arising from within the organization?"

It was during pilot interviewing that Medi's problem of employee fraud was first raised as a critical issue. As mentioned earlier, we later discussed this issue in a conversation with Medi's CEO, and jointly agreed to refocus the study specifically on the threat of employee fraud at Medi. Thus, our second stage of interviewing focused exclusively on Medi and employee fraud. The CEO of Medi (who was also a member of the top management team for Insurance Corporation) and his direct report (who was responsible for crisis and safety management for Insurance Corporation as a whole, including Medi) helped us select a preliminary list of Medi employees to be interviewed. The CEO's direct report also helped us coordinate a schedule of interviews with these employees.

The preliminary interview list consisted of Medi employees who had direct responsibility for managing insurance fraud for Medi or who had direct line responsibility for a division of Medi that had the potential to encounter employee fraud. We asked these participants to recommend additional interviewees, enabling us to develop a significantly broader snowball sample. In total, we interviewed 23 Medi employees, including all members of Medi's senior executive team, all department heads, individuals formally responsible for tracking and resolving frauds, and those involved in security functions.

As in the pilot phase, the same series of questions were asked in the same order of all of the interview participants. The interviewer started each of the interviews with a general topic: "Please tell me a bit about how your department fits into Medi. What are your professional responsibilities within this department?" These questions had multiple purposes. First, as in the pilot phase, they were intended to give interview participants a chance to "warm up" to the interview. Second, answers to these questions enabled us to learn about the different sections of Medi, participants' formal roles and work activities, and how insurance claims and other pieces of business flowed through the system.

Next, the interviewer asked: "Give two examples of your worst case scenario for potentially bad news you might receive. Give me two examples of your best case scenarios". The interviewer then asked a pointed question about the participant's role in managing employee fraud: "What is your role in managing employee fraud?" These questions were intended to provide data on two related issues. First, we hoped to determine whether participants believed that employee fraud was a significant issue for them personally or for the organization. Second, we hoped to gain insight into the extent to which participants believed that they were primed to sense warning signals of employee fraud and to respond quickly and appropriately to suspicions of fraud.

The interviewer then moved to questions intended to determine how information about a possible fraud flowed through Medi. First, the interviewer asked: "How do you find out about potential employee fraud? Who is likely to find out about potential employee fraud first? How? Would you give some examples?" These questions were designed to solicit information about the initial detection of employee fraud. Then, the interviewer probed for information on how a possible fraud might be handled: "After you've heard about a potential employee fraud, what do you do with the information?"

The next series of questions asked about the processes and resources at Medi for handling employee fraud: "What formal procedures are there at Medi for relaying information about a potential employee fraud? Are there better ways for relaying such information? Do you train subordinates in how to detect potential employee fraud? What types of resources do you rely upon for gathering information on a potential employee fraud? Are there times when information on a potential employee fraud might be concealed from you or not revealed soon enough? Tell me about these times. Is there anyone at Medi who is formally responsible for tracking employee fraud? Does upper management support/reward active 'signal detection' at Medi? How?"

The interviewer asked follow-up questions throughout each interview to clarify and build on what participants said. The interviewer also allowed participants time at the end of the interview to ask questions and add additional information or insights of their own.

*Archival data and public documents*
We examined confidential organizational documents that comprised the complete archival records of incidents of employee fraud at Medi over a 14 year period. While ten employee-perpetrated fraud acts were detected at Medi during this period, four fraud incidents were still under investigation at the time of this study. Our concern was with the full process involved in successful detection and resolution. Thus, we did not examine documents concerning these four frauds still under investigation. In addition, one fraud committed in

1988 was poorly documented. Thus, we eliminated this fraud from our analysis.

Fraud files were developed and maintained by the director of auditing for Insurance Corporation. The director documented each of the incidents from the time that it was first suspected to the time of final resolution. Each of the files contained a range of supporting documentation such as depositions, written confessions, internal memos, and FBI transcripts.

Much of the documentation established the status of fraud schemes over time, highlighted inferences made by investigators, described roles of relevant individuals (i.e. managers, employees, police officers, bank tellers, medical providers, and beneficiaries), and detailed additional decisions and actions associated with each fraud. File memos were usually addressed to the CEO of Medi from the auditor, and sometimes were distributed to a few additional Medi managers and investigators. Some files included notes reflective of the auditor's questions and findings, media coverage, affidavits, and transcribed interviews with suspects.

In addition to examining the fraud files, we collected published and unpublished documents concerning Insurance Corporation and Medi. These documents included annual reports, government guidelines on program integrity, press coverage, and rules and procedures for handling insurance claims.

*Interactive Session*

We conducted a half-day interactive session following a preliminary analysis of our other data sources. The twenty-two participants included Medi's CEO, top managers, and key fraud investigators of Medi – all individuals considered by Medi's CEO to be central to the detection and resolution of employee fraud. An additional colleague worked with us to facilitate the session. The interactive session had twofold goals. First, we sought to validate, correct, and build on our preliminary analysis of the data we had collected. Our second goal was a practical one: to help guide managers, executives and fraud investigators to improve fraud management processes at Medi. Similar sessions with company staff have been used in the past to build case study data (e.g. Dutton & Dukerich, 1991). We collected participants' contributions to this session through several means – groups summarized their insights on flip charts, individuals edited a graphic model of our preliminary findings, and scribes assigned to each group recorded all discussions and later transcribed their notes.

The half-day session involved a series of exercises and discussions. First, we asked participants to generate a list of the strengths and weaknesses they perceived in Medi's methods for managing employee fraud. We hoped that this exercise would give us further insight into factors that make effective fraud detection and resolution more or less likely. Next, one of us presented a map (created through a preliminary analysis using the other data sources) that depicted how employee fraud occurred at Medi. The map provided many specific pieces of information. First, it demonstrated how insurance claims and other data flowed through the operational system. Second, it demonstrated how prior employee fraud had occurred (or could occur) at different points in this system. Third, it identified methods for detection and resolution already in place at different points in the operational system. Finally, it identified areas of vulnerability in the system where adequate detection and resolution methods were lacking.

We continued by dividing participants into small groups of about 3–4 people and giving each group a copy of the map. We directed groups to "tear the map apart", meaning that we wanted groups to correct inaccurate information and conclusions appearing on the map. After groups completed their task, each group shared their results. We saved the amended maps so that we might change our preliminary conclusions based on participants' additions and corrections. This feedback provided valuable information that, according to Miles and Huberman (1994), we could use to validate and extend our interpretations and conclusions.

Next, each group drew upon its members' specific expertise to imagine particular instances of employee fraud that could be perpetrated at Medi in the future, and to design ways to identify and resolve these hypothetical situations. This exercise was primarily meant to be of practical value to participants. However, results of the exercise also provided us with additional data on factors that might help or hinder the effective detection and resolution of fraud. Finally, participants generated a list of specific, realistic action steps to improve Medi's employee fraud management capabilities. Again, while this exercise was designed to provide practical insights for participants, we were able to use data generated from it to add to our insights about factors that can help or hinder effective resolution of fraud.

### Data Analysis

In this section we describe how we moved from raw data to the development of a model depicting the process by which employee fraud incidents are effectively detected and resolved, and to the creation of a categorization of factors that might help and hurt an organization's ability to detect and resolve employee fraud. We followed a grounded theory approach (e.g. Strauss & Corbin, 1990), building process models from the raw data. In the following sections of the data analysis section we describe the procedure we used to build each of these models.

### Development of a Process Model

We sought to depict the processes involved in effectively resolving incidents of employee fraud in an organization. To build this model we analyzed two primary types of data: archival records depicting Medi's responses to five prior fraud incidents, and public documents relevant to these incident responses. We chose to focus on these two data sources because they provided verifiable facts about what actually took place. We also collected comments from interviews relevant to the specific fraud incidents of interest to us. We used these comments to supplement our two primary data sources.

Our analysis followed a two-step procedure. The first step was to build descriptive pictures of detection and resolution of each the fraud cases at Medi. Later, once these descriptive pictures were built, our second step was to develop a conceptual model of how employee fraud is successfully detected and resolved in organizations.

At first, we read all of the fraud files and other relevant public data. This first reading allowed us to become generally familiar with what happened in each of the fraud cases. Next, we read through each of the fraud files (and other relevant public access data), one-by-one. For each file, we recreated what happened in words and also developed a graphic representation. In reading the contents of each fraud file, we identified critical incidents occurring from the start to the end of the cases. In drawing pictures of what happened for each case, we represented critical incidents as circles or ovals and provided a description of the happening or event within the circle/oval. We also identified "if/then" links, which we defined as causal or determinant connections between different happenings and events in the case. We represented if/then links through lines and arrows linking the circles/ovals. By working back and forth between data and the descriptive picture we recreated the progress of each case from start to finish.

The next step was to move from the individual descriptions of the unfolding of each fraud case to a conceptual model of steps involved in effective detection and resolution of employee fraud. To do so we relied on Turner's (1981) concept card technique. Concept cards are literally flashcards, pieces of paper, or document computer files. Each concept card represents a different theme in one's data. At the top of a concept card, the theme is identified. Under this theme title, data are listed which illustrate the theme.

The themes we sought to identify in our data concerned the process steps leading to the effective resolution of an employee fraud. Thus, each concept card was intended to represent a potential step in the process. To build these concept cards, we relied on the descriptions and pictures already developed for each fraud. All of our concept cards were created and stored on computer document files.

As a first step, we compared descriptions across all of the cases to identify common themes, then listed evidence from each of the fraud incidents illustrating the theme. Within this step, we started by identifying a common theme highlighting how a case started to be given notice at Medi. We then sought to identify the next step in fraud resolution by looking for what happened just following the point that a fraud was noticed. We continued to follow this process until we reached the final concept card, which we labeled closure.

Next, we reviewed the descriptions contained within each of the concept cards to ensure that the descriptions all represented one general theme, and that each card represented a unique theme in comparison to other cards. Some changes were made as a result of this review. Then we sought to tease out sub-themes within each of the cards. We did this by focusing on one card at a time and looking for ways to break the descriptions contained within a card into sub-categories. Sub-themes were evident for some of the concept cards, but not all of them.

### Development of Categorization

All of the data sources were used to develop insight into factors helping or hindering successful resolution of fraud. As before, our concept cards were created and manipulated as computer files. Using the same series of steps described above, the concept card technique led us to identify factors helping or hindering successful resolution of fraud.

### Integration of Prior Research

In the final stage of this analysis, we went back and forth between the concept cards and published research on deception, fraud, antisocial behavior, and related topics that seemed relevant to each of the themes identified in our data. As a consequence, we drew from research crossing disciplinary and theoretical lines to help us interpret our data.

# A PROCESS OF THE RESOLUTION OF EMPLOYEE FRAUD

The process model that resulted from our analysis of Medi's responses to five employee fraud incidents indicates that three steps appear to be involved in the successful resolution of fraud. The first step is the appearance of information indicating a suspicious or unusual situation, which draws the attention of organizational officials. In the second step of the process model, investigations are undertaken in which a variety of tactics are employed (e.g. cooperation with external stakeholders and law enforcement agents, computer audits of claims data, and interviews with suspects and employees who may reveal pertinent information). A third and final step in the process model involves successful closure of a fraud case. We identified two types of closure: one in which perpetrators' actions are curtailed and they are held accountable for their actions; and another in which new fraud prevention measures are developed to help protect the organization from similar employee fraud in the future.

*Step 1: Suspicious or Unusual Information Prompts Attention*

The initial detection of employee fraud schemes occurred when suspicious or unusual information came to the attention of one or more company officials. Prior research suggests that attention is triggered when there is a discrepancy between the perceived and expected ("normal") situations (e.g. Cowan, 1990; Kiesler & Sproull, 1982). According to our data, this also seems true of fraud detection:

> Generally, we can tell when something is out of the ordinary by looking at reports because we are familiar with this, and how they typically look (interview participant no. 10).
>
> In one situation, someone called that owed us money because Medi had no records of receiving their payment . . . an examiner is trained to look critically for aberrations on claims . . . (interview participant no. 08).

People first became aware of unusual or suspicious information via a range of channels. In two cases, suspicions were raised when a Medi employee or someone outside of the firm blew the whistle on the illicit activities of one or more Medi employees. An anonymous tip, in one of these cases, also prompted the attention of company officials to the situation. In another case, Medi was first contacted by law enforcement officials investigating suspected drug abuse of a provider. Based on initial information provided by these law enforcement officials about the case, Medi investigators started to suspect an employee accomplice. Finally, in two other cases, suspicions of auditors were raised when routine quality assurance checks performed by Medi's computer systems "flagged" irregular insurance claims data.

While initial detection occurred with aberrant and unexpected information, recognition of and attention to possible employee fraud also seemed to require the "stamp of approval" from company officials with managerial or employee-fraud related responsibilities:

> An employee may get a call . . . [and] it will be reported to the head of Program Integrity. The head of Program Integrity is usually the first to recognize the fraud case (interview participant no. 12).
>
> I take information [on a potential employee fraud] to the head of Program Integrity. Before I do that, I investigate it . . . I find out how bad things are, and then approach him after I have put the situation into perspective . . . (interviewparticipant no. 07).
>
> I try to confirm that it is actually a problem situation. When it concerns a check, I will consult Program Integrity with evidence . . . After they have confirmed that it is a potential fraud problem, I will bring it to my boss (interview participant no. 22).

It seems that company officials, especially those located in Program Integrity, (the area of Medi responsible for investigating fraud), had an important influence over how people treated signals of fraud. Time and attention seemed to be devoted to signals to prepare them for Program Integrity's viewing. Investigations seemed to be triggered when Program Integrity officials labeled the situation as a possible employee fraud.

### Step 2: Investigations Reveal Details of the Employee Fraud

Step 2 involves successful investigation of suspicions about an employee fraud. Investigators relied on an array of methods, tactics, and serendipitous circumstances to generate evidence and data. Each appeared to serve a specific purpose. Medi's information technology systems monitored the quality of claims processed. Thus, this technology was helpful in identifying clues and evidence of false or manipulated claims. Linkages with internal stakeholders (e.g. corporate legal counsel, human resource specialists, managers of areas involved in a fraud) and external agents (e.g. police, FBI) provided a system of clues and evidence that allowed an investigation to proceed and losses to be stemmed. Interviews with informants provided Medi with circumstantial evidence of fraud. Clarifying rules and policies of the organization allowed Medi to determine possible vulnerabilities in its system. Covert monitoring of ongoing fraud activities allowed investigators to wait for additional evidence of foul-play.

Investigators deftly moved between Step 1 and Step 2. Signals of wrongdoing led to investigation. Information generated, collected, and discovered through this investigation provided clues and evidence that created new insights and opportunities for investigators to further their investigation. Thus, investigation surfaced more signals, and these signals highlighted new paths for investigation. Sometimes, lines of inquiry led to dead-ends, and investigators' success with the case arose because they redirected their efforts. Creative methods and tactics were needed to redirect in more productive directions. This allowed investigators to identify new signals. And so on.

We provide an extended example to illustrate this iterative nature of signal detection and investigation. In one of the five cases we examined, an auditor who noticed an irregularity in data being reviewed for quality control purposes first detected this fraud. Specifically she spotted a mismatch between a claim appearing on her computer screen and a microfilmed version of the claim. This discovery prompted the auditor to contact the Medicare provider identified on the claim. The provider said that he had never performed the services for which reimbursement was being sought. This suspicion provided evidence of wrongdoing. In the same time frame, further analysis of the suspicious claims allowed the auditor to identify a possible suspect. Once a suspect was identified, the suspect's supervisor was contacted for additional information. The additional information allowed the auditor to run "profiles", or claim analyses that could identify additional irregularities or trends. At this time, the FBI was also contacted for the suspect's license number. This number was used to allowed the auditor to run additional profiles targeted toward the suspect. With the help of the FBI, analyses of these profiles led to the identification of 69 fraudulent claims worth more than $300,000 and 10 perpetrators – two employees as well as eight non-employee co-conspirators.

As illustrated in this case, successful investigation allowed Medi to uncover details of an employee fraud such as perpetrators, accomplices, monetary losses, and how the fraud was accomplished. The successful investigation of these fraud cases allowed Medi to move to the point of closure, which is the last step in our model.

### Step 3: Case is Brought to Closure

The last step in successful resolution of a fraud is closure. Two types of closure were most evident in the five frauds studied. First, perpetrators' actions were curtailed and accountability for their actions was sought. Second, Medi's operational systems and procedures were modified to help protect the organization from a similar future attempt at employee fraud.

*Perpetrators' Actions Curtailed and Accountability Sought*
A first type of action allowing for closure was that Medi investigators blocked suspected perpetrators from attempting further fraudulent activity (thus protecting Medi from further losses) and held these individuals accountable for their behavior. A method used by investigators for such damage control was to remove a suspect as soon as possible from physical access to Medi. In two of the cases we examined, perpetrators were either suspended or terminated as soon as Medi officials had sufficient evidence to strongly suspect their involvement in illicit activities. In one of these cases, Medi officials discovered that an employee (who officials suspected was stealing checks from Medi) had a prior felony conviction, thus making the employee ineligible for employment. This finding served as an excuse to immediately remove the employee from having further access to checks, which he had been stealing.

In all five cases, Medi held perpetrators accountable for their actions. However, Sparrow (1996) discusses that one of the challenges that limit the control of employee fraud is organizations' reluctance to take legal action against perpetrators. Unless dollar losses are significant, Sparrow (1996) explains that many organizations choose to take minimal action. This seems to be true of Medi as well. In all of the cases Medi employees were terminated or suspended from the organization. This action seemed to be the extent that Medi held employees personally accountable for their actions. While in several cases the U.S. government took legal action because money stolen by perpetrators was government property, Medi never sought legal retribution. Thus, while perpetrators were held accountable, as Sparrow (1996) discusses, minimal action seems sufficient to allow Medi to reach successful closure.

*Modification and Adaptation*
Closure also involved the modification and adaptation of Medi's operational systems and procedures in all of the fraud cases studied. These changes represented an attempt to protect the organization against employees who might attempt to commit the same type of fraud in the future. It also allowed Medi to improve its ability to detect employee fraud schemes by building structures for monitoring and gathering information. The particular types of modifications and adaptations made within Medi for each of the five frauds substantially differed from one another with regard to the types of changes made as well as the degree of change implemented.

# POSSIBLE INFLUENCES ON RESOLUTION SUCCESS

In this section, we describe influences that helped or hindered successful resolution of employee fraud at Medi. We found that six categories of influences seemed able to affect the degree of success in resolving employee fraud: values and assumptions regarding employee fraud, methods and procedures used to track and respond to employee fraud, employees' knowledge of how to exploit Medi's operational system, and the degree that other individuals feel responsible for reporting suspicions and helping with investigations.

## *Values and Assumptions Regarding Employee Fraud*

Shared values are "important concerns and goals that are shared by most of the people in a group . . . that often persist over time even with changes in group memberships" (Kotter & Heskett, 1992: 5). Assumptions are taken-for-granted, invisible preconscious beliefs that guide behavior (Schein, 1985). Research suggests that shared values and assumptions encourage certain forms of activity and discourage others – signaling what ought and ought not to be (Kotter & Heskett, 1992; Schein, 1985).

A most important assumption evident at Medi was that employee fraud was not an important problem. Rather, as the following quotes illustrate, employee fraud tended to be treated casually:

> A lot of people take [employee] fraud for granted (interview participant no. 22).
>
> An "it's not our money" mentality – and a belief that fraud doesn't hurt our pocket book – is a weakness at Medi (generated during the interactive session as a weakness in Medi's approach to managing fraud).
>
> There is a lack of management concern regarding raising awareness and accountability across the board (generated during the interactive session).

Other evidence supports these sentiments. For example, security desks were reported unmanned, and employees reported checks left unattended and unsecured in the check dispersal room.

The reasons why employee fraud might be taken for granted at Medi seemed varied. First, employee fraud was rarely detected at Medi. Thus, as with other rare but significant threats, employees and managers assumed that employee fraud was not a real problem of immediate concern. Some interviewees reported that day-to-day work demands were so significant that they didn't have time to worry about unlikely employee fraud.

Second, as suggested in a previous quote, managers and employees tended to see the money flowing through Medi as someone else's – in fact, it belonged to the U.S. government. Moreover, since monetary losses due to fraud did not immediately effect Medi's bottom line, managers and employees appeared to view employee fraud as an unimportant problem. To increase vigilance, Medi would need to increase managers' and employees' sense that the money mattered, as one participant stated (above).

Third, employee fraud was assumed to be a taboo topic – something that should not be openly discussed in the organization – and this may have fueled a lack of awareness and concern at Medi:

> We need to be careful about talking about fraud "awareness" issues around employees. We don't want them to think that they are viewed as untrustworthy. We don't want to suggest that lots of fraud is taking place (interview participant no. 02).
>
> We don't tell employees that people [other employees] will be punished if they do something. We want to give an aura of trust (interview participant no. 07).
>
> A lot of people want me to be hush-hush about an employee fraud situation in my area . . . I don't know what the outcomes would be [if I said something] . . . whether other areas would get the impression that my area is a bunch of thieves (interview participant no. 19).

To us, these quotes suggest that impression management concerns drove employee fraud to be treated as a taboo topic at Medi. These concerns seemed many and varied. First, there appeared to be a fear that Medi's external reputation would be tarnished if people knew that Medi had problems with employee fraud. Second, some managers seemed to believe that managing impressions about employee fraud was also important to employee relations. As suggested above, some participants seemed to harbor fear that trust between employees and managers would be undermined if managers raised employee fraud as an issue. Finally, the last quote (above) suggests that impression management concerns stimulated concerns about hiding employee fraud that had occurred in one's department or area of the organization. The fear expressed in this quote was that revealing such information would lead others to associate one's department with thievery. In sum, fear of bad reputation or loss of good-will between managers and employees may have driven employee fraud underground and rendered it less visible as an issue.

While employee fraud was not at the top of managers' list of priorities, high performance standards, defined as efficiency and quality, were a most important shared value at Medi. High standards for performance were driven by the intense competition between Medi and other organizations, each wanting to maintain its status as a Medicare contractor. Managers wanted to minimize problems that might influence evaluations on Medi's all-important contractor evaluation. To fit in, as one employee stated, employees needed to regularly rise to the challenge of perfection:

My feeling is that you have to be perfect to fit into Medi . . . . My feeling is that if we don't achieve maximum points [100%], that we are a failure. If I achieve 97%, I am personally dissatisfied (interview participant no. 13).

One might expect that this orientation would counteract Medi's lax attitude toward employee fraud. However, our study suggests that values favoring high performance and quality at Medi may have actually had an opposite influence, for several reasons. First, high performance standards may have encouraged employees to circumvent systems in place to minimize fraud losses by encouraging employees to break safety standards and rules in order to maintain productivity. Haynes and Prasad (1997) have noted that work culture has an important influence on whether safety standards and rules are abided by. Their analysis suggests that safety rules and standards may be rendered ineffective because a work culture encourages employees to ignore or actively work against them.

In the case of Medi, there is some evidence to suggest that this may have occurred. As a Medi security officer stated: ". . . some people give their own identification numbers to others who aren't supposed to have access to it. I think they do this because they have work overloads – they want others to complete their work". This type of behavior opens the door to employee fraud. The first fraud perpetrated at Medi was in part made possible because employees faced intense pressure for efficiency (measured by how many insurance claims they processed per day). As a part of his plea-bargain, the perpetrator described how he carried out his scheme by offering to help employees and managers who were getting behind in their work. In so doing, he learned how to correctly enter insurance claims into Medi's computer system, and also gained access to create false claims. Following this fraud case, Medi's security manager responded by creating confidential employee identification numbers. Employees needed to use these numbers to be able to do work on their computers. However, once again, some employees circumvented this precaution in order to compete their work. Medi's security officer reported to us that she had recently discovered information that employees shared their identification numbers. Again, employees shared this confidential information to help colleagues catch up on work.

Second, our data suggested that the messenger of bad news, who reports suspicion of fraud, may be penalized in Medi for coming forth:

I get the impression that some managers feel that they should keep their nose clean, and keep in their own business – there is a culture created of this. Some managers "shoot the messenger" (interview participant no. 16).

If managers overreact, employees won't tell them .... With [the head auditor for
employee frauds], what happens to the messenger of bad news depends on his mood
(interview participant no. 07).

Employees may have a range of reasons to expect punishment if they report
observations of possible fraud. However, in Medi's case we speculate that
cultural norms and values for perfect performance may have an influence.
Specifically, the message sent by the perfection standard at Medi is that
mistakes and problems should be avoided. To admit to a mistake or a problem
is to acknowledge that one is not performing at 100%. Thus, one would expect
employees to avoid being associated with mistakes and problems, even if they
did not cause them. Further, as the above quotes suggest, some employees may
have experienced managers' wrath in the past when problems or mistakes
occurred.

Third, faced with a shrinking budget, our evidence suggests that Medi's
management may have intentionally sacrificed better fraud control, detection
and resolution mechanisms in order to maintain the ability to keep up with high
performance concerns. Resource scarcity acts as a constraint on an organization's ability to respond to risks or concerns (Kunreuther & Bowman, 1997).
Trade-offs may be made, for example, in the allocation of resources to
organizational safety in an effort to decrease costs (Mitroff, Pearson &
Harrington, 1996). Companies may value safety as desirable, but temper
decisions about investments in safety measures as a means of addressing
stronger values, for example profitability (Marcus, Nichols & McAvoy, 1992)
or efficiency. At Medi, organizational goals that were immediately pressing,
such as efficiency, were given top priority. As summarized by a Medi executive,
"looking out for potential (employee) fraud and abuse may be low on
everyone's list when compared to productivity issues".

### Methods and Procedures to Track and Respond to Employee Fraud

Earlier in this article we described some of the specific methods and procedures
used by Medi to track and respond to employee fraud. In this section, we
describe important defining features of these methods and procedures. We also
provide a critical analysis of these features in terms of their possible impact on
the successful resolution of employee fraud.

Medi's methods and procedures focused on identifying insurance claims
frauds through its process controls (i.e. auditing procedures). As we described
earlier, Medi's computer system audited insurance claims, after entry into
Medi's the computer system, for quality and accuracy. If claims violated
specific parameters, the computer system "flagged" them for further review by

a high-level auditor. After review, the auditor was supposed to contact the Program Integrity department if the claims seemed suspicious. Representatives of this department would then review the flagged claims a second time. Investigations were initiated if their suspicions were also aroused. This system has three defining characteristics that may affect its success, as we describe next.

## Reactive Rather Than Proactive

First, this system was primarily set up to be reactive rather than preventative:

> Right now, it's an "after" type thing. We monitor, so we will catch a person if they are [already] doing something . . . (interview participant no. 15).
>
> There is almost nothing you can do up front to deter employee fraud. You can't deal with it until after it happens (interview participant no. 20).

Once an ongoing fraud was discovered, Medi was prepared to respond quickly. Investigators located in the Program Integrity department and Insurance Corporation's lead auditor were ready to serve as primary investigators on cases, and actively worked to solve cases when they arose. In contrast, Medi had minimal methods and procedures to prevent employees from committing fraud in the first place (with the exception of its practice of rotation and separation of employees' duties).

## Built Through Experience

Medi tended to build its systems directly from its experiences with prior employee fraud:

> We use past frauds and abuse to inform us about future possible acts. We use the information to implement tracking systems on our [computer] systems (interview participant no. 11).
>
> We have learned and taken corrective action from past experiences (workshop participant).

Kunreuther and Bowman (1997) discuss this type of response, evident at Medi, as indicative of a shift in reference point used to sense and interpret organizational vulnerability. Medi became aware of "worst case" scenarios by experiencing specific incidents of employee fraud, and used its learning to adjust its control systems to minimize perceived vulnerability.

This practice helped Medi deter, detect and investigate similar subsequent acts. However, its practice of building systems from experience may have had some negative effects as well. First, the system tended to be oriented toward detection of false or manipulated insurance claims because Medi's early experiences were with this type of fraud. A problem with this limited approach is pointed out by Sparrow (1996: 20): ". . . the number and type of fraud schemes that become visible depends as much upon the effectiveness and biases of detection systems as upon the underlying patterns of fraud . . . ." Thus, organizations tend only to discover the types of frauds that their systems are set up to detect. If systems are limited or focus on one type of fraud, then fraud discovered is also likely to be limited.

At Medi, evidence suggests that this problem may be occurring (though the nature of this problem makes it difficult to demonstrate). Of the prior fraud acts successfully resolved at Medi, the only ones that came to light as a result of Medi's own detection efforts were those where systems already existed. Specifically, Medi found out about insurance claims manipulation and falsification because it had computer systems in place to detect clues. All other employee frauds were discovered by chance, for example, as a result of a whistleblower's information.

### Innovative and Creative Methods for Investigation

As we described earlier, Medi's methods for investigation seemed to be highly flexible, able to shift and change based on the complex nature of an employee fraud and as new facts came to light. Investigators needed to be able to identify a range of appropriate methods for discovering different types of information, so that needed facts and evidence would be generated. This strategy seemed vital to the successful resolution of employee fraud. Through this approach investigators discovered new facts, redirected their efforts when they were stymied, and considered a wide array of possible leads. Thus, our research suggests that no one method was sufficient to successfully investigate fraud at Medi. Medi's approach to investigations was adaptable and responsive, and this seemed important to the successful resolution of employee fraud.

### Employees' Knowledge of Operational System

Our analysis revealed that perpetrators used knowledge and insight gleaned from their individual work experiences at Medi to identify vulnerabilities in Medi's system, to manipulate the system, and disguise fraud:

> If someone knows the system, they could beat it (interview participant no. 05).
>
> [A fraud can be perpetrated] if a perpetrator has access to beneficiary histories, knows the billing procedures, knows audit parameters, knows when to stop and start, is a trusted employee [who is] above suspicion, keeps his [or her] mouth shut, and is willing to do it (list generated during interactive session).

Court transcripts and FBI interviews revealed how the ring-leader of the first fraud manipulated his knowledge of the system to perpetrate fraud:

> . . . seeing that I didn't do enough work, [managers] were always eager . . . to train me in new systems. So, I was able to learn how to instigate batches [of claims] and how to put

claims through [the system] . . . . I would go to one of the [claims] operators. They were purely innocent. I would ask, "can you help me out? I want to get this paid fast". That was the normal procedure if someone had a friend rather than going through the complete process, you can hand the claim to someone and they would transact the claim for you [more quickly] (Perpetrator's testimony to a Federal Grand Jury).

[The perpetrator] said that no one ever questioned why he was processing claims . . . On one occasion, his supervisor stopped by and congratulated him [for his hard work] while [he] was inputting the false claim information which he had written on a scrap of paper . . . (FBI transcript).

In other situations, employees committed fraud by pilfering checks that came through the mailroom. Again, an illusion of normal activity was possible as employees stole incoming checks while appearing to perform standard mail processing duties:

During the time I worked for Medi, I took approximately four checks payable to Medi. I took the checks during a four month period, [and] I took both the checks and the envelopes the checks were in during my normal duties . . . (confession of employee perpetrator).

This employee avoided being caught because she could disguise her activities as part of her normal mail-opening routine.

In another instance of fraud, an employee's responsibilities were to answer questions about the completion of Medicare claims. In this situation, the Medi employee conspired with a provider by informing him how to submit claims that would lead to inflated reimbursement rates in return for kickbacks:

In the preliminary audit it appeared that it would be difficult or highly unlikely that [the doctor] could have made the visits [as described] . . . . Using code 3 billing code yields a greater return on claims and the claim is secondly a more costly charge . . . . [The employee perpetrator] could have given information to [the doctor] or [his assistant] to show him how to circumvent the system by entering false/fraudulent entries . . . . [The suspect's] position is dealing with providers regarding billing problems . . . she is capable of giving information on how to circumvent the system . . . (legal affidavit).

These cases illustrate that fraud at Medi was made possible when an employee disguised his or her illicit behavior to appear as if it were legitimate, used insight and knowledge about inner-workings of Medi's operational system (and its vulnerabilities), and took advantage of role responsibilities to engage in certain illicit activities. Nelkin (1994: 373) aptly summarizes the essence of the dilemma thus created for Medi:

The location of [work-based crimes] in the midst of ordinary business and occupational activity both facilitates their achievement and helps prevent their detection by colleagues and superiors as well as by outside authorities. In contrast to ordinary crimes such as burglary, the perpetrator has every justification for being present at the scene of the crime. Indeed . . . unlike ordinary crimes, where presence at the scene is a crucial clue, with white-collar crimes, the problem is not so much to identify the culprit as to discover whether there

has been an offense . . . . The [offending] behaviour . . . is often indistinguishable on its
surface from normal legal behaviour.

At Medi in particular, role specialization and experience provided employees
with knowledge about how to commit fraud without detection. For example,
claims processors knew how to create fake claims that looked real. Experience
on the job allowed employees to garner knowledge about areas of the
organization that might be vulnerable to exploitation, or how to beat the control
systems. Some Medi employees took advantage of a lack of monitoring in the
mailroom and, thus, stole incoming checks without detection. Further,
relationships among employees and between employees and outsiders made
detection of fraud difficult. These relationships were in part defined by the
structuring of job responsibilities within the organization. For instance, an
employee responsible for provider relations formed a relationship with a
provider, and together the two abused the claims reimbursement process. The
employee's role allowed her to mask her behavior as legitimate, because
"employee relations" fit within this employee's formal organizational role. As
suggested by Croall (1992), each of the various facets of an individual's job
make it possible for illegitimate employee behavior to be less visible to
outsiders, thus facilitating fraud.

### *Stakeholders Who Feel Responsible for Identifying, Reporting and Tracking Fraud*

In every case of fraud at Medi, the cooperation of stakeholders was key to
revealing the nature of an emerging incident and to containing the effects of the
event. Medi relied on stakeholders' abilities to evaluate and relay pertinent
information, and to act swiftly on early signals of potential employee fraud.

With regard to detection of signals, internal or external stakeholders
identified a number of the detected fraud schemes as a function of their role
responsibilities. Within Medi, auditors were likely to detect fraud because of
their role in ensuring quality and validity of claims. In addition, some of the
fraud schemes detected at Medi were identified by whistleblowers external to
Medi – a representative of a local bank in one instance and a State investigator
exploring prescription drug abuse in another – who encountered suspicious
information as a part of their role responsibilities and alerted Medi officials to
an irregularity.

The cases we examined demonstrate that detection was made more likely
when certain individuals were structurally positioned within or outside of Medi
such that they were exposed to discrepant or unusual information. Their
positioning made it more likely that they would become aware of warning

signals indicative of possible fraud. Further, external whistleblowers tended to have organizational roles that made them feel responsible for reporting suspicious information (even though they didn't have formal responsibility for tracking fraud).

# IMPLICATIONS

Our study had two goals: to build a model depicting how fraud is successfully addressed in an organization, and to identify a range of factors likely to help or hinder this process. To pursue these goals we examined qualitative data from Medi, an organization that succeeded in dealing with a series of fraud incidents that spanned more than ten years. The major strength of inductive research like ours is in its ability to raise important questions and insights. However, it has limitations as well, including its inability to provide evidence able to fully validate concepts and theories. This task is left for scholars who wish to continue research in the area of employee fraud. An additional limitation of our study concerns the generalizability of its findings. We investigated employee fraud in one company, and relied in part on historical and retrospective accounts of responses to specific fraud incidents. Opportunities for extension beyond our research are abundant for those interested in studying how organizations successfully (or not so successfully) address employee fraud.

As a next step in such research, scholars might devote additional investigation to the types of variables influencing successful detection and closure of cases of fraud. At a most basic level, our research suggests that organizations with formal methods and procedures in place for detecting warning signals of specific types of employee fraud are more likely to reach closure and stem losses from these types of fraud. Similarly, those organizations that have created methods and procedures for investigation also seem more likely to reach closure and stem losses. Company officials are more likely to respond quickly and to successfully reveal details of an employee fraud faster than if these investigative procedures were not in place:

> Proposition 1a: Organizations lacking methods and procedures to detect warning signals of specific types of employee fraud are less likely to successfully reach closure on particular fraud cases.

> Proposition 1b: Organizations lacking methods and procedures to detect warning signals of specific types of employee fraud are more likely to incur greater losses attributable to employee fraud.

> Proposition 1c: Organizations without methods and procedures for investigation prior to the occurrence of a particular employee fraud

incident are less likely to reach successful closure on a case of employee fraud.

Proposition 1d: Organizations without methods and procedures for investigation prior to the occurrence of a particular employee fraud incident are more likely to incur greater losses due to such fraud.

Our research also suggests that organizations need to think strategically about the methods and procedures used to resolve cases of employee fraud. In particular, it suggests that organizations with methods and procedures focused solely on damage control, rather than also including a focus on employee fraud prevention and early detection, are likely to incur more losses due to employee fraud. In addition, our data suggest that an organization needs to build methods and procedures from experience, but also to move beyond past experiences to imagine other possible types of employee fraud. Finally, our research suggests that organizations need to revisit and revise procedures on a regular basis, before fraud is detected:

Proposition 2: Losses to employee fraud are likely to be greater if an organization's methods and procedures for resolving employee fraud focus exclusively on damage control than if they also address fraud prevention and early detection.

Proposition 3: Losses to employee fraud are likely to be greater if an organization's methods and procedures for resolving employee fraud cases are based only on past experiences with particular types of fraud than if they also address other possible types of employee fraud.

Proposition 4: Losses to employee fraud are likely to be greater if an organization's methods and procedures for resolving employee fraud are not updated regularly than if these procedures are revised to respond to new vulnerabilities.

While an organization's methods and procedures for resolving employee fraud are crucial, our research suggests that other factors are also of vital importance. Specifically, our findings indicate that shared values and assumptions within an organization are likely to have three important effects. First, they can influence whether and how quickly warning signals are detected. Second, they may influence the degree to which and how quickly investigations detect employee fraud. Third, they may influence whether methods and procedures for controlling and responding to employee fraud are used appropriately (or abused).

Our study identified two types of values and assumptions that seem to exert effects on the detection and closure of cases of fraud. The first had to do with the importance attributed to employee fraud as an organizational issue. Our findings suggest that managers and employees who see employee fraud as an unimportant problem may be less likely to look for employee fraud and less prepared to respond quickly when investigation may be necessary. If employees believe that fraud losses do not have a negative impact on the organization, they also may be less likely to report suspicions of fraud. Unless an employee has as a strong moral compass guiding his or her actions, or believes that reporting fraud is part of his or her job responsibility, perpetrators' actions are more likely to be observed with some degree of complacency, making it less likely that witnesses will report wrongdoing:

> Proposition 5: Resolution of employee fraud is likely to be delayed or unsuccessful, and losses are likely to be greater, when managers and employees believe that employee fraud is an unimportant problem.

Our research suggests several reasons why fraud might not be taken seriously. First, when fraud is rarely detected, employees' day-to-day work demands are likely to take precedence. Second, employees who fail to understand that employee fraud has financial (or other negative) impacts are less likely to take such fraud seriously. Finally, employee fraud may not been taken seriously if it is treated as a taboo topic not to be openly discussed with employees. Together, these factors suggest a need for top officials and managers to clearly explain that employee fraud is an important problem, and to articulate that employee fraud leads to organizational losses:

> Proposition 6: Losses due to employee fraud are likely to be less significant when top officials and managers have provided clear and ongoing communication about employee fraud as an important and costly organizational problem.

The second type of values and assumptions likely to affect detection and resolution of fraud has to do with the performance standards shared among organizational members. Our findings suggest that placing value on high performance standards may work against effective resolution of employee fraud, for several reasons. High performance standards may encourage rule-breaking behavior. In addition, employees may avoid reporting suspicions of employee fraud or anomalous information if there is fear that managers will interpret the information as a problem or mistake, or if punishment is expected. If employees decide to come forward, they may delay doing so. Or, employees may filter the information to make it appear more positive that it is in reality. Thus, managers may hear about a possible fraud later rather than sooner, and receive distorted rather than fully accurate information. In addition to delayed detection, investigation attempts may also be stymied if employees fail to volunteer information when asked by officials, actively hide such information from investigators, or filter the information for fear of raising problems. Finally, when faced with a shrinking budget, an organization valuing high performance above all else is likely to devote resources to ensuring this performance rather than to looking out for employee fraud.

> Proposition 7: Resolution of employee fraud is likely to be delayed or unsuccessful, and losses are likely to be greater, when managers and employees believe that conveying bad news should be avoided.

> Proposition 8: When employees are under significant pressure to maintain high work performance (especially productivity), they are more likely to circumvent or ignore procedures and methods for fraud prevention and detection.

> Proposition 9: When faced with limited resources, managers will choose to overlook employee fraud concerns to address stronger values, such as maintaining performance.

In addition to shared values and assumptions, two other factors likely to influence closure and losses were identified through our research. A first factor is employees' knowledge of their organization's operational system. Our results indicate that employees who develop knowledge and insight into the inner-workings of their organization are more likely to be able to figure out how to commit a fraud, and how to mask their behavior or make it appear legitimate. Albrecht and colleagues (1995) suggest several methods that can be used by an organization to prevent employees from developing this knowledge or hinder employees' ability to mask illicit behavior. First, security features such as hidden cameras are likely to be effective in uncovering illegitimate actions. Employees may also be less likely to engage in such behavior if they know they are being monitored. Second, rotating employees between job responsibilities ensures that employees do not build the insight associated with employee fraud. Third, segregation of duties (i.e. breaking up job duties such that one employee cannot carry out a fraud without collusion from other employees) is another method.

> Proposition 10: Losses to employee fraud are likely to be less significant when an organization practices rotation of duties, segregation of duties, and employee monitoring techniques.

Finally, our research suggests that internal and external stakeholders are critical to successful resolution of employee fraud. Specifically, our findings indicate that warning signals of fraud may be detected more quickly, investigations of fraud more swift, and successful closure more likely when stakeholders are involved at all stages.

Proposition 11: Detection, investigation, and closure to an employee fraud are likely to be facilitated when fraud investigators build cooperative relationships with internal and external stakeholders.

Proposition 12: Stakeholders are more likely to detect and report employee fraud if their job responsibilities involve enforcement of rules or regulations, reporting fraud, or engaging in responsible or ethical behavior.

## ACKNOWLEDGMENTS

We extend our gratitude to members of Insurance Corporation, Medi, and Dr. Ian Mitroff who paved the way for this project. We are also indebted to Sandra Waddock and Jean Bartunek who provided feedback on earlier versions of this manuscript. This project was supported by the Center for Crisis Management at the University of Southern California.

## REFERENCES

Albrecht, S. W., Wernz, G. W., & Williams, T. L. (1995). *Fraud: Bringing Light to the Dark Side of Business*. New York: Irwin.

Anonymous (1997). Six million dollar man is sitting on a desk new you. *International Journal of Retailing & Distribution Management, 25*, vi-vii.

Bourque, A. J. (1995). Getting smart about employee fraud. *The National Public Accountant, 40*, 29.

Cowan, D. A. (1990). Developing a classification structure for organizational problems: An empirical investigation. *Academy of Management Journal, 33*, 366–390.

Croall, H. (1992). *White Collar Crime: Criminal Justice and Criminology*. Philadelphia, PA: Open University Press.

Dutton, J. E., & Dukerich, J. M. (1991). Keeping an eye on the mirror: Image and identity in organizational adaptation. *Academy of Management Journal, 34*, 517–554.

Glaser, B., & Strauss, A. (1967). *The Discovery of Grounded Theory*. Chicago: Adline Publishing Company.

Greenberg, J. (1997). A social influence model of employee theft: Negotiating "the line" between taking and stealing. In: R. W. Griffin, A. O'Leary-Kelly & J. Collins (Eds), *Dysfunctional Behavior in Organizations* (Vol. 2). Greenwich CT: JAI Press.

Giacalone, R. A., & Greenberg, J. (1997). *Antisocial behavior in organizations*. Thousand Oaks, CA: Sage.

Guercio, J. P., Rice, E. B., & Sherman, M. F. (1988). Old fashioned fraud by employees is alive and well: Results of a survey of practicing CPAs. *The CPA Journal, 58*, 74–77.

Gup, B. E. (1995). *Targeting fraud: Uncovering and deterring fraud in financial institutions*. Chicago: Probus Publishing.

Haynes, T., & Prasad, P. (1997). Patterns of "mock bureaucracy" in mining disasters: An analysis of the Westray coal mine explosion. *Journal of Management Studies, 34*, 601–624.

Hays, D. (1998). Rms can tilt odds against crooked workers. *National Underwriter, 102*(14), 28.

Hooks, R. L., Kaplan, S. E., & Schultz, J. J. (1994). Enhancing communication to assist in fraud prevention and detection. *Auditing: A Journal of Practice and Theory, 13*, 86–117.

Johnson, P. (1996). The impact of fraud on small businesses. *Accountancy Ireland, 28*, 32–33.

Johnson, P. E., Grazioli, S., & Jamal, K. (1993). Fraud detection – intentionality and deception in cognition. *Accounting Organizations and Society, 18*, 467–488.

Kiesler, S., & Sproull, L. (1982). Managerial response to changing environments: Perspectives on problem sensing from social cognition. *Administrative Science Quarterly, 27*, 548–570.

Kotter, J. P., & Heskett, R. (1992). *Corporate Culture and Performance*. New York: Free Press.

Kunreuther, H., & Bowman, E. H. (1997). A dynamic model of organizational decisionmaking: Chemco revisited six years after Bhopal. *Organization Science, 8*, 404–413.

Loebbecke, J. K., Eining, M. M., & Willingham, J. J. (1989). Auditors' experience with material irregularities: Frequency, nature, and detectability. *Auditing: A Journal of Theory and Practice, 9*, 1–28.

Luizzo, A. I., Luizzo, F. A., Van Nostrand, G., & Luizzo, P. F. (1996). The fraud prevention jackpot. *Security Management, 40*, 70–75.

Marcus, A., Nichols, M. L., & McAvoy, G. E. (1992). Economic and behavioral perspectives on safety. In: B. M. Staw and L. L. Cummings (Eds), *Research in Organizational Behavior* Vol. 15, (pp. 323–355). Greewich, CT: JAI Press.

Miles, M. B., & Huberman, A. M. (1994). *Qualitative Data Analysis*. Thousand Oaks, CA: Sage.

Mitroff, I. I., Pearson, C. M., & Harrington, K. (1996). *The essential guide to managing Corporate crises*. New York: Oxford University Press.

Nelkin, D. (1994). White-collar crime. In: M. Maguire, R. Morgan & R. Reiner (Eds), *The Oxford Handbook of Criminology* (pp. 355–392). New York: Oxford University Press.

Pearson, C. M., & Clair, J. A. (1998). Reframing crisis management. *Academy of Management Review, 23*, 59–76.

Randle, W. (1995). When employees lie, cheat or steal. *Working Woman, 20*, 55–56.

Schein, E. (1985). *Organizational Culture and Leadership*. San Francisco: Jossey-Bass.

Security (1997). When the boss is the crook. *34*, 32–33.

Souter, G. (1995). A policy against employee fraud. *Business Insurance, 29*, 25.

Sieh, E. W. (1993). Employee theft: An examination of Gerald Mars and an explanation based on equity theory. In F. Adler and W. Laufer (Eds.), *New Directions in Criminological Theory* Vol. 4, (pp. 95–111). Greenwich, CT: JAI Press.

Sparrow, M. K. (1996). *License to Steal: Why Fraud Plagues America's Health Care System*. Boulder, CO: Westview Press.

Spencer, S. (1996). Inside job. *Jewelers Circular Keystone, 167*, 112–115.

Stavros, J. A. (1998). The forgotten factor in preventing employee fraud: Employee screening. *Pennsylvania CPA Journal, 69*, 30–33.

Stuart, P. (1995). HR attacks health-care fraud. *Personnel Journal, 74*, 28–33.

Strauss, A., & Corbin, J. (1990). *Basics of Qualitative Research*. Newbury Park, CA: Sage.

Trevino, L. K., & Youngblood, S. A. (1990). Bad apples in bad barrels: A causal analysis of ethical decision making behavior. *Journal of Applied Psychology, 75*, 378–385.

Turner, B. (1981) Some practical aspects of qualitative data analysis: One way of organizing the cognitive processes associated with the generation of grounded theory. *Quality and Quantity, 15*, 225–247.

Yin, R. (1984). *Case Study Research*. Beverly Hills, CA: Sage.

# EMPLOYEES' REACTIONS TO CULTURAL DIVERSITY IN THE MANAGEMENT TEAM

Gayle Porter

## ABSTRACT

*This study is an analysis of open-ended survey responses to questions posed to non-managerial employees about cultural diversity among the managers of a U.S. manufacturing facility. Responses are categorized and demographic covariance is noted to uncover major patterns in respondent reactions. Findings indicate that the majority of respondents assigned positive value to diversity among management, citing a variety of benefits including moral obligation, business necessity, opportunity to broaden perspectives, and a positive influence on the organization's culture. Examples of less supportive comments included references to quotas, concerns about communication difficulties, and ethnocentric statements.*

## INTRODUCTION

Studies on peer-level diversity reactions have shown evidence of both positive and negative potential. For example, Raghuram and Garud (1996) found that

**Advances in Qualitative Organization Research, Volume 3, pages 189–203.**
2001 by Elsevier Science Ltd
**ISBN: 0-7623-0772-2**

diverse groups bring multiple perspectives to tasks, generate more ideas, and are more innovative than homogeneous teams. Conversely, the authors also cited studies showing that diversity is associated with weaker affective ties among team members, generates higher turnover, and sometimes generates stereotyping. Jackson (1992) had earlier published similar conclusions. While heterogeneity facilitates performance on some types of tasks, it generally discourages cohesiveness among group members.

The present study expands on this past research by looking beyond peer reactions and focusing instead on employee reactions to cultural diversity among management. There are important reasons why diversity among managers might induce positive reactions among subordinate employees. For instance, the presence of managers who have obvious dissimilarities demonstrates that all kinds of people can achieve higher positions. In this way there is a symbolic value of having many cultures represented on the management team. At the same time, diverse managers serve as role models, demonstrating how to navigate the path between fitting in and maintaining individuality.

In very real terms, a diverse management team can lead by example. As other employees struggle to accomplish tasks – in spite of language, custom and value differences – each individual is daily forming opinions on whether any added inconvenience is worth the trouble. If managers form a solid, well-functioning team of leaders, in spite of these same hurdles, they are providing evidence for the value of the effort. If the total facility also begins to accomplish more than its counterparts in the larger organization, issues formerly viewed as hurdles may be recast as a part of a process toward greater achievement.

Despite these potential gains, employees might react negatively to diversity among managers. For example, employees might feel compelled to change their own style of interaction – an extra demand on their time and energy. Employees might see a less cohesive management team and develop concerns about whether strategic direction and organizational values are still as firm as in the past.

In light of these possibilities, the following study took as its starting point three basic questions: When exposed to it, do employees value cultural diversity in a firm's management? What are employees' specific positive or negative reactions to diversity at higher organizational levels? Are there demographic patterns in responses regarding management diversity? Open-ended questionnaire responses were categorized and demographic data analyzed in order to provide tentative answers. The results of these assessments are reported below.

# METHOD

## *Research Site and Respondents*

My study took place in a new facility of a large, multinational firm in the electronics industry. The company's decision to build the facility in the U.S. was a choice that some felt contradicted then-current wisdom, due to cost favorability and success records of overseas sites. However, once the decision for a U.S. plant was made, attention focused on how to ensure the new facility would meet or even exceed the productivity and quality standards established by equivalent operations in other parts of the world. Toward this goal, the company assembled a management team of talented individuals, all of whom were male. Nearly all came from within the parent company. Some of the managers' careers had been based solely in the U.S. but others were brought in from successful sites in other countries. The total management team (19 for start-up, then decreasing to 13 for ongoing operations) represented several national cultures: Japanese, Chinese, Korean, and U.S. For the first time in the company's history, a Japanese manager held the top leadership role for a U.S. manufacturing plant.

My involvement with this management team began at the time the plant started production. To reach that point, the managers had worked together through months of preliminary set-up. They were excited about the new venture and determined to succeed. The managers themselves considered the diversity of the management team to be a positive contributor to this success.

Each manager had been selected for his skills and experience. The managers' combined technical expertise was certainly a strength for leading this organization. They also believed they could learn much from each other regarding management styles and philosophies drawn from the different cultures. Their workforce included people of many cultures, in particular, groups of technical employees from Japan that made up a noticeable segment of the population (approximately 10% of the total but positioned in only a few functional areas).

In initial conversations with me the managers expressed two concerns. The first stemmed from the company's approach toward organizational learning. When this facility succeeded, which the managers fully intended and expected it would, other locations could only build on that success if there was some attempt to document the important factors contributing to that success. They hoped that my study would help in this documentation. The second, related concern came from acknowledgement that the managers did face certain challenges in working together as a multicultural team, and most of them were facing this situation for the first time. Would they recognize an impending problem early enough to avoid it becoming a detriment to their operations?

During its start-up, the company built a workforce that could be classified in three segments. Approximately one third of the employees transferred from a similar existing facility located nearby in the same city. An equal number of employees came from another division of the company. Although their previous workplace had focused on different products and customers, they were familiar with the parent organization. The remaining third of the workforce were new hires to the company.

This combined group included 323 non-managerial employees, 297 of which completed questionnaires. Respondent ages ranged from 18 to 59 years, with more than 70% under the age of 40. Approximately 75% were male. The largest ethnic or racial category was White/Caucasian at 58.6%; thirty-seven individuals (12.5%) identified themselves as Black/African-American. Fifty-five people (18.5%) were Asian, Asian-American, Pacific Islanders. Ninety-five percent of the respondents had more than a high-school education, with 18% listing at least a four-year college degree and another 23% reporting some graduate education or a graduate degree.

*Procedure*

My study used data collected with an employee survey that was administered approximately 10 months after the facility began production. Employees completed the survey on work time. Managers strongly encouraged participation, to the extent of monitoring attendance at the data collection sites. However, written and verbal instructions emphasized that completing any or all of the survey was voluntary. This resulted in a response rate of 92%.

The survey and written instructions were provided in both English and Japanese. To ensure confidentiality, no company employees at any level were allowed to handle the completed surveys. The content of the survey included a large number of questions on work-related attitudes, self-concept, team implementation and general interpersonal relations among employees. Although there were many diversity-related questions, it did not give the overall impression of being a "diversity survey."

The last entry on the survey stated, "One of the unique features of [this facility's] top management team is the cultural diversity. How important is this to you?" Instructions asked that they circle one of the following responses: not at all; very little; somewhat; very much. That was followed by the simple question, "Why?" Responses to these questions served as data for the present analysis.

Of the 297 total responses, slightly over 64% indicated that cultural diversity was either somewhat or very important. This proportion seemed to indicate that the workforce generally valued having diversity on the management team. Of more interest were answers to the question of "why". To summarize for feedback meetings with both the managers and the employees, these explanatory comments were listed anonymously in groupings based on the importance noted in part one of the question. A common reaction during feedback meetings was surprise at the fact that many people who indicated that cultural diversity was of little or no importance often seemed to be making comments under "why" that could be interpreted as pro-diversity. To allow a more in-depth examination of the employees' attitudes, the following re-categorization was based on the content of their remarks and framed within the context of demographic patterns and characteristics.

### Categorization of Comments

My original sort of responses resulted in three major categories: statements of why this was not an issue for discussion, pro-diversity sentiments, and comments that were not supportive of diversity. Within each major category I created several second level distinctions, and often there was a third level of separation. I identified categories by key phrases or words common to groups of responses and assigned representative titles.

A graduate student working as a research assistant reviewed a randomly selected sample of 27 comments (slightly over 10%). Her independently derived categories easily fell within my first level categorizations for 26 of the 27 comments, plus substantial agreement with second level categorizations. To check the finer distinctions of the third level, she completed a series of seven worksheets, each of which required her to sort between 27 and 37 items spanning 4 to 6 different categories. Two other raters were asked for judgments on all cases where her selection differed from my categorizations. Initial levels of interrater agreement ranged from 77% to 93%. After clarification of the categorization scheme, interrater agreement increased to between 88% and 100%.

## RESULTS

My work with the team of managers began because of my experience working with teams; I did not go into this project as an expert on cultural diversity. Although I worked with surface-level familiarity of diversity topics in my teaching, I had not previously done in-depth study of work on cultural differences. Thus, all categories emerged from the data; none were a priori conceptualizations.

For each category, a few examples are given of the actual comments taken from the surveys. Demographic patterns that appear meaningful are briefly noted as results are reported in this section.

### *Importance of Diversity is Not the Issue for Discussion*

A total of 225 different comments were sorted into response categories. Of that total, 58 people replied in a way to suggest they did not feel diversity was the issue to be discussing. These answers were put into three groupings.

#### *Diversity Does Not Exist*
The first group of five answers simply said that diversity on the management team did not yet exist:

> "even though there is a diverse management team, they tend to separate into U.S. and Asian groups – interactions *between* groups is much more limited"
> "no blacks"
> "not just religion and ethnicity is it? What about a male culture? Where are the women in the [facility] top management?"

All five of these respondents were male; three of the five identified themselves as White and two as Black.

#### *Diversity Makes No Difference*
Twenty-six people made comments to the effect that diversity on the management team makes no difference. Seven of these made very general comments of no difference, for example:

> "it makes no difference"
> "shouldn't matter too much."

Seven more people made similar comments but from a more personal viewpoint:

> "because I can get along with everyone"
> "It doesn't matter to me who my boss is. I get paid by the company to get along with everyone and work hard."

Another group of seven seemed to express that there was little difference because of their limited interactions with the top management team:

> "I very seldom have contact with upper management."
> "We don't communicate with top management."

Similarly, five more people indicated either organizational hierarchy or the company culture overrode any difference that might pertain to cultural differences on the management team:

> "they're all the same at the top. It doesn't matter what culture they're from"
> "doesn't seem to make much difference in decisions/policies. The [company] culture/norm is the biggest variable."
> "cultural diversity does not matter at all. [The facility] manager is the one that makes the decisions and that is what is going to happen."

Of the 26 people who said diversity on the management team makes no difference, none of them had indicated "very much" importance placed on the managers' cultural diversity. Two of the seven making very general statements about no difference had said that the managers' cultural diversity was "somewhat" important, but the predominant answers were "not at all" important (12 people) and "very little" importance (12 people).

### *Diversity is Not What's Important*
Twenty-seven people discounted the importance of diversity in favor of focusing on people's performance or qualifications for the job. For example:

> "I am convinced that you should hire the most qualified, independent of race, color, or creed."
> "People need to be judged on performance not race or culture"
> "It doesn't matter what cultural beliefs you have. The most qualified person should get the job.".

This particular type of comment is one that caught the attention of the managers themselves as they reviewed survey results. Only one of these 27 people fell within the group saying that the managers' cultural diversity had high importance; most (23 people) said little importance or not at all. The managers read the narrative comments to mean that even though cultural diversity was not particularly important to these individuals, they still expressed fairly pro-diversity sentiments in saying that the best person should be in the job regardless of race. Of these 27 responses, most were from White males (20 White males; 2 Asian males; 4 White females; and 1 Black female).

### *Pro-Diversity Sentiments*

Sixty-one percent of all the comments were classified as pro-diversity sentiments. These responses have been separated into seven different types of comments, with a further level of definition within some of those types.

*Moral/Ethical Imperative*

Eleven people referenced ideas of goodness, fairness, justice or equality in their explanation for the importance of diversity:

> "morally and ethically it's the right thing to do"
> "we have different ethnic groups of people with different religious background, and each needs to be recognized as individual"
> "to understand each other, cultural respect, and just maybe we can end hate."

Ten of these eleven people said that the cultural diversity on the management team was either somewhat or very important to them (5 of each response; 1 said not very important). There was notable dispersion across gender and ethnic groups – 5 female and 6 male; 4 White, 2 Hispanic, 2 Asian, and 1 Black. In education, everyone with this category of response had more than a high school education (which is true of 94% of the sample); respondents ranged throughout the remaining categories of some training beyond high school up through those with graduate degrees.

*Personally interesting or enriching to work amid diversity*

Fourteen people referred to their own interest in different cultures or a belief that it added an interesting dimension to the workplace:

> "It is interesting to work with different cultural backgrounds."
> "It makes for a more interesting work place."
> "I like being exposed to a variety of cultures."

These 14 respondents all indicated that diversity on the management team was either somewhat or very important. Gender was split with 8 females and 6 males. Twelve of the 14 were White; one was Asian, one Black.

*Diversity is source of learning and understanding differences*

Twelve statements referred to the value of diversity for learning about and understanding different people:

> "You get the benefit of looking at the world through other 'cultural eyes'. Once you do this, you realize the differences between groups is very small and the similarities are greater."
> "learn from each other's thoughts and experiences."
> "It gives each of us an understanding of us and understanding of each other. This shows to me how much we have in common rather than differences we have as a human race."
> In this grouping, there were more male respondents (9 vs. 3 female); only 5 were White (4 Black; 2 Asian; and 1 Hispanic).

*Benefit from Access to Diverse Input*

Twenty-eight people made statements pertaining to how diversity generally broadens ideas and perspectives:

"Different people with different ideas may contribute to the total picture without bias and being closed minded."
"We get many different views on one topic."
"Expands the mental boundaries cultures tend to set"

A group of nine responses offered a little more specificity in mentioning skills, knowledge, experience, or methods, rather than general ideas/perspectives:

"brings many skills together from different backgrounds"
"sharing of special knowledge"
"different ways to conduct business."

Another nine specifically referenced decision-making and problem solving in their statements about the benefits of diverse input:

"It gives us a broader base from which important decisions are made."
"Different cultures have different means/training for problem solving – we can learn from each other."

Two more people phrased their response in terms of creativity or innovation:

"If we are to continually improve, we need ideas from a diverse group to be creative and innovative in our work."
"We need cultural diversity to be the 'best we can be' with new ideas, creativity and innovation created by diverse backgrounds."

Across those groups that mentioned the benefit of diverse input, everyone rated diversity on the management team as either somewhat or very important. The two people referencing innovation (both White males), were among those saying very important. Race, gender, education and age show no apparent pattern across these response categories.

*Diversity in management as a business necessity*
Earlier discussion highlighted employees who spoke of valuing diversity without particular mention of the business outcomes or business needs that might link to that value. Among the people who did make reference to business necessity, two individuals made very general statements. For example, "It's not unique, because it's necessary for top management." Other responses of this category were more specific about the business need being addressed. Some mentioned the need to match external conditions:

"We live in a very diverse country; the workforce should also reflect that."
"The people that we serve are diversified."

Others mentioned the internal workforce composition and expressed that diversity on the management team was necessary for effective leadership of that diverse workforce:

"only because so many people reporting to the management are of cultural diversity."
"Since [the company] employs people of different cultures, it's important to understand individual cultures and be able to work as a team for the benefit of the company as a whole."

Some respondents anticipated or hoped for a business advantage as an outcome of diversity – a means to get ahead rather than just keep up:

"This ensures the success of [the facility] and perhaps I'll have an opportunity to be promoted."
"Being diverse allows us to achieve in areas normally impossible."

*Global Business Necessity*

Although it is highly related to the general topic of business necessity, references to global business necessity seemed distinct in that focus and thus were segregated as another category:

"We live in global economy. We must be able to communicate with and influence members of many cultures."
"It is a global company and we must be able to quickly move our people resources around for efficiency. To move around the globe easily, cultural diversity is necessary."
"An effective management team needs a diverse set of backgrounds, experiences, and skills. Cultural diversity does not ensure success (although cultural diversity does facilitate the forming of a successful team). Remember, the global marketplace is where we compete."
"[the company] is a global company."

With two exceptions, the people citing business necessity or global business necessity all said the cultural diversity was somewhat or very important. For business necessity, the gender comparison was roughly the proportion of male and female respondents overall – 13 men and 4 women. On global business necessity the comments came from 13 men and only 1 woman. The business necessity responses seemed to represent a racial mix somewhat proportional to the overall sample with 10 Whites, 4 Asians, 2 Blacks and 1 Native American. In contrast, references to global business necessity came from only Whites (8) and Asians (6). On business necessity, 13 of 17 respondents were between the ages of 30 and 50; the other four were in their twenties. On global necessity, only three of the 14 were more than 30 years of age.

*Benefit to the organizational culture*

Twenty-one people gave responses that concerned the benefit diversity provided by signaling or contributing to a change in the organization's culture. Five people referred to diversity on the management team as being a break from the established patterns:

> "I think it greatly relieves the regimented behaviors that are prevalent in organizations that are predominantly controlled by white males."
>
> "Coming from another part of [the company] I know of the gross, unfair prejudices that obviously prevail among old style management, causing the high potential of certain individuals to never be realized, as they are squelched early on."

Four others mentioned the positive influence on their general working environment:

> "It is a little better for working circumstance."
>
> "The work environment is completely professional if, strangely, the people are from different backgrounds rather than the same."

Another five people viewed it as being symbolic of equal opportunity in the workplace:

> "It shows equal opportunity for everybody."
>
> "because it reflects on the idea that anybody can be a part of top management"
>
> "belief that I will more likely get judged by ability than if not so diverse"

Finally, seven comments seemed to reflect views of people for whom diversity on the management team has special meaning, because they identify themselves as outside the mainstream:

> "from a different ethnic background myself, I feel more comfortable approaching people like me (non-Americans) which helps in effective communications."
>
> "Because I am female, cultural diversity is extremely important to me. The white, male, U.S. born culture is very strong here and without respect for cultural differences my chances for contribution and advancement are not good."
>
> "I have worked in non-diverse cultural environment where a manager continuously *corrects* my English and other insensitive cultural behavior. I will *never* allow myself to be subjected to such insensitive treatment ever again. I would form my own company with diverse culture before I'll let this happen again."

Of the 5 people who mentioned it as a positive by breaking established patterns, all 5 were White and 4 of the 5 were male. In that grouping and the comments about general working environment, respondents had all said the diversity among managers was either somewhat or very important, with about an even mix between the two answers. Of those who commented about equal opportunity and desirability for people outside the mainstream – 12 in all – every one of them rated the importance of cultural diversity on the management team as very important.

The people classifying themselves as outside the mainstream consisted of one White female, 2 Asian females, 3 Asian males and 1 Black male. Ages in this group ranged from mid-twenties to 51, and the education was at the higher end of the scale: 2 graduates from two year college programs, 1 with a 4 year degrees, and 4 people with graduate degrees.

## *Not Supportive of Diversity*

In any organization – regardless of training, leaders' emphasis, or prevailing social trends – -there will be some people who speak out against a particular action. In this sample, 18 people, approximately 8%, gave replies that seemed clearly not supportive of diversity.

Three individuals' responses were examples of ethnocentric thinking:

> "I think Americans can run this company just fine."
> "We do not have to have the Japanese to be successful."
> "I am disappointed in the trend toward Japanese top management and fear that the company is and will be influenced too heavily by Japanese-style decisions. This is not good for an American company."

Another 4 people chose to focus on the communication difficulties involved in having a culturally diverse management team:

> "not important to get the job done, causes communications problems."
> "I feel people need to fully understand, read and write and talk in a standard language. People who can not do this make it very hard at the workplace".

Of the 7 people whose answers are in these two groupings, 6 of them also indicated that having a cultural diverse management team was of little or no importance. Both groups had male and female respondents, but all seven identified themselves as White.

A variety of cynical attitudes were expressed about the attention to diversity. Four people referred to affirmative action or quotas, as if those were synonymous with diversity:

> "One should seek the best person for the job – -not fill a quota."
> "I don't believe in quotas, just how well is the job getting done."
> "Affirmative action is nothing but reverse racism."

These responses were predominantly from White males, although one was from an Hispanic male. All were midrange on education, and ranged from ages 25 to 50.

Three people gave answers that seem to be in direct opposition to the earlier categories relating diversity to business or global business necessity. These individuals perceive that the attention to diversity as not contributing to the company's business focus:

> "The [facility] top management team is culturally diverse for the sake of claiming cultural diversity, but the organization does not benefit so much from this."
> "Don't force diversity where it is not naturally occurring. Diversity for diversity's sake is stupid."

In a few cases employees simply stated they had no opinion, or they made comments about the management team that had no apparent relationship to the diversity issue. Nearly one fifth of the sample chose not to respond to the question of why they did or did not feel the cultural diversity among the management team was important.

## DISCUSSION

This study capitalized on an opportunity to study employee reactions in an organization where they were exposed to working for a culturally diverse management team. The initial question was whether employees in this situation value that diversity. It seems that a majority of this sample did, because 64% said it was either very important or somewhat important. Second, I explored their specific positive or negative reactions to this diversity at a higher organizational level, through categorization of their written explanations. Similar to findings of earlier research on peer interactions, the range of responses represented both positive and negative reactions. As the categories developed, results seemed to suggest that many of the perceptions and attitudes are basic enough to human nature that they appear similarly when dealing with diversity at any organizational level. For example, meeting business needs is a positive aspect of diversity and communication difficulty is a negative aspect.

The literature on diversity, as well as diversity training, frequently mentions the importance of acknowledging different perspectives, points of view, or ideas and talents (Cox, 1993; Gordon, DiTomaso & Farris, 1991; Jackson, 1992; Thiederman, 1991). By that reasoning, the opening of organizational processes to more diverse input increases opportunity for deriving the best possible solution. Increased global competition has brought home the lesson that one country or culture does not have all the best ideas. This enhancement of increased input and broader perspectives is likely to be the argument for diversity most commonly promoted in organizations. Forty-eight people in this sample mentioned benefits of diverse input, either in a general sense or with specific reference to skills and knowledge, decision-making or problem-solving, or creativity.

Nearly all of the respondents in this study indicated they had received some type of formal diversity training. They had not all been through identical training, as they had come to the current job from a variety of previous situations. A survey of articles about diversity training reveals that trainees are usually exposed to a variety of reasons for promoting diversity: legal implications, productivity increases, reducing conflict, or as a boost to recruiting the best new talent (e.g. Bacon, 1990; Thomas, 1990). There may be some reference to diversity as the "right" thing to do (e.g. Cox, 1993). However, moral judgments are less common and typically framed in a business context pertaining to equal opportunity, community relations, or acknowledging the reality of changing workforce composition. Therefore, when people respond that diversity is important for moral reasons, it seems more likely to stem from a personal value that goes deeper than the training they have received as part of their professional development. Nonetheless, eleven people gave moral or ethical references in their reasons for the importance of diversity on the management team.

In this study there were indications that some employees would rather avoid the communication difficulties or other inconveniences of dealing with a diverse group of managers, and those people made no mention of benefits that might make the effort worthwhile. Barry and Bateman (1996) described social traps related to the management of diversity in organizations. These "diversity traps" refer to the trade-off between short-term convenience and long-term benefit. In their discussion, a manager might avoid bothersome confrontations with diverse employees, which consequently sacrifices long-term benefit. This would seem to also apply in the opposite direction, the focus of this study. The employees may create long-term difficulties in the organization by limiting upward communication that is, initially, somewhat awkward on a day-to-day basis.

The mention of communication difficulties is not a surprise in a group where native languages differ. Focusing on intercultural communications, Wiseman, Hammer and Nishida (1989) discuss the concept of a cross-cultural attitude as including dimensions of stereotyping, ethnocentrism, and social distancing behaviors. This provides a link between the willingness to work at communication and the ideas expressed in ethnocentric comments and cynicism about diversity. All seven of the people making ethnocentric comments or citing communication difficulties identified themselves as White respondents. This places them as majority group members and most likely native-English speakers.

Although the pro-diversity reactions indicate this organization is moving in the direction of diversity being well accepted, not all responses were positive. Even with a relative small number of unsupportive comments, it is important to consider that some of those who did not respond to this particular question on the survey may have shared their sentiments. The non-respondents did not differ in any identifiable pattern of demographics. However, during survey administration, there was a great deal of surprise expressed that the company had allowed an outsider to come in and survey employee attitudes. Along with that surprise was some skepticism that the researcher was truly as independent as the introductory information said. It is impossible to determine whether those skeptics were less likely to respond to this portion of the survey, or whether the non-respondents might have held back because their comments were non-supportive.

In closing, it is important to note that the facility of the current study may have some unique features that limit generalization. It was a greenfield site and all employees knew from the start they would be working for managers from different cultures. This was an opportunity to set the initial culture at a more diversified stage, rather than attempting transition in an established facility. Also, in this high-tech industry, the specific expertise of the individuals may be a more readily accepted justification for change. Still, the fact that this selection of managers varied from the traditions of the parent organization did not go unnoticed. Evidence is seen in the comments about the importance of the multicultural management team as a benefit in changing the culture. It is unclear whether diversity is the causal factor in culture change, or whether having diverse managers is a signal that the culture has changed or is changing. In either case, the employees commenting on the benefit of diverse management as a shift in the culture saw this change as one that had some meaning to them in their work lives.

# REFERENCES

Bacon, C. L. (1990). *Celebrating Diversity: A Learning Tool for Working with People of Different Cultures*. Washington, D.C.: American Association of Retired Persons.

Barry, B., & Bateman, T. S. (1996). A social trap analysis of the management of diversity. *Academy of Management Review, 21*, 757–790.

Cox, T. Jr. (1993). *Cultural Diversity in Organizations: Theory, Research and Practice*. San Francisco: Berrett-Koehler.

Gordon, G. G., DiTomaso, N., & Farris, G. F. (1991). Managing diversity in R&D groups. *Research-Technology Management, 34*, 18–23.

Jackson, S. E. (1992). Team composition in organizational settings: Issues in managing an increasingly diverse workforce. In: S. Worchel, W. Wook & J. Simpson (Eds), *Group Process and Productivity* (pp. 138–173). Beverly Hills, CA: Sage.

Raghuram, S., & Garud, R. (1996). The vicious and virtuous facets of workforce diversity. In: M. N. Ruderman, M. W. Hughes-James & S. E. Jackson (Eds), *Selected Research on Work Team Diversity* (pp. 155–178). Washington, D.C.: American Psychological Association.

Thiederman, S. (1991). *Profiting in America's Multicultural Marketplace: How to do Business Across Cultural Lines*. New York: Lexington.

Thomas, R. R. Jr. (1990). From affirmative action to affirming diversity. *Harvard Business Review, 68*(2), 107–117.

Wiseman, R. L., Hammer, M. R., & Nishida, H. (1989). Predictors of intercultural communication competence. *International Journal of Intercultural Relations, 13*, 349–370.

# VENDOR-MANUFACTURER PARTNERSHIPS IN THE SUPPLY CHAIN: AN INDUCTIVE CASE STUDY FROM NEW ZEALAND

Terence H. Wilson and Jayaram K. Sankaran

## ABSTRACT

*A critical tenet of the field of supply chain management (SCM) concerns the importance of developing "partnerships" between members of the supply chain, consisting of enduring relationships based on collaboration, mutual trust, and the sharing of information. Published research on vendor-manufacturer partnerships focuses for the most part on the automotive industries of Japan, Korea, the U.S., and elsewhere, which are structurally different from process flow industries, such as forestry, that altogether comprise the majority of manufacturing operations in many other countries. In light of this limitation, we report an in-depth, inductive case study of a vendor-manufacturer partnership located in a process industry in New Zealand.*

## INTRODUCTION

In the traditional arm's length approach to supplier management, the buyer plays off a large number of suppliers against each other to gain price concessions, allocates amounts to suppliers to keep them in line, and uses

Advances in Qualitative Organization Research, Volume 3, pages 205–251.
Copyright © 2001 by Elsevier Science Ltd.
ISBN: 0-7623-0772-2

short-term contracts or spot purchases to structure vendor-manufacturer relationships (Spekman, 1988). The underlying logic is that the buying firm maximizes its bargaining power by minimizing its dependence on any one supplier (Porter, 1980).

A contrasting approach is the partner model (Dyer, Cho & Chu, 1998), for which the success of Japanese automobile firms, notably Toyota, provided the initial impetus (Cusumano & Takeishi, 1991; Dyer & Ouchi, 1993; Nishiguchi, 1992). Over the years, vendor-manufacturer partnering has emerged in the automotive industries of the U.S. (Dyer, 1996b), the U.K. (Carr & Ng, 1995; Leverick & Cooper, 1998), continental Europe (Bensaou, 1999), and Australia (Langfield-Smith & Greenwood, 1998). In this approach, suppliers are given implicit (and sometimes explicit) guarantees on future business, and in return, make relation-specific site, physical, and human asset investments to enhance the buyer's productivity by facilitating inventory reduction, quality improvement, and rapid product development (Dyer, 1996a). Vendor-manufacturer partnerships are a primary focus of Supply Chain Management (SCM), as both a field of academic research and an area of business activity. They have been defined as "tailored business relationship[s] based on mutual trust, openness, shared risk and shared rewards that yield a competitive advantage, resulting in business performance greater than would be achieved by the firms individually" (Lambert, Emmelhainz & Gardner, 1996: 2).

The point of departure for the present article consists of the finding of the New Zealand (NZ) replication of KPMG's *Global Supply Chain Benchmarking Study* that New Zealand's local manufacturers are lagging behind their overseas counterparts in many key areas of SCM, including the formation of vendor-manufacturer partnerships (Maller, 1998; Newman, 1998). To explore the implications of this finding in greater depth, we conducted a case study of supplier partnering in NZ. We chose an unusual industrial context, forestry, in which to conduct our investigation, for two important reasons. First, forestry comprises the third largest export sector for NZ, whose economy is highly dependent on exports for growth in light of its tiny domestic markets. This led us to suspect that SCM deficiencies highlighted in the NZ *Benchmarking Study* should be readily evident in practices in the forestry industry. Second, 80% of New Zealand manufacturing is oriented towards process flows (Macquet, 1997), as in the forestry industry, as opposed to the fabrication/assembly of discrete parts that characterizes the automobile industry (the corresponding figures for Australia and the world over are 70% and 50% respectively). The distinction between process industries and fabrication/assembly industries is well-established in the operations management literature (e.g. Silver, Pyke & Peterson, 1998). As we planned our study it appeared to us that this distinction might also shape or influence the formation of vendor-manufacturer partnerships. We hoped to discover empirical evidence that might explicate or contradict this supposition.

Our article is laid out as follows. In the next section, we discuss the research process of our study, with special emphasis on the inductive nature of the methodology and the techniques used for data analysis. Subsequently, we present a case description of the vendor-manufacturer partnership that is at the heart of this paper. We then address the New Zealand-specific aspects of the case as well as the features that set this process-industry-based case apart from those in discrete-part fabrication/assembly industries.

## METHODOLOGY

Swamidass (1991), among others, has decried the lack of inductive, field-based studies in the operations management literature, arguing for a deductive-inductive equilibrium. Our choice of methodology in the present study is partly an attempt to address this imbalance. The investigation is primarily qualitative in nature, involving constant iteration between data gathering and data analysis (Strauss & Corbin, 1990). Our approach partakes of grounded theory development inasmuch as the grounded theory approach is "an inductive, theory discovery methodology that permits the researcher to develop theoretical accounts of general features of a topic while grounding the account in empirical observations or data" (Martin & Turner, 1986: 141).

### *Key Informant Selection*

With reference to inter-organizational research of the kind reported here, Kumar, Stern, and Anderson state that gathering information from key informants "is appropriate when the content of inquiry is such that complete or in-depth information cannot be expected from representative survey respondents. [Informants] are chosen because they are supposedly knowledgeable about the issues being researched and able and willing to communicate about them" (1993: 1634).

Initially, we approached the Procurement Director of the manufacturer's parent company to gain understanding of the appropriate persons within the manufacturer who might act as key informants. We refer to the manufacturer as Alpha, and to the parent company as Phi. The Procurement Director of Phi identified the Procurement Manager and the Partnership Manager of Alpha as suitable candidates.

The Procurement Manager, David, had held his current job in Alpha for several years, and was the original Partnership Manager. This experience appeared to render him the ideal candidate to speak knowledgeably on the history of the partnership and on the context in which it was formed. The current Partnership Manager, Susan, was selected because the Procurement Director of Phi had indicated that she would be the most appropriate person to speak about current and future partnership issues. We restricted the number of informants interviewed at the manufacturer to two, because although the success of the partnership was well known within Phi, in-depth knowledge was, for all intents and purposes, restricted to the Procurement department.

The second phase of the data-gathering process entailed contacting the vendor's Commercial Manager, John, who was also Susan's "opposite number" at the vendor organization, which we refer to as Beta, to identify those people in Beta who would be best positioned to participate. John as well as Paul, the Technical Services Manager, and Alan, the Manufacturing Manager, had been in Beta prior to the partnership, and were therefore able to provide insight into several aspects of the partnership, including the context within which it originated. Due to the small size of Beta, several executives, including John, served dual roles. For example, the Managing Director, Ray, doubled as the Marketing Manager. Therefore, Ray could potentially throw additional light on the dynamics of the partnership. Table 1 lists all the informants for the research, including their affiliations and designations.

***Table 1.*** List of Informants and their Roles/Designations at the Partner Organizations.

| Name | Organization | Role/Designation |
|------|--------------|------------------|
| David | Alpha | Procurement Manager and former Partnership Manager |
| Susan | Alpha | Current Partnership Manager |
| John | Beta | Commercial Manager and also Manager of Beta's partnership with Alpha |
| Paul | Beta | Technical Services Manager |
| Alan | Beta | Manufacturing Manager |
| Ray | Beta | Managing Director, also Marketing Manager |

## Data Collection

The issue of what constitutes an appropriate degree of theoretical formulation prior to data gathering in qualitative research has been debated upon at length. One set of authors, including Lofland (1971) among others, maintains that ideally, data collection should commence from a "blank state." However, for reasons similar to those cited by Miles & Huberman (1994), we followed their recommendation of commencing data collection with a rudimentary conceptual framework of sorts.

In our context, a "mundane" reason (Miles & Huberman, 1994: 17) for doing so was that the principal source of data was interviews with senior executives of both the manufacturer and the partner supplier. To minimize our imposition on their time and to simultaneously get the most out of the interviews, we saw fit to do some prior homework. This took the form of, among other things, taking stock of the salient literature on supplier partnering. To illustrate, questions probing asset-specificity ("What degree of expenditure has there been on re-tooling Beta around Alpha's products?") and trust ("Do you [Beta] consider Alpha to act fairly and do you expect unfair treatment if Alpha has the chance?") were derived respectively from Bensaou and Venkatraman (1995) and Dyer, Cho and Chu (1998). In practice, while the literature provided a set of themes to initially guide fieldwork, the inductive nature of the research meant that several questions were derived from emerging concepts (we clarify this point when describing our analytic process).

Data were collected in two phases. Phase One consisted of four interview sessions with David, the Procurement Manager, and Susan, the Partnership Manager, at Alpha's head office, over a month-long period in late-1999. Each session ranged between one and two hours in duration. The respondents also furnished supporting documentation, such as the partnership agreement between Alpha and Beta. The time between interviews enabled us to iterate, in the spirit of induction, between emergent theory and data.

Phase Two consisted of four interviews conducted over a day at Beta's head office in Wanganui, NZ. We engaged John (the Commercial Manager/ Partnership Manager), Paul (the Technical Services Manager), Alan (the Manufacturing Manager), and Ray (the Managing Director/Marketing Manager), in sessions that were between one and two hours long. Besides confirming information and insights derived from Phase One, we also explored issues that were quite specific to the vendor (such as waste management processes), which could affect partnership dynamics. At the close of the interview sessions, John conducted a tour of the production and research facilities for our benefit.

## Data Analysis

We employed open coding (Strauss & Corbin, 1990) to organize the vast amount of interview data in a conceptually coherent manner. Following Strauss and Corbin (1990: 61), we define *concepts* as "conceptual labels placed on discrete happenings, events, and other instances of phenomena." A *category* was "a classification of concepts", which was identified "when concepts are compared one against another and appear to pertain to a similar phenomenon." An *indicator* was defined for our research purposes as an event or happening that fits into a concept.

As part of our coding, we scanned the interview transcripts from start to finish, at all times searching for themes that began to manifest in the data with the potential to recur. We illustrate with reference to the following extract, in which "FA" refers to the first author, and "PM" refers to the Procurement Manager of Alpha. Gamma was another supplier that competed with Beta for Alpha's business.

> FA:  Probably a bit of a strange question, but why was Beta chosen over Gamma?
> PM:  We went through a fairly rigorous evaluation process. I sent you a copy of the criteria that they were judged on. The RFP itself we sent out comprised of 40-odd pages. Well, lots and lots of questions focused around the type of culture they had. The RFP was not, if you like, the end point. We had the RFP out, gathering information about both companies. We had both companies do presentations of their RFP's to quite a large team who rated them on how they came across, the information that they had provided, etc.

A theme/pattern (concept) that emerged from the above extract was Alpha's thoroughness in the selection process, of which two indicators are: *the comprehensive nature of the RFP* (40-odd pages); and *the use of multiple methods* ("The RFP was not, if you like, the end point"). Such an emergent concept was filled upon the analysis of subsequent text, failing which it was explored through subsequent data gathering. In that manner, we subsequently uncovered further indicators of *Alpha's thoroughness*, such as: *the prolonged selection process* ("The whole process took 2–3 months"); Alpha's having *"no fixed conclusion when they went in[to the selection process]"*; and Alpha's *professionalism and integrity* ("They [Alpha] didn't give away that they were preferring anyone over anyone . . . A lot of integrity in the whole process . . . . They didn't really let on that we [Beta] had the inside running or anything").

In the manner of the *constant comparisons method* (Glaser & Strauss, 1967), upon the gathering and analysis of subsequent data, a concept could well be redefined or relabeled, perhaps as not one but several (lower-level) concepts. It was vital to ensure that at all times, each one of the indicators of a concept truly constituted a manifestation of the pattern or theme that was referred to by the concept's label. Thus, not only had the indicators of a concept to cohere with the label that was assigned to the concept, but also the various indicators (e.g. 'the comprehensive nature of the RFP's'; 'the use of multiple methods'; etc.) had to stand in relation to each other as being different representations of the same pattern or theme ('thoroughness in the selection process').

As we analyzed the data inductively and uncovered various concepts and their associated indicators, it became clear that further classification was required to organize the multitude of concepts coherently. We then identified four overarching categories: 'the background [context] to the partnership', 'Alpha's selection of partner', 'implementation of the partnership', and 'evolution in the partnership'. Table 2 reports the categories and their included concepts/subcategories. The following case description is an elaboration of these categories and their included concepts.

### *Validation*

Once we completed data gathering and analysis, we prepared the first draft of the case study and gave copies to Susan and John for review. The first author then presented the case description and analysis at the semi-annual supplier review meeting held at one of Alpha's manufacturing sites. During this meeting, we distributed additional copies of the first draft and solicited feedback. While a few minor changes were made with regard to factual data, both parties – Alpha and Beta – indicated that the case description was "a really good account of the partnership", one that was true and accurate. We attribute the endorsement of our case description directly to the inductive nature of our investigation in which, in keeping with the ethos of much qualitative research, we sought to "forge interpretations in terms of their [the respondents'] own natural language" (Bryman, 1989: 137).

## CASE CONTEXT

### *Alpha*

Alpha is a wholly owned subsidiary of Phi, and is one of New Zealand's larger manufacturers. Alpha produces a broad range of products at several manufacturing sites in New Zealand and Australia, with nearly 60% of revenues earned in overseas markets. While the years prior to 1995 had been prosperous for Alpha, the years ahead provided management with concern.

As outlined in an internal, confidential document furnished by Alpha, three events would simultaneously shape the manufacturer's future. First, the New

*Table 2.*     Concepts and Categories Emerging from Open Coding of
Qualitative Data.

| CATEGORY | INCLUDED CONCEPT |
| --- | --- |
| Background/Context | Alpha's history |
| | Beta's history |
| | Reengineering at Alpha |
| | Chemical supply |
| Partner Selection | Manufacturer's motivation and expected benefits |
| | Alpha's considerations in partner selection |
| | Motivation for supplier to enter into partnership |
| | Benefits from partnership envisaged for supplier |
| | Mutual benefits envisaged for both parties |
| | Reasons for partner's not wishing to be Alpha's sole supplier |
| | Selection process methodology |
| Partnership Implementation | Barriers to overcome in the partnership |
| | Facilitators of the partnership |
| | Complications during the transition to the partnership |
| | Seamless, interorganizational development, planning and control |
| | Interpersonal interactions |
| | Communication and sharing of information between partners |
| | Guiding principles to the partnership |
| | Trust |
| | Mutual goodwill |
| | Benefits realized by the manufacturer |
| | Benefits realized by the vendor |
| | Mutual benefits accruing to both parties |
| Evolution in the Partnership | Continuous improvement |
| | Ongoing challenges |
| | Maintenance of the partnership |

Zealand dollar experienced a dramatic resurgence in relation to the currencies of Alpha's key customers. During the period between January and April 1995, for example, the Japanese yen lost 15% of its value against the New Zealand dollar. Second, the onset of the 'Asian Crisis' (which was a major reason for the recession in the NZ economy in the first half of 1998) and a downturn in the Australian building industry saw a drop in customer demand, and consequently lower prices. Third, manufacturing capacity was being increased in the Asia-Pacific region, fuelled mainly by start-ups in low-cost environments of Indonesia and Thailand. A consultant to Alpha noted in a confidential report, "This was not another short-term situation to be met with incremental measures, but a deep-rooted crisis that threatened to overwhelm Alpha's core businesses. The speed with which events were overtaking the company had caught Alpha off-guard."

## Beta

Beta (NZ) Ltd is a subsidiary of Beta Industries, which is one of the largest of its kind in the world. The New Zealand subsidiary operates two manufacturing facilities, one in the South Island (near Invercargill) and the other in Wanganui. The latter is the main site and the focus of the present case. This plant specializes in the manufacture of various chemicals for New Zealand's forestry industry.

Beta commenced operations in NZ as Theta, a small producer of chemicals in Auckland. While Theta had a vision to grow in New Zealand, it lacked the resources and the technology to compete with the incumbent, Gamma. In the late 1980s, Beta was approached by Theta to supply technology for a new NZ-based chemical facility that supplied the forestry industry. John remarks, "Beta had a global vision, . . . so obviously New Zealand with the amount of forests available, its protected wood harvest, . . . was a long-term prospect."

Several other factors attracted Beta to the New Zealand market. John recalls "a survey of our [Beta's] customers, they were all talking expansions and most of those expansions happened between 1991 and 1996." Growth in the forestry sector was inevitable despite demand shocks such as the 'Asian Crisis'.

Paul explains further, "It is a case of use it or lose it, you can't just have a forest sit there and do nothing. They are all coming to maturity from about 2005 to about 2015, and . . . the companies that own them would much prefer to turn them into something rather than into woodchips or logs."

Another consideration was the monopolistic behavior of Gamma, the incumbent chemical supplier to Alpha. Until the entry of Beta/Theta, Gamma had been the sole supplier of chemicals to the forestry sector in NZ. With regard to Gamma, the Managing Director of Beta, Ray, remarked, "Once you start to extract abnormal profits from a market, then obviously it becomes attractive. Going back over time in New Zealand . . . what attracted first of all Theta, but also Beta, into the New Zealand market was that margins on chemicals for forestry in New Zealand were very, very attractive because one company [Gamma] was taking advantage of a monopoly situation."

The early part of the 1990s saw a doubling of manufacturing capacity in that sector of forestry in which Alpha operates, through the entry of new investors and the expansion of current producers. The dramatic downturn in demand had potentially very significant ramifications for Alpha and Beta. Paul recalls, "I must tell you, that Alpha was not looking good . . . . It was said that if some miracle didn't happen then they wouldn't be operating in 12 months' time . . . sales were down, the factory was only 60% utilized in terms of capacity, and they just could not make money at all."

### Reengineering at Alpha

In reaction to the changing business environment, in early 1996 Alpha decided to reengineer the structure of the organization to move away from a traditional hierarchy to a flatter company that had a supply chain focus. Alpha also reorganized its operations into four main areas: Demand Generation, Order Fulfilment, Product Supply, and Procurement, with each area charged with developing strategies to support 'Operational Excellence'.

For Procurement, this meant understanding the drivers of Alpha's market in more detail. David stated that in the past the Sales and Marketing team had focused on providing superior customer service at a premium that customers were willing to pay for. But when Procurement went to the market, they learned that customers actually demanded DISOTIF ('delivery in specification, on time, in full') without a price premium.

This realization caused Procurement to define its own Operational Excellence, "moving away from being all things to all people, and refocusing on providing the lowest cost yet best quality solution." The first task in achieving this goal was to reduce waste within the organization. Best-practice studies by the team convinced its members that this goal could be reached through the development of an explicit supply chain vision, with strategies focused around partnerships with a reduced set of suppliers, managed by specialist supplier teams. For this to happen, however, three main tasks needed to be undertaken.

*Identification of key suppliers.* The suppliers targeted in the initial review comprised vendors of key supplies such as chemicals, wood, energy, and process consumables. A number of "excellent" supplier relationships existed even prior to the reengineering effort. The relationships with the supplier of wood (a sister company of Alpha) and of another category of consumables were acclaimed as heading towards partnerships.

*Reduction of suppliers to a manageable level.* The main driver for supplier reduction, besides being a key feature of the best practice studies, were costs to Alpha of a few hundred million NZ dollars, distributed across roughly 3600 suppliers. In the past, a lack of understanding about the contribution of procurement to the organization had resulted in a very decentralized process of purchasing that focused mainly on 'lowest price'. Such an approach led to instances where different plants had different suppliers for the same products, and in some instances different plants had different prices with the same supplier. A study conducted during the reengineering initiative found that the cost of processing each invoice averaged in excess of $NZ 50. Such examples of waste led the procurement team to realize that by centralizing the selection and management of vendors, as well as buying the total spend under a single supplier philosophy, Alpha would gain greater leverage on the supply network and reduce total costs considerably.

Four strategies were considered by Alpha for the procurement of key components: self-manufacture, preferred supply, competitive bidding, and partnerships. Of these, the partnership route was considered the only option that could achieve both a reduction in total costs and world-class DISOTIF, within an allowable period of time.

*Building a case for action.* The team still needed to convince itself and others within Alpha, and those outside the company, of the need to move towards partnerships. A great deal of time was spent 'selling' Procurement to the company. David recalls, "Initially it was going to take up a lot of resources for the return conveyed back to the company . . . . We spent a lot of time up-front going around each of the sites and communicating what Procurement's objectives were . . . because it was going to be quite a large change in the way we managed our suppliers for the future."

## Chemical Supply

For much of the time prior to 1990, the dominant party in the New Zealand forestry chemicals industry was Gamma, which consequently was the sole supplier of chemicals to Alpha. Gamma had been able to dictate the terms and conditions under which chemicals were sold to the market. The manifestations of this power were typical of a company enjoying the benefits of a monopoly situation. One interviewee at Alpha grudgingly revealed that this extended to arbitrary price increases, leading to healthy returns for "the incumbent supplier." John observed, "Their [Gamma's] profits were . . . much healthier than they are now. The industry has saved 10% of chemical costs since the other company [Beta] came in, maybe even 20%." Even in 1998, when Beta controlled the lion's share of the chemical market, Gamma continued with prices similar to that of the old monopoly. Ray remarked, "When we opened the South Island facility, the price of chemicals provided by our competitor dropped a significant amount overnight the day that we started to supply into that market. To me that was a situation of a company taking advantage of its lack of competition."

At the time of Beta's entry to the NZ forestry chemicals industry, the demands of the forestry industry were not technologically driven. Paul explained that since "there wasn't pressure to improve the environmental properties of the chemicals, it was relatively straightforward to manufacture a chemical that performed well for the manufacturer." This lack of technological drive, coupled with satisfactory financial performance, meant, in John's words, "technology was a bit slower in coming" from Gamma.

The entry of Beta shifted power from the vendors to the customer-manufacturers. This shift also highlighted one aspect of the earlier monopoly that was often taken for granted, namely, the attitude of the incumbent towards its customers. When power shifted back to the customer-manufacturers, Beta appeared to be more customer-focused than Gamma. John clarified, "When you realize that customers are your bread and butter, you have to change your focus, and we were quite early in that . . . . We [Beta] had a natural advantage in that we are customer-focused by the sheer fact of a small customer base . . . . If you have got 4 or 5 major customers, you can't help but be customer-intimate . . . . Whilst they [Gamma] had the same number of customers, they still treated their customers like they had 100 customers." (Unlike Beta, whose staple business was the manufacture of chemicals for forestry, Gamma operated numerous businesses in NZ for a variety of industries; forestry chemicals made up only a portion of its total New Zealand operation.)

Alan believes, "The difference between the two chemical companies was technology and customer service. We weren't just selling a product, we were willing to say the product will do this, and if you have a problem with it we will do this and this. But that is really a company thing, we have always been like that. We have had to be because when we started we had 0% of the market, so we really had to focus on customer service."

Despite inevitable change in the chemical industry, Gamma embarked on an aggressive campaign to hurt the new player as much as possible, including, as John recalls, "locking Beta's future partner (Alpha) into a supply contract . . . . They dealt with Alpha on an open-book pricing, low-margin basis to keep Beta out." Low margins were accompanied by a system of volume rebates that eventually became unsustainable for Gamma: "They lost a lot of money, so they pulled out . . . . That was when we got in there."

From then on, Alpha effectively split its purchase of chemicals between the two companies. Gamma kept supplying chemicals to the Murupara plant that manufactured product-category A, and Beta supplied chemicals for the Kawhia plant that manufactured product-category B. The rationale for this strategy was two-fold. Firstly, Alpha could effectively control the price it paid for chemicals by playing off one supplier against the other, and secondly, by supporting Gamma's competitor, Alpha would ensure that it was not faced with a dependent relationship similar to that of the past.

The price reduction strategy effectively reduced the margins of the chemical suppliers, especially as additional capacity for chemical manufacture was being installed to take advantage of the projected increase in their customers' capacity. When this growth did not occur, both Gamma and Beta found themselves with excess capacity and negative margins. By 1996, Alpha was facing the prospect of downsizing and both Beta and Gamma needed additional volume to run their over-capacity plants.

# PARTNER SELECTION

### *Manufacturer's Motivation and Expected Benefits*

Alpha was looking for "long term sustainable reduction in TC (total costs) and achieving world class standards in DISOTIF (delivery in specification, on time, in full)" to support the demands of its own customers: DISOTIF of product without a premium price. The TC philosophy takes an alternate perspective on price determination. Ray explained, "The main difference with our arrangement with Alpha is that right from day one it was developed around a TC [concept], where we looked at the costs right across the board and focused on that rather than the price of chemicals. My interpretation of it is that cost = price + performance, and if you take performance out of it, you have cost = price. [This second] relationship in my view doesn't hold because I can supply you with something that is cheaper but doesn't necessarily work as well and you will have a cheaper price but your costs could very well go up. We have seen that in some of our other partnership arrangements, that where the focus has been totally on price, the costs have actually gone up, and eventually those sort of arrangements tend to flounder."

Chemicals represented a significant supply cost for Alpha. Analysis by Alpha during the opportunity assessment stage showed that chemicals ranked as the second largest raw material cost. Therefore, as David confirms, "Our partnership selection is fairly important to us. Getting it wrong could have cost us quite a lot of money."

Alpha stood to receive benefits beyond the achievement of TC reduction and DISOTIF. By instituting the consignment-stock policy, Alpha could effectively reduce its investment in inventory of chemicals to zero, with the added benefit of a reduction in stock monitoring. This policy was implemented from the first day of the Beta partnership, with assistance from Phi, Alpha's parent company.

Another motivation was, as John described, a reliance on the vendor "to provide technology to help them [Alpha] [in] their business . . . . They see us [Beta] as a technology provider now, not just a chemical supplier." One of the more fundamental benefits that would accrue to Alpha was that a partnership for chemicals would provide the company with expertise that it simply did not have, as Susan observes: "We [Alpha] have one person on our staff who has some understanding of chemicals, but very little, so we needed a company that could provide that for us." In a similar vein, John noted, "You can't be experts at everything and their [Alpha's] expertise is probably in manufacturing product-category A, but a really integral part of that is: can they get the right chemicals?"

Alpha also needed "support to meet the changing requirements of the customer." Meeting these requirements, in light of a lack of expertise at Alpha, meant that the partner for chemicals would take responsibility for new product development. With reference to the current partnership, Susan alludes to the level of responsibility given to Beta: "We want a high-quality final product [one that is 'green' for instance, and that has various structural properties], so it is up to Beta to develop the solution, working in conjunction with our people as far as organizing trials and that sort of thing goes."

Through partnership, Alpha could also enjoy access to the latest technology from the vendor at differential prices compared to competitors. Ray clarified how new developments were shared with the market: "Anything that is initiated by Alpha that we get involved in stays with Alpha. If it has been initiated by us for the market as a whole, and if the development work is done with Alpha in the first instance, then obviously they get a lead on everyone else." In cases where there has been spillover of technology from Alpha to the wider market, a differential is applied, as clarified by David: "Alpha will receive the chemicals at one price, our competitors will receive it at a higher price." Susan remarks, "It [having the vendor supply competitors] also helps to reduce our cost too. If they are supplying only us with specialty chemicals, the price is much higher than if they are developing huge volumes."

Through the initial fact-finding and subsequent visits and communications, a partnership for chemicals would allow Alpha to better understand the vendor's capabilities, especially for the supply of new chemicals. David explains, "With Beta, they have a number of batch sizes. They can make a minimum of three tons [of chemicals] at a time, they can manufacture [up to] 18 tons, and their standard is 12 tons. So if we are looking at introducing new chemicals and we want to avoid waste, we have to understand what their capabilities are. Once you understand what their capabilities are, then you can look at potential improvements."

## Alpha's Considerations in Partner Selection

The location of the plant of the supplier of chemicals, with respect to Alpha's major plant at Murupara, was an important consideration with potential to impact significantly on the TC for chemicals, and the eventual choice of partner. John explains, "Transport accounts for 10–15% of the price of chemicals, but potentially if Murupara were Kaitaia, then it would be 20–30%. So location is an important factor."

Beta was at a natural disadvantage by being in Wanganui (a four-hour truck journey from Murupara), while Gamma stood to benefit from its location at Gisborne, which was only a two-hour truck journey from Murupara. David explains, "By going through Gisborne, if your truck is configured correctly, you can cart chemicals in one direction [Gisborne to Murupara] and finished products in the other [Murupara to Gisborne]. Gisborne is one of our major export ports . . . so you effectively reduce the delivered cost per ton because of back-loading capability. None of our product goes out through Wanganui so invariably there are specialty tankers that come over full [to Murupara] and go back empty [to Wanganui]. So it is a longer distance and you don't have the economies of back-loading."

Beta's transport company, Omega, has worked to negate these effects through the effective coordination of movements. Alan explains, "The four-hour thing [travel time between Wanganui and Murupara] means that the guys can get to Murupara and back within their eleven hours, so they can actually do a return trip . . . . [The] tanker system works on a 24 hour a day basis, so that has offset that [higher transport costs] a little bit for Omega."

The eventual partner for chemicals also had to be passionate about its business. As noted earlier, Gamma operated numerous businesses in New Zealand and chemicals for forestry made up only a portion of its total New Zealand operation. Beta, however, operated facilities that specialized in chemicals for the forestry industry. David clarifies, "Whilst Beta didn't have the lowest prices because of their relative location to our major plants in comparison with Gamma, we assessed they would make a better partner than Gamma would because they were actually passionate about chemicals for forestry and the development of such chemicals. We saw that as a real need in respect of where we were going as a company."

The choice of partner had ramifications beyond the sphere of the supply of chemicals: Alpha needed to consider the impact of its decision on the wider parent organization, Phi. David expanded: "In the [Gisborne] region in which Gamma operates, there are a number of Phi companies so if we had an impact on Gamma in their local environment, we could ultimately affect the other operations of Phi." As the interests of Phi focused mainly in the primary manufacturing sectors (such as forestry), its operations tended to be located in regions where it was often the largest employer. Alpha's being seen to put people in Gamma and other group companies in Phi out of work could have negative outcomes for the Phi group.

The partner for chemicals also needed to share with Alpha a common ground of growth. David remarked, "If we chose a supplier of chemicals we would want them to grow with us, not just grow in size but rather in terms of technology. By making sure that they remained at the forefront of their own industry, we ourselves wanted to be at the forefront of our industry." According to Paul, Alpha is the only manufacturer in New Zealand capable of producing its entire product range to the strict new standards that took effect in mid-2000 of one of its major export markets, and "that wouldn't have happened unless there was the close working relationship [between Beta and Alpha]."

David noted that the partner for chemicals also had "to meet all our needs at all manufacturing facilities [Murupara and Kawhia]." Besides capacity issues, Alpha needed to consider the compatibility between the two production processes, i.e. balancing Alpha's requirements with the batched nature of production of chemicals at Beta: "So for example if we want 10 tons of chemicals, that sort of fits somewhere in between [Beta's capabilities]. Now we know that is going to cause difficulty for them to produce. Further, in certain instances, the chemical has a very limited shelf life."

The partner's organizational culture was also a consideration. David concedes, "We [Alpha] had very much a corporate culture . . . . We had reached a position where we could not continue our business or doing our business in the way that we had done previously. We had to change the culture of Alpha, and that was one of the criteria that we used in terms of selection." In this context, Ray implied that in comparison with Beta, Gamma had more layers of bureaucracy as a result of its larger size and diversity. David concurs: "Beta had more of the type of culture that we wanted within our own organization, whereas Gamma on the other hand had a very similar culture [to where Alpha was at the time]. So it was easy to help us in our decision making in terms of the way we wanted to go forward." In this context, John observes, "Sometimes people don't appreciate how good small companies are – less bureaucratic and can do things quite quickly, and people say 'Oh wonderful Beta', but . . . it is a consequence of our size."

Ray describes Beta's culture as being team-based: "We have a very good team, we talk about it quite a bit . . . . We are a bit like a family, we have our disagreements, we have our squabbles but at the end of the day, we function very well as a unit as well as individuals." He also notes the lack of pretension that is latent in Beta's organizational culture and the fit thereof with Alpha's aspirations: "We have felt that we shouldn't try to be something that we are not . . . . We have taken that approach with our customers. With Alpha, that approach has been very readily accepted . . . . We have other customers where our approach has not gelled . . . and we do very little business, if any, with them."

The biggest requirement from Alpha's new partner for chemicals was the willingness to have a partnership based on openness and honesty. Paul expresses that "what tipped the scales was that we wanted to be open and honest with them [Alpha] and work with them as a partner. They knew they could trust us."

### *Motivation for Supplier to Enter into Partnership*

When pressed on Beta's motivation for entering into a partnership with Alpha, John responded instantly: "Survival . . . [If Beta had not secured Alpha's business,] we would have had to shut down the larger facility [at Wanganui] or downscale it big time, I mean, big time. We were committed to the second, smaller facility [near Invercargill] but we could have been on a day-only operation here at the larger facility [in Wanganui], probably lose 20 or 30 jobs, mothball a lot of plant." Although being quite small by global standards, Beta ranked in the top twenty of employers in its region. Hence, a loss of 20–30 jobs was not insignificant.

At the time, securing the volume of one of the largest customers in NZ would go a long way in meeting ROI (return on investment) commitments that would otherwise prove difficult to achieve. John remarks that, "We [Beta] had built so much plant capacity we could supply the New Zealand market twice over." David agrees, "Both companies [Beta and Gamma] could see that with the extra capacity that was being installed in the chemical industry, they would have some difficulties in meeting some of their own ROI commitments."

The partner for chemicals had the potential to pick up not only business for chemicals, but to become a 'total chemical solutions' provider as well. David explains, "Because there is some similarity between a producer of chemicals and a user of chemicals, we were looking at perhaps our supplier of chemicals also looking after or managing our total chemical requirements by combining our requirements of all chemicals with theirs to provide better purchasing leverage with their own suppliers." However, at the time of the interviews (late-1999), such joint procurement had not transpired. John suggests that while it could be possible, the volumes of in-common chemicals that Alpha requires are insufficient enough for Beta to justify adding the necessary resources to effect Alpha's earlier expectations. Moreover, "Firstly you have to get to the information sharing stage and then you can maybe do some deals together . . . . We are still at the information gathering stage."

### Benefits from Partnership Envisaged for Supplier

By being appointed as the sole supplier of chemicals for Alpha, Beta would enjoy "long term security . . . [having] got a committed customer who is in for the long haul." The partnership would also enable the partner for chemicals to become a technology leader. According to David, "Most R&D plants are in laboratories and they are minor-scale. We have actually provided Beta with a full-scale R&D plant, so they can undertake research and development trials using a full production facility. That gave them very much a lead over their competitor."

By becoming a partner with Alpha, the vendor of chemicals could take advantage of other partnerships implemented by Alpha. Susan clarifies: "An electricity contract that we might have, we may be able to negotiate something that allows Beta to benefit from." At Alpha, electricity ranks as the fourth largest commodity in terms of Alpha's procurement costs, and the company has negotiated favorable contracts for the procurement of electricity. This combined with New Zealand's flexible electricity market means that a joint contract with the same energy vendor is possible through the partnership, and affords increased leverage to both partners. John responds, "We didn't go with Alpha's preferred company in the end, but certainly the information helped us evaluate the different offers we had. It was better on a commodity basis, we went for the cheapest company in a way."

### Mutual Benefits Envisaged for Both Parties

The partnership would allow each company to be at the forefront of its respective industry. The increased volume of business for Beta from Alpha would justify a Center of Excellence, which provides Alpha with the optimal chemicals to meet its own customer needs effectively and efficiently.

A question that arises here is whether this would not also apply to Gamma and one of Alpha's competitors. In this regard, Ray relates his experience concerning relationships with other manufacturers: "Our competitor and likewise ourselves have entered into other so-called partnerships. None of the ones that we have been in (and I don't believe that the ones that our competitor [Gamma] has been in) are quite on the same level as the one that we have with Alpha, and likewise they don't work as well . . . . The so-called partnering arrangements that we have entered into with other customers have carried with them all the baggage of previous arrangements. They have not been about furthering the interests of both businesses."

For both Alpha and Beta, as alluded to earlier, possible synergies could be realized through the joint procurement of commonly used raw materials and services such as energy. Although the potential is not yet realized, John believes such synergies are possible at least in the case of some commodities: "We had two preferred suppliers for some of the other commodities and one of them has got a lot of history with Alpha. So . . . if we know that they supply Alpha's requirements, then we know that in terms of their thinking, they will be good for us as well."

### Reasons for Partner's Not Wishing to be Alpha's Sole Supplier

In an interview with David, he made the interesting comment that "assuming that a vendor wants all of your business sometimes is not a correct assumption." His remark reflected Alpha's experience with Beta: "They [Beta] had previously indicated that they didn't want to see a single supplier situation established, they were a bit reluctant to become a sole supplier to Alpha. They saw it having some adverse effects on the chemical industry themselves, like the possibility of one supplier going belly-up." John clarifies, "We thought that it [partnering with Alpha] wasn't very wise to do in fact because it was going to make the market a mess . . . . The winner was going to have a huge share of the business and the loser was going to have to chase the rest. We thought it was going to be quite disorderly and that it was going to cause problems in the New Zealand market."

He explains the impact of the transfer of a large amount of business in the highly concentrated chemical industry, thus: "The market has a way of balancing itself out. If one supplier doesn't have enough business, they will go out and chase some. The customers seem to have a conscience. Zeta decided that they had to give more business to the other competitor [Gamma] at their mill to even up the market, to keep both companies viable . . . . Some of our other customers would definitely feel very threatened if they saw only one supplier there."

Ray reiterated this issue: "The sector of the forestry industry in New Zealand to which we supply, wished to have at least two suppliers. They didn't wish to go back to a monopoly situation. If they felt that one chemical company or the other was getting too big, then they would take steps to correct that imbalance. The market seems to be comfortable with between 60/40 and 50/50 [split of market share]. You go out of that as we did for a while and very quickly you come back into line." Ray also added that "most of them [customers] like [a] major-minor [pair of suppliers]. Having a major supplier and a minor supplier to keep it [the major supplier] honest."

Further, in Beta's view, it needed competition to be innovative and competitive with regard to price and service. Paul explains, "It [a monopoly] is a bad thing . . . . Competition forces us to continue to develop, to be innovative, to look for cheaper TC and cheaper chemical solutions for our customers." Besides, as Ray observed, "anyone who tries to take advantage of a monopoly situation leaves themselves wide open for a new player to come into the market." Thus, such a situation would be unsustainable in the long run. Beta also feared the increased risk ("putting all your eggs into one basket") to which it would be exposed by being the sole supplier to Alpha, as Ray clarifies: "If the relationship doesn't work out, then half your business can disappear overnight."

*Selection Process Methodology*

The selection process for the partnership was rigorous and comprehensive, taking approximately 2–3 months. Alpha's Request for Proposals (RFP) was extensive, comprising 40 pages, to gain understanding of each potential partner's capabilities. "The RFP was not, if you like, the end point", and Alpha engaged multiple methods in the selection process, including a number of presentations by chemical suppliers to Alpha's management, frequent visits to the facilities of Alpha, Beta, and Gamma, as well as references from other customers of Beta and Gamma. In the early stages of the process, the Procurement team of Alpha undertook a thorough industry analysis, which was later used as an improvement platform.

As the eventual chemical supplier needed to provide Alpha with substantial value, the suppliers of chemicals were assessed on a number of factors, such as: capability (in terms of capacity and technology), cost (identified TC savings), partnership development, strategy compatibility, performance, cultural fit, and information systems. Alpha also had to go back to each supplier, probing for further information to gain "understanding [of] the material costs of their operations, understanding what capacity did in respect to their overhead cost, and/or even their direct costs – things like electricity and labor" [David].

John remarks that Alpha conducted the process with professionalism: "They had no fixed conclusion when they went [into the selection process] . . . . They didn't really let on that we had the inside running or anything . . . . [There was] a lot of integrity in the whole process."

A fall-out of this methodical process was that the selection team was better able to 'sell' the selection of the partner to stakeholders and managers, adding credibility to the choice of partner and facilitating buy-in from senior management. According to David, "The real benefit was that it provided focus . . . . Whilst it took a long period of time, we believe it helped us reach the right decision. By shortcutting it, we could have made the wrong decision by overlooking things and the wrong decision could have resulted in lower savings than expected."

# PARTNERSHIP IMPLEMENTATION

## *Barriers to Overcome in the Partnership*

Beta confirmed it had early suspicions about the partnership, which were driven partly by a history of 'old pricing behavior' by Alpha. David admits, "Within the organization [Alpha], it was still price, price, price, get the lowest price. 'Make sure that the quality was alright, but get the lowest price'." Further, Beta was less than satisfied with the level of information shared. John explains the relationship prior to the partnership, thus: "There were some issues with technology. There was still quite a good working relationship. We still got on pretty well, but you never knew what was going on. We found some people not very helpful with information in some places." He suggests that the lack of information sharing might have been related to Alpha's doing business with two vendors: "When they had Gamma and Beta, Alpha always felt some responsibility to keep quiet . . . . They didn't want to give all the secrets away from one company to the other."

Nevertheless, in light of such prior experience, Beta was ignorant of Alpha's "real motivation [for the partnership], which you don't really pick . . . from a tender or evaluation." Hence, Beta "were a little reticent to start with and a little bit suspicious of Alpha's motives." As a result of its experience during its process of selecting the partner for chemicals, Alpha has taken a modified approach with all its suppliers. David observes that in general, Alpha now "had to explain [to suppliers] the reason why we had to reduce the number of suppliers as a way of strengthening the overall Alpha supply chain, and where we saw the benefits."

The asymmetric nature of information-sharing during the evaluation stage provided further barriers, as John recalls: "They [Alpha] just asked for every little bit of information that you can provide and [were] not really providing that much information back. It seemed like we were bearing our soul to someone who wasn't really bearing their soul at the time."

A compounding issue was Beta's lack of previous acquaintance with the Procurement team from Alpha. John recalls, "There were new people at the time, David wasn't that well known to us, [the Procurement Director] wasn't known to us at all. Traditionally we dealt with the people at the sites more than the people in the head office." Beta also feared potential resistance from Alpha's sites about "how things were done, because it (the partnership) was really a head office initiative (at Alpha)."

*Facilitators of the Partnership*

The above barriers were countered by several facilitators of the partnership, such as the exit of individuals who would have been at best indifferent to the partnership, and the repositioning of individuals who would favor it. Paul recalled that Alpha had an Operations Manager who looked after product-category A and who was very friendly with Gamma, which consequently supplied chemicals for product-category A. Over time, that individual was replaced by someone more friendly towards Beta: "The relationship that I had with [the new manager] was a lot stronger . . . . When [the operations manager overlooking product-category A at Alpha] left, that opened product-category A up to us because then [the new manager] had more of an 'in' to product-category A, and . . . we went on from there. That is what helped us in a lot of ways to get the partnership in the first place."

Beta believes itself to be more open than the chemical companies of yore (e.g. the 1970s), and that this openness has facilitated the partnership. Paul clarifies that "previously chemical companies were very closed – closed doors, closed ranks, can't get any information out of a chemical company about its processes or pricing, anything." Paul notes that by 1996 however, Beta was "open to outsiders looking in . . . . We would open our books. There wouldn't be a hidden agenda about what we were going to do."

Support from Alpha's senior management has served to nurture the partnership, a fact recognized by Beta. According to John, "The key thing is that the senior management at Alpha have supported the partnership. The CEO of the division is pretty good, and the MD at Alpha, and in our [Beta's] case, Ray is quite supportive as well. If that level dropped off, you might see some danger. The Procurement group have been well resourced and are highly encouraged in Alpha." John believes that "the hardly any resistance from the sites . . . goes down to a lot of communication from the likes of David."

As a result of the lack of bureaucracy at Beta, the company is more responsive to Alpha's needs. John expresses it thus: "We [Beta] are not bound by procedures and disciplines . . . . We can be reactive because we are not big . . . . We don't have hundreds of customers where you have to stand away, so we can be flexible in a lot of ways . . . . We are small, we can pick these things up really fast and run with it, and definitely are receptive to doing new things." Ray concurs: "Alpha have had their eyes opened up on occasions, that small companies tend to do things far more simply than a large company." The simplicity of operation is reflected in production scheduling at Beta. Alan remarks, "We [Beta] actually run our production schedule on a whiteboard so we can physically change numbers by a duster and a marker pen . . . . While we have tried lots of different, more efficient ways (e.g. using computerized databases and other programs), for us that is the most efficient way . . . . [The in-plant] could ring today and say I want this sort of special chemical, could you do it by Wednesday. We could probably on most occasions say yes, we would just bump someone else down the order and slot their one in."

The multi-faceted nature of the relationships between both organizations has ensured that the success of the partnership does not hinge on a few individuals. John elaborates, "They [relationships between Alpha and Beta] are at lots of different levels and different areas, so it doesn't really matter if one or two people fell away . . . . People have left, and we have had different partnership managers. I wasn't the initial manager [at Beta], there was another guy, and when he left, we did not have a drop off in our communications."

The abundance of resources in terms of plant and people at the vendor also facilitated the partnership. John observes that in fact, "We [Beta] were probably over-resourced as a company at that time [during the formation of the partnership]."

*Complications During the Transition to the Partnership*

During the transition into partnership, a number of issues arose for both companies that demanded careful management. From Beta's perspective, as John recalls, "We were a little concerned that we had to jump into supplying eight products from four . . . . We had to get these new products accepted quickly . . . . We had been out of Murupara [which made product-category A] for a little bit of time, as they were being supplied by Gamma, so we didn't have that much experience." Concerns were also raised about whether the in-plant would be in place in time, a situation borne from Beta's desire to select the right person, and not "the first person we came across." The development of trust was another issue: "Just developing a level of trust, it takes a bit of time."

From the manufacturer's viewpoint, the transition from a twin supplier situation to one of a single supplier needed to be managed carefully so that, as David put it, it had "minimal effects on the supplier that we were leaving. We had to leave in such a way that if we had to go back at sometime in the future, then there wouldn't be any bad feelings because of the way that we had exited from the previous supplier arrangement." To incorporate Gamma's two-three months' timeframe for enforcing redundancies, Alpha had to slowly, as opposed to abruptly, decrease the amount purchased from Gamma over that time.

*Seamless, Inter-Organizational Development, Planning, and Control*

The collaboration between Beta and Alpha spans development, planning, and control. For example, they jointly develop the annual business plan. One topic that is frequently discussed is the future volumes of Alpha, as Ray elaborates: "We [Beta] periodically . . . sit down and talk about the volume requirements and product requirements of Alpha, because that goes into our production planning. Some of our raw materials are imported. Obviously we don't want to have a warehouse full of something that is costing $NZ 2000–3000 per ton. Equally, we don't want to be in a stock-out situation and have Alpha knocking on our door saying we want that product, so we work quite closely in that area."

Through collaboration, they effectively manage the production, storage, distribution, and consumption of short shelf-life chemicals. John remarks, "We do get their (Alpha's) assistance to make sure that product is used up."

Beta is actively assisting Alpha in the procurement of component C (an imported raw material used by both companies), as described by John: "Alpha are thinking about doing their own [procurement of component C]. We are helping them do a market study and helping them to evaluate different machinery, etc."

Beta also assists Alpha in process design. Paul recalls, "I wrote [a major portion of the production process] for them. I write all their technology, all their process development, for them." Paul is also closely involved in Alpha's "development of new products for new markets."

Likewise, Alpha, while lacking the same level of expertise in chemicals as Beta, has taken leadership in development projects at Beta. According to Paul, "We are so close with Alpha that I actually had their Technical Manager leading one of the chemical development projects here. He would come and review the chemical development project (the recipes, etc.) with our chemists who he had working for him on that project."

The seamless nature of the relationship between Alpha and Beta manifests in various ways. Paul remarks: "We work for Alpha, and Alpha work for us. It is a really funny thing, you have to remind yourself who pays the bills sometimes." Alan confirms: "We are much more open with Alpha on just general information than any other customer. In fact, for some of our guys, that probably caused a problem because they have to remind themselves that they are talking to Alpha and not other people."

### Interpersonal Interactions

Collaboration between Alpha and Beta is enabled by extensive interactions between individuals of both organizations. Beta's in-plant presence in Alpha at Murupara plays a key role, acting as a primary point of contact for the day-to-day management of the partnership. John describes the role of the in-plant representative thus: "There is the fundamental role of just taking the production schedules . . . and then translating them into orders for chemicals. There is a monitoring role to ensure the chemicals are being put to the best use. Then there is a trouble-shooting role to help Alpha out with their plant problems or projects that they have on their plant." Susan remarks that "having the in-plant is critical [at Alpha] . . . because you have someone in our organization [Alpha] that fully understands the processes of Beta, and she manages that totally. She receives our schedules and ensures we get chemicals to meet those schedules." Alan further clarifies the value to the partnership of the in-plant: "Basically she deciphers it all [Alpha's production schedule] and then just puts in an order for chemicals, so we don't get involved in the specifics of quantities of final products. She converts all of that into x tons of chemicals due on a particular date."

Each company has a Partnership Manager [Susan at Alpha and John at Beta] who has direct responsibility for overseeing the success of the relationship. As a result, the two managers are in frequent contact. The Managing Directors and other senior management personnel meet with each other at least twice annually to discuss the long-term direction of their companies, in addition to the periodic partnership appraisals.

Alpha has also had in-plants who worked inside Beta. David observes that, "[Alpha's] technical people may go down and spend a couple of weeks working in the labs on R&D projects .... It is a lot about providing development for our own people, it provides them with an opportunity to work outside of Alpha in an industry which is fairly critical to Alpha."

Paul spends a great deal of his time at Alpha's sites working with the manufacturer on chemical and product development, in addition to "an R&D group here [at Beta's site in Wanganui] of scientists and a few support people. At least a quarter of them are on Alpha-related work." Alan and other members of the Beta team have also had sessions with Alpha's planning team, and "even at the operator level, the interchange between the two plants is very good. We have had quite a bit of interaction with the operators from Murupara, we have had two lots of our guys go over as well."

### Communication and Sharing of Information Between Partners

Information between the two organizations is shared at all levels, including that of the CEO's. Susan of Alpha observes that, "Our Managing Director has said that there are very few people who have open access to his schedule but Ray [the Managing Director of Beta] does."

She also noted that, "They [Beta] attend all our staff forums where we put all our figures on the table and discuss our issues." In those forums, as John remarks, "We [Beta] show them our prices, margins, market share, raw materials, etc .... We don't supply it every month, but it is available on request and we certainly don't hide anything." In addition to such monthly exchanges, each company shares end-of-year financial information and, as David clarifies, "If it is necessary, we go through the review process [where] the progress of both Beta and ourselves [Alpha] can be openly discussed."

During the regular review meetings, there is free and open discussion on topical issues within each business. Paul explains, "I sit in on the business unit teams which is for senior management. At those meetings, we discuss the most sensitive issues of Alpha in terms of new product development, new markets, pricing strategies, etc." Ray noted that, at least initially, the organizational cultures were discussed at length: "When we first went into our partnership with Alpha, the cultural differences of the two organizations were discussed very openly and there were quite significant differences. By talking very openly about where there were differences or a potential for clashes in advance, we were by and large able to avoid negative situations." As noted earlier, Alpha and Beta have also shared information on prices, markets, and potential suppliers of [component C].

### Guiding Principles to the Partnership

Central to the relationship between Alpha and Beta are the Guiding Principles and Statement of Intent, documents that embrace the spirit and philosophy behind the partnership. The most salient of these principles is the collaborative approach to conflict resolution. David elaborates, "There perhaps have been times when one would question whether we have been fair and reasonable, but if that question is asked by the partner, we will then sit down and review the situation, and say well, have we been unfair? Or have they been unfair and unreasonable? And we find by discussing it we can rapidly reach a decision which may have appeared initially to be unfair but is then seen as entirely fair to both organizations." Susan adds that, "It [any conflict] doesn't really get down to negotiation. It is just 'let's settle this and move on'."

This view is also shared by Beta, as John expresses: "We have all learned to step back and really analyze it [any conflict or problem] for what it is worth and find the true causes and try and work through solutions for the future. People in Procurement are pretty mature at things like that; they don't tend to jump to conclusions. Sometimes site people who are quite new to things tend to jump and blame the supplier straight away. Chemicals are a soft target in products made by Alpha; if things go wrong, they just blame the chemical. We have learnt not to over-react and get too defensive ourselves . . . . We say we will come and help you out and we will look for solutions . . . . At times we have been to blame for things, sometimes we have provided chemicals that was not what the customer expected for different reasons, but we haven't had that many. If it was a weekly occurrence it might be different, but it only happens once or twice a year, and again identifying the causes is not that simple."

Such collaborative resolution is a reflection of the principle, expressed by David, that "when you are in a partnership, you can't actually dictate, you actually have to compromise . . . . We will be fair and reasonable to one another at all times, so in respect to what we do ask them, we have to be reasonable." Ray concurs: "[The partnering arrangement with Alpha] involves compromise from both parties [in contrast with other partnerships]." David reports an example of this compromise: "Whilst we [Alpha] would have preferred that Beta run pure ABC [activity-based-costing] costing models, so they know exactly what the costs are for each product they manufacture, for us to request that type of information from them is perhaps unreasonable. It's unreasonable for us to assume that they would have such a financial reporting model operating within their business. So the approach is to understand how they collect their internal information and then to use that as best we can."

In keeping with the spirit of compromise, Alpha does not seek details of its competitors through Beta. David clarifies, "We do not expect Beta to share the information they get from our competitors . . . . We might want to know these questions, but in respect of Beta and the trust we have in them, we expect they would show the same sort of values with their other customers, so whilst we would like to know, we do not ask." While there is a possibility of spillover of technology from the partnership to other customers of Beta, there is a clear definition of when this can and cannot happen. According to David, "Our understanding with the supplier is that if there is something that is developed specifically for us, we will have the opportunity to create a competitive advantage."

Another central guiding principle is that of openness, as summarized by David: "The more open we are with our partner, the greater the return is back to us."

*Trust*

Each partner appears to reciprocate with regard to openness and trust. For example, John noted that, "Once we saw that [trust reposed in Beta by Alpha], we were very open ourselves, and it [trust] builds on itself. David put a lot of time and effort into it initially. They probably came down once a month, we would meet up pretty regularly really, so we could see what sort of commitment they were going to put into the partnership, so we obviously reciprocated as well."

From the very first day, Alpha dispensed with checking invoices and the tools to do so. John recalls that, "David straightaway said we are not going to check the invoices . . . . We are not going to review your prices all the time. We are going to trust you to deliver the right product at the right place at the right time."

The "sharing (of) information to the level we do" is an indicator of trust between the two parties that has already been discussed at length. The absence of a legal document that is binding in court is another indication of trust. According to David, "We have a governance document which explains how the partnership is to work. We stay within that document because there is a requirement in certain cases to appease directors and/or shareholders to have some contractual arrangement . . . . It was more of a comfort factor for the other parties." John corroborates David: "The spirit of the partnership has probably overridden everything that is written down in a way. It has just embraced a spirit of co-operation and that has been quite important."

As the partnership has progressed, the frequency of performance reviews has been reduced, as David states: "Last year [1998] . . . they were conducted quarterly, this year [1999] on, they will be conducted six-monthly."

## *Mutual Goodwill*

The mutual goodwill between the two companies manifests, for instance, in Beta's willingness to share its cost savings with the manufacturer, as Paul explains: "We profit-share on our chemicals. If technology allows us to remove an ingredient out of our chemicals, or it reduces the cost of the ingredients in the chemicals, then we will go halves with them on the savings of that. We obviously have to pay for the costs of a technology center and sixteen scientists in there doing the work, we have to recover those costs, but basically we will go halves with them." Ray assents: "We have tried to share those benefits (from reducing TC) between the two parties . . . . [There is] an openness about 'yes we have made a savings there' and a sharing of the benefits."

Beta is also perceived by Alpha to be a critical supplier. Susan notes: "They [Beta] are happy to provide Alpha with very direct and honest feedback, something that suppliers would not generally do, because they try to be nice to their customers and don't want to lose their business . . . . [Beta] come up with more improvements for us than we come up with for ourselves." Likewise, Beta positively views feedback from Alpha, as Susan remarks: "It would be fair to say that last year [1998] when we tracked their performance in terms of the review, relative to other companies, we saw Beta actually going backwards from where they started. Now that had been raised and they were well aware of the problem. They took no offense, as they said at the time 'Obviously we have become complacent, we need to get back on track and it is because you have been able to show us and tell us where we have been going wrong which will help us get back on track'. And back on track means continuing on an upward and forward fashion."

Alpha's goodwill towards Beta is reflected in its desiring Beta to be a healthy and successful company. David remarks, "We want Beta to grow, that's part of our commitment. If they do something with us then we would expect that ultimately they would be able to reap the benefits of that by offering it to a much larger market than Alpha. We [Alpha] must be realistic. It [NZ] is a very, very small market and the other competitors in the New Zealand market also compete in the international markets with us. So we have to take a much broader view and say our competition is outside of New Zealand, not within New Zealand. So we are a bit more relaxed about the transfer of chemical technology that may have been developed in one area through to our competitors. There is the odd occasion where we would have a limited technical advantage for a period of time, even on the domestic market, but after that, no." Ray assents, "Obviously from a company point of view, if we [Beta] develop something and spend money doing so, then we want to recover that money as quickly as possible, so in that sense it is in our interests to sell it to the wider market rather than just one company [Alpha]."

Some relevant facts help clarify this point. Alpha and its major rival largely dominate the local (NZ) market for product-category A. Each of the companies held approximately 40% market share as of mid-2000, and other locally based manufacturers vied for the remainder. In terms of exports, Alpha realizes about 60% of its sales in export markets (including 30–40% of total sales that emanate from Australia). Alpha's nearest rival relies on exports for nearly 50% of its sales, with nearly 30% of its total sales originating from Australia. Despite the level of activity in exporting (a third manufacturer exports 90% of its production), all the NZ-based manufacturers in Alpha's sector of the forestry industry together account for less than 1% of the global market.

Likewise, Beta also needs Alpha to be a healthy and viable company. The instance described previously when Alpha was facing imminent closure was partly resolved by Beta's seconding Paul to Alpha for a period of three months where he developed new, high-value products to boost revenue. As he explains, "There was a huge turnaround, but that had to happen because if they went down, in many respects, we would go down with them. It is in Beta's best interests to see Alpha be successful and grow their business, because in theory, it generates more volume for us."

Alpha, through the Phi Group, have similarly assisted Beta (and themselves in the process). Ray explains: "We have another raw material, component D, which is produced by Y. Y is the largest supplier of component D in the world, certainly in the non-captive area of the [global] market. They are the only suppliers in NZ, so they have a monopoly situation. They are powerful enough on a global basis [that] they can block others from delivering component D into NZ. We went to Y and said, 'You are not in the short-term going to disadvantage us, because we simply pass on the cost of component D in our products. But you are going to stifle growth in the forestry industry because you are going to make the NZ forestry industry a high-cost industry relative to its competitors'. We hammered them on this for several months. To Y's credit, they approached Phi and spoke to a couple of analysts within Phi, who basically confirmed the point that we were making that if Y was going to screw us, in turn we [would] pass that on to our customers who are going to get screwed in the international marketplace to the point where they couldn't grow their own forestry businesses, and new investors in the forestry industry were not going to come to NZ, they were going to go to Malaysia or Indonesia or China, but not NZ with its high-cost environment."

Alpha has been willing to share with Beta its own internal initiatives and experiences with management practices. Susan remarks, "They [Beta] tried to set up their own Procurement strategy, and Alpha has assisted them in doing that. They haven't had exposure to Procurement outside of the relationship with Alpha . . . . Recently we introduced a benchmark to the Baldridge awards [for quality management] . . . . Again, Beta were willing participants, they wanted to send all of their directors for the focus day. So they are very receptive to what we do."

Negotiations regarding uneconomic lot sizes are conducted with similar mutual concern. John clarifies, "Susan and the Procurement Group don't want to destroy value for us. We have had some revisions to the partnership agreement to specify things like minimum order sizes, and policies on returning chemicals that are outside their shelf date."

### *Benefits Realized by the Manufacturer*

The Alpha/Beta partnership has generated numerous benefits for Alpha: reduction in delivered costs of chemicals, zero stocks of chemicals, reduction in invoices (to just one invoice per month from Beta), reduced management costs (negotiation, supplier management, issue resolution), site representation (immediate availability of expertise), a template for the partnership process (i.e. the proven design allows other supply partnerships to proceed faster), and access to other products and services.

The objective of reducing TC has been, and continues to be, reached. In this context, Paul observes, "They (Alpha) are leading everybody in terms of their cost reductions. I can say that because I do know a lot about their [other customers of Beta] capabilities and their costs of manufacturing."

From Alpha's perspective, Beta is measuring up to the responsibility for new product development. As noted earlier, Paul has been providing technical support for Alpha and has also been involved in the R&D and product development groups, extending as far as developing new products for Alpha, which, according to Susan, "created a huge amount of value for the company [Alpha]." Ray highlights the customer-focused nature of Beta's technology: "We work very closely with Alpha on their product development program, we get actively involved in the development of products for their customers, even to the point of meeting with their customers, including customers in major export markets."

Alpha believes that its reputation can grow overseas only as a supplier of environmentally friendly products from 'clean, green' New Zealand because, as John clarifies, "A lot of people see forestry products as a generic thing, they just see New Zealand made, not necessarily Alpha's made. With what we [Beta] call [Grade 1] chemical, there has been a recognition that the products our other customers are making, are not quite making a Grade 1 standard. I think as a trade group the companies belonging to the composite product-category-A group decided they needed to change that to make sure they were consistently Grade 1, . . . because otherwise if we had a disparity in products from New Zealand, Alpha would suffer if New Zealand forestry was perceived as not being environmentally friendly."

From Beta's perspective, additional benefits have accrued to Alpha, such as the improved handling of customer complaints. John explains, "There have been a couple of customer complaints that Alpha have had where Paul has been sought for advice on how to overcome them." The collaboration between Alpha and Beta on technical issues means that customer and technical problems are handled with expertise, such as the ideal combination of raw materials and the overuse of chemicals.

Alpha has also benefited from Beta's handling of problems relating to material shortages and non-availability. Ray recalled, "We had a situation 18 months ago where one of the imported raw materials [component C] that we both use was in extremely short supply. By working together we were able to overcome a shortage within Alpha and then assist them to set up a longer-term arrangement with a common supplier."

Alpha enjoys preferential treatment from its vendor in a variety of ways. It receives "different prices" compared to other customers of Beta. In many instances, Beta has made concessions on price to allow Alpha to gain entry into particular markets.

The manufacturer is also given priority on the production plan. John explains, "We have sort of promised them [Alpha] first crack at most things . . . especially if Alpha has a heavy program of trials and new products." Alpha is also favored with a shorter lead time, as Alan reveals: "We tend to put pressure on other customers to order earlier ahead; we ask for a week's advanced ordering from other customers whereas with Alpha, we would ask for a day or something like that."

Beta also appears to regularly go the extra mile for Alpha. John concedes, "I guess we are probably too obliging at times, and we lose the value-added because we say yes to most things, but I guess if it is a one-off, we would be prepared to suffer a loss." Susan endorses his remark, "If anything at times, I have to say 'Well, how about we pay for this part of it?' More often than not, they are willing to pay for more than I think is their share at times."

David succinctly sums up the benefit to Alpha from the partnership: "We should have created the partnership years ago."

### Benefits Realized by the Vendor

The most notable benefit to Beta has been an increase in market share. Paul notes, "When I started here we had 25% market share of forestry chemicals in this country, and we peaked in 1997–1998 with 85%. A lot of that has been from new products developed with Alpha."

Of further benefit to Beta was the holding of inventory on a consignment basis, that is, holding (and retaining ownership of) chemicals at Alpha's factory that would be invoiced only as the chemicals were used. David admitted, "It would be fair to say that Beta did have some reservations to start off with [about holding stock on a consignment basis] but they fully support the move now." John acknowledges that the benefits from the vendor's holding consignment stock "does depend on the type of business of course, but it is ideal for this company with chemicals that have short shelf-lives."

By operating consignment stock, Beta enjoys the benefits of logistical postponement (Bowersox & Closs, 1996). Susan explains how this is put into effect with the supply of chemicals: "Beta are responsible for monitoring the tanks and ensuring that the chemicals don't go to the 'pavlova' stage just before it goes off. They can return the chemicals to their plant, rework it, and dispatch it again." Such control has been made possible by the use of an in-plant at Alpha's product-category A site, who has direct responsibility for measuring stock levels of chemicals, thereby allowing Beta better control over its own production, a point echoed by Alan.

According to David, "it gives them [Beta] the advantage of managing their own production, to move the product around the country from customer to customer." John clarifies that the management of inventories of chemicals on a consignment basis has also improved the efficiency of partnership logistics: "The ability to be able to manipulate/stagger the bulk (chemicals) that you supply all the time, to leave room for specialty ones is quite great for our business. We can get trucks coming in when we need them and not turning up all at once, so you know there are a lot of efficiencies by controlling the ordering."

Beta's transport provider, Omega, has also reaped the benefits of improved efficiency, which in turn has positively impacted on TC, as John and Alan attest: "Our transport company can be a lot more flexible in their delivery requirements .... They don't have to have people working at midnight on a Saturday night for example ... because we can control the schedule and they [Omega] can control the movements, it is more effective for them." As a consequence, Beta has been able to negotiate lower rates with Omega. The increased volume of business has also enabled better service: Alan confirms "the truck and trailer that Omega put on round-the-clock was purposely built for the Alpha run."

The close relationship with Alpha has provided Beta with the opportunity to learn from the manufacturer, which is supported by Alpha's well-resourced parent company, Phi, in terms of management direction. John clarifies, "We are a little bit isolated in New Zealand, so ... we don't follow all the new management themes that are being employed around the world. Often we see that Phi are pretty high on the uptake on those sorts of things .... We learn from their mistakes as well .... Phi seems to be leading edge (in NZ) on human resource initiatives, and [we] picked up a few things from that .... We have picked up on [supply chain management] and we are managing our suppliers along the same lines as Alpha do now .... It [the partnership] means that we can plan for the future ... we can target our R&D and our resources here better ... it does provide a lot of direction." Ray concurs: "We have got benefits of improved management practices, which we have incorporated into our operations and which have saved us a lot of money .... In more general terms, how we interact with our other customers and also our suppliers has been influenced by what we have learnt from the partnership with Alpha."

The partnership has also allowed Beta to pursue more effective development of new chemicals, through the dedicated research facility. Paul explains, "What we really have is fairly good pilot plant facilities here, so that we can continue to develop chemicals in our laboratory and then trial them in the lab, making products under the similar conditions that prevail at Alpha's plant in Murupara. So that when we do come up with something, we have a good idea of whether it will work prior to us going to the plant. In the past, you would develop a chemical and then cross your fingers and hope that it would make product in the plant, and that wasn't always the case." Alan explains how the development of new chemicals works in the partnership: "If it was Alpha that wanted a new chemical, what our guys will do is work with their R&D people as that is about to come on-line. So we will actually do some trials in the lab to make sure that we can actually make it, and that is from a materials handling point of view through to storage/logistics, to pumping it out. We don't want to make a 15-hour batch when we could be making eight-hour batches because that is the same as a loss of production, so there are lots of considerations that we are involved in."

The partnership has afforded Beta the opportunity to trial new product, furthering the goal of technology leadership to the benefit of both parties. Ray states, "The co-operation we get from Alpha . . . speeds up the development of new products for us and likewise for Alpha."

The partnership has led to a change in the work ethic at Beta, as Alan observed: "It [the partnership] has had quite a big impact on the people here at work as well, to look at things a little bit differently and say we can work a little bit smarter by setting things up, putting it out in front of people, and saying hey as long as we have these type of agreements, we don't have to spend time chasing around everyone else."

### *Mutual Benefits Accruing to Both Parties*

The partners' improved understanding of each other' business has been mutually beneficial. Alan remarks, "Before, there would be a lot of negotiation over why they [Alpha] wanted it in that amount and the implications for us. Now there is a much better understanding of some of the problems that we have, remanufacturing or reworking product, . . . and us understanding their process to see how they could run it more efficiently as a trial or whether the product means an upgrade or a downgrade [compared to existing products] . . . . [We have] good insight into the problems they have, whether it is being market-driven or production-driven or warehouse-driven . . . . Better understanding of how each plant is working, not just the manufacture of product-categories A or B or chemicals, but also some of the other things that come into it."

With regard to TC, Ray notes that his company [Beta] is "very comfortable with the way that it has worked with Alpha. Both parties have made savings right across the board in terms of invoicing, sharing of information, and the development of new technology . . . . We have . . . entered into arrangements with other forestry companies, whereas with Alpha we have seen that the long-term benefits accrue. With the other companies, by and large it has just been another attempt to price gouge and we haven't seen the long-term benefits."

Both companies are learning from each other's experiences. Ray explains, "If you take the secretiveness that often prevails between a supplier and a customer away, it opens up a lot more opportunities . . . . When you have a very open relationship like the one we have with Alpha, you are able to share a lot more experiences that go way beyond the supply and use of chemical."

The closeness of the current partnership and the level of information sharing have enabled both parties to benefit from each other's capabilities outside the bounds of the supply agreements, most notably in times of crisis. David provides an illustration: "Perhaps one of the strengths of the relationship was a situation about 12–18 months ago [i.e. in early-mid 1998] when they [Beta] had manufactured some specialty chemicals for WW [a competitor to Alpha]. The WW [mill] went down with a strike. The strike lasted longer than the shelf life of the chemicals, or was expected to last longer. By working with our technical people, we were able to utilize that high cost chemical (it had a very high cost, because it had a very high content of component C). We [Alpha] were able to take it into our Murupara plant at the same price as the standard chemicals, so in effect we were assisting Beta. [In this] situation, they could have been faced with writing off perhaps $NZ 500,000 of chemicals, and then also the problems of disposing of that chemical (we have to go to a specialty dump). But by us utilizing that chemical, at least they recovered something like 70% of the actual cost of manufacture, so it was another of those win-win solutions." John confirms that this was not an isolated example; there have been similar other occasions where other customers have expected the chemical supplier to accept returns of unused products, and Alpha has adjusted its production schedule to ensure the returned product does not become waste. Alan confirms, "The secret is good production planning and good communication over order sizes [to] make sure that there isn't any waste."

# EVOLUTION IN THE PARTNERSHIP

### Continuous Improvement

The quest to reduce TC involves constant attention to continuous improvement. David notes, "We are continually looking at ways of improving our chemical, reducing the TC through de-engineering where we have over-engineered products, or similarly improving the properties and the machinability of the final product itself."

The nature of chemical production leads Beta to pursue a very active environmental policy, one that is reflected in the company's maxim, "We would rather see chemicals in a product than in the ground." Beta has achieved ISO 14001 certification, which represents the environmental part of the ISO series of standards. Besides detailing processes for the handling of waste, it has targets for waste reduction. This system functions to the extent that, as Paul remarks, "We don't have waste. In fact, any wastewater or water material that we do have – we tend to analyze it, and then use that in our chemicals. Very little goes off this site, the only time is if you get a massive storm and you get a bit of runoff." (In fact, the environmental policy is promoted in the local business community, when, as Ray expresses it, "we [Beta] bring the local business community together, talk about our environmental and business matters, giving them a tour of the plant if they want.") John affirms that each year, Beta writes off less than one half of 1% of total production.

As an example of waste reduction, on one occasion, a chemical was being delivered to a customer site into a tank that was reading as empty, when in fact it was full. The truck driver went away while it was filling, only to return to see the tank pouring into the overflow catchments, which also contained "quite a bit of other rubbish in it." Paul believes that "in some industries, that would have gone down the drain." However, the chemical was pumped up, returned to Beta where it was reprocessed, and delivered to the customer. The ability to do this has been partly due to in-house procedures at Beta. Paul clarifies: "Our quality system requires a quality plan to go with how you are going to dispose of unused chemicals in a manner that is responsible. You have to have the chemistry and the rework done, how you are going to cook it off and make it into something that is more commercially saleable."

John envisions that the company will continue to play a part in Alpha's downstream supply chain initiatives: "You look at the supply chain initiatives, they are being taken to the customers as well, not just a procurement strategy, now it is a marketing strategy and we can help in that area. Again it will mean that we will have to be involved right from the product development stage right through . . . . That fits in pretty well, we have shown flexibility and capability of working in a partnership or a supply chain pretty closely." In the same vein, he observes that "in recent times Alpha have shown they are heading towards customer intimacy maybe, customizing solutions more, and we can help in that area as well, developing product (that is) specific for customers."

*Ongoing Challenges*

As the Alpha/Beta partnership matures and moves forward, it faces several challenges. A major challenge is diminishing support for the procurement team at Alpha, as noted by John: "It (the support) is dropping off now to be honest . . . . I guess that in any of these companies, it is always a bit of a power struggle, which department has got the most influence. The procurement people have had a good crack of the whip at Alpha particularly, whether that continues I am not sure."

The potential for shifts in the balance of power is always present. John also observed "it [support for the partnership] depends at times on where the power base is . . . . You might get new site people, new head office people that have a different view, different allegiances, different history. So if I had a fear about the partnership that would probably be it, that someone at Alpha might have a different viewpoint." David echoes that view: "The partnership . . . may not be able to go further forward because of changes . . . . For example, if the Beta business was sold to another corporate body, they may have an entirely different view on how the business is to be conducted, and also the way that they would do business with their customers."

New entrants to both organizations need to be schooled in the partnership concept. John points out that "with new people you have to remind them of that [the guiding principles of the partnership], you really have to work on new people in particular; otherwise you might lose."

The commodity nature of both the chemical and forestry industries means that often, TC reductions can be difficult to identify in the face of rising raw material prices and exchange rate fluctuations. John elaborates: "If you measure value [added by the vendor] on historical cost levels, it is not going to be right because it depends on a lot of commodity costs that we are buying. We are buying commodities that represent 60% of our pricing, so when those go up in value it looks negatively on the partnership, which is nothing to do with the partnership." Thus, Beta might find it difficult to continually attain high levels of performance with regard to TC, which John describes as "very hard to measure", especially when compared to the relatively straightforward measure of DISOTIF.

*Maintenance of the Partnership*

In various ways, Alpha and Beta continue to sustain the partnership. Both companies openly display the certificate that bears the Mission Statement. Within both organizations, the partnership is the subject of widespread and on-going discussion. John affirms, "I guess we just talk about it [the partnership] a lot. [It] is quite useful to have the odd partnership meeting and technical meeting. We tend to re-iterate things again and again . . . . We have used it [the partnership] a lot in our communications with our corporate people, how well it is working and what the successes have been." Beta is also gratified by the open endorsement by key personnel at Alpha of the partnership: "David has been pretty public and open about demonstrating the successes of this partnership. It has been used as a bit of a model within Phi so that is great and we appreciate that."

The "enthusiastic" in-plants have also helped nurture the partnership. John notes that the in-plants "can stretch themselves in the area of trouble-shooting and helping Alpha with their problems and just being a good communicator between the two companies. So we have had good people, we have been lucky, but we have supported those people a lot with training and help."

From Beta's perspective, Alpha's dynamism, which contrasts with its competitors, has been a key factor in the continued success of the partnership. For example, Alpha's support of the technology leadership strategy is operationalized by its setting aside plant capacity for trials and new product development. John notes that in contrast, "some of the other companies are full up plant capacity wise ... [and] seem to be reluctant to try new things at times." Alpha is more willing to innovate, such as by trying out new, environmentally-friendly chemicals despite initial cost penalties.

Alpha is perceived by Beta to be more willing to suffer failures and as having more of an understanding of Beta than Beta's other customers. John affirms, "If we (Beta) fail, some of the other companies kick us in the (behind) big time." The degree of understanding and flexibility evinced by Alpha is highlighted in John's response to the WW strike discussed previously: "We could have charged the customer [WW] for it [the chemical that was going off] but they would probably never buy from us ever again, they are pretty unforgiving like that, I don't know why. The expectation was there that we would take the product back and that would be that."

Alpha is perceived as being more realistic about its own abilities. John explains, "They (Alpha) see that they are not experts in every area, and where they need help, they ask for help and get it. Some [other] companies are a little bit arrogant and think they know everything themselves and they like to play off chemical companies to get what they want at times."

## THEORETICAL INSIGHTS FROM THE CASE STUDY

As one would expect, in various ways the case study reaffirms findings of prior research on vendor-manufacturer partnerships. Empirical evidence suggests that high trust vendor-manufacturer relationships tend to be high performers: high trust is associated with higher delivery frequency, higher percentage of vendor sales to the manufacturer, greater assistance from the manufacturer (Dyer, 1996c), lower quality defects, lower cycle time and higher return on assets (Dyer, 1996a; Kalwani & Narayandas, 1995), and organizational learning (Lincoln, Ahmadjian & Mason, 1998). Lack of trust has been found an important cause of partnering failure (Ellram, 1995).

In the present partnership, trust is manifested for instance in Alpha's dispensing with the checking of invoices, the "sharing (of) information to the level we do", the absence of a legal document that is binding in court, and the diminishing frequency of performance reviews. In return, both parties have gained: Alpha with regard to, for example, cost reductions and superior product performance; and Beta in terms of, for instance, increased market share.

The case also strongly supports the notion that mutual dependence is conducive to the formation of trust (Kumar, 1996). The small size of the NZ market means that Beta is dependent on Alpha for volume, while the manufacturer depends on Beta to provide technical expertise and assistance in making products that meet its customers' expectations. Alpha's dependence on Beta is similar to the buyer-product specificity described by Nooteboom (1993) and the mutual adjustment relationship identified by Bensaou and Venkatraman (1995), where the supplier produces leading edge technology that the manufacturer requires and considers non-substitutable.

While qualitative data such as that reported here provide empirically well-grounded insight into partnership-related phenomena and processes such as the development of trust, the purport of our case study has really been to understand how the process industry nature of the partnership and the New Zealand context influence partnership dynamics. Accordingly, we now discuss these influences.

### The Process-Industry Nature of the Partnership

Below, by turn, we describe the various ways by which the process-industry context of the partnership (as distinct from a fabrication/assembly context, which characterizes the automobile industry) impacts on partnership dynamics.

*The changed relevance of supplier proximity.* Dyer, Cho and Chu (1998: 71) state that in a vendor-manufacturer partnership, the vendor must deploy relation-specific investments in terms of site, physical, and human assets "to co-ordinate effectively with the buying firm and customize the component." The first of these, site asset specificity, or the proximity of the supplier's site to the manufacturer's, is likely to be important in a process-based partnership, but for different reason(s). When Dyer, Cho and Chu (1998) remarked that site specificity was important because of the need for frequent face-to-face interaction and the coordination of interdependent tasks, they were speaking to the automobile industry and suchlike. In such industries, vendor proximity also enables just-in-time deliveries and the reduction of inventories.

However, in a process industry relationship, the raw material supplied by the vendor partakes of the nature of a commodity with a characteristically low ratio of value-to-weight. To clarify, information provided by Alpha suggests that the average price of chemicals supplied by Beta is several hundred dollars per ton. Similar 'strategic' components in the automobile industry such as electronics, air-conditioning systems, and body panels average several thousand dollars per ton in value. This difference, of an order of magnitude, suggests that in process industry relationships, *vendor proximity is important because transportation costs reflect a higher proportion of the delivered cost.* This is supported by David's assertion that if the shipping distance between Beta's facility at Wanganui and Alpha's plant at Murupara doubled, the landed cost of chemicals would increase by as much as 10–15%.

*Coordinated procurement of (common) raw materials.* Commonality in raw materials between the vendor and manufacturer appears more likely in process industry contexts. Indeed, "because there is some similarity between a producer of chemicals and a user of chemicals", one synergy in the partnership was the coordinated procurement by both vendor and manufacturer of common raw materials (e.g. component C) and possibly services; energy costs are a higher proportion of total manufacturing costs in process industries (at Alpha, electricity represented the fourth largest spend).

*Improved waste management.* Silver and Peterson (1985) note that process manufacturers are likely to produce a higher number of by-products than a discrete-part fabricator/assembler, some with commercial value and some with potentially harmful side-effects. The case illustrates how "in a variety of ways," both Alpha and Beta have stood to gain from the partnership by "seeing chemicals in a finished product than in the ground."

*Benefits from vendor's management of consignment stock.* In many vendor-manufacturer partnerships, it is quite typical for the vendor to hold consignment stock on behalf of the manufacturer. However, empirical evidence (e.g. Holmlund & Kock, 1996; Kalwani & Narayandas, 1995) suggests that where the buyer is dominant, suppliers are often forced to carry inventory either as part of the contract or to qualify for selection: "it seems that most of the costs are the suppliers' and most of the benefits are the customers' " (Waters-Fuller, 1995).

Interestingly, in the present partnership, owing to the perishable nature of chemicals and the batched nature of production, both of which are more likely to occur in process industry contexts, Beta stands to gain in at least three respects by managing and holding consignment stock:

(1) "By controlling the ordering (manipulating/staggering the bulk chemicals that we supply all the time, to leave room for specialty ones)", Beta "can get trucks coming in when needed, rather than all at once, so you know there are a lot of efficiencies."

(2) Beta can "make sure the [short-lived] chemicals do not go off, and rework them if necessary." Such control is facilitated by the in-plant, who has direct responsibility for monitoring stocks of chemicals at Alpha's facility in Murupara.

(3) Owing to the generic (commodity) nature of chemicals, Beta can realize the benefits of consolidation of stock for chemicals, especially for those chemicals with short shelf lives, by practicing logistical postponement (Bowersox & Closs, 1996), which is "the advantage of moving the product [chemicals] around the country from customer to customer."

*The relative insignificance of Electronic Data Interchange (EDI).* Dyer et al. (1998) and Bensaou and Venkatraman (1995) have presented relationship structures that heavily utilize EDI for the sharing of information such as production schedules. The batched nature of manufacturing of both chemicals and product-category A reduces the need for information sharing through EDI, which consequently plays no role in the Alpha/Beta partnership. Production schedules are fixed in the short-term and thus the frequency of transactions is low. In contrast, a discrete-part assembler, such as Toyota, employs mixed-model scheduling to avoid high inventories of any one model (Chase, Aquilano & Jacobs, 1998) and changes the schedule in the very near-term (such as the same shift), thus necessitating EDI.

*The relative insignificance of physical asset specificity.* Dyer et al. (1998: 66) note that in the U.S. context, "in part due to low levels of trust, suppliers' investments in relation-specific assets are low relative to Korean and Japanese suppliers." In relationships with low trust, increased levels of asset specificity contribute to a higher perceived risk of the manufacturer's switching suppliers, while in high trust relationships, the opposite is likely to occur (Mudambi & Helper, 1998).

In the current partnership, the investment that is most relationship-specific, that is, the dedicated tanker used for transporting chemicals, is actually owned by a third party. The low level of investment in physical assets reflects not the lack of trust. Rather, it proceeds directly from the commodity nature of both forestry products and chemicals. In the present partnership, the relation-specific investments are in the form of human assets (e.g. the in-plant).

## The New Zealand Context

We now describe various aspects of the partnership that reflect the distinctiveness of the NZ business environment.

*The impact of overcapacity in process industries.* The projected increase in forestry products' capacity during the 1990s meant that chemical companies had installed sufficient capacity of their own to meet future demand. When the anticipated increase in demand did not occur, the chemical companies found themselves in a situation of overcapacity ("we could supply the NZ market twice over"), a situation that is more likely in a country such as New Zealand that lacks sufficient domestic demand to absorb downturns in export markets. Overcapacity made it difficult for both Beta and Gamma to meet ROI commitments, and provided stronger motivation for either supplier to become the partner (and sole supplier of chemicals) to Alpha.

*The acceptability of spillover of technology to the manufacturer's competitors.* In their study of vendor-manufacturer partnerships in discrete-part fabrication/assembly industries, Kalwani and Narayandas (1995) remark that in joint development programs, the supplier should not share developments with the manufacturer's competitors; the cost of development is offset by increases in volume from the manufacturer through the consolidation of business. In contrast, technological developments quite often spillover to Alpha's competitors, reflecting Beta's concern to meet its ROI commitments in a small market, as expressed by Ray: ". . . if we develop something and spend money doing so, then we want to recover that money as quickly as possible, by selling it to the wider market rather than just one company." Alpha reconciles to the spillover by taking a five-fold, "much broader view":

(1) Beta's growth is "part of our commitment."
(2) "NZ is a very, very small market. Our competition is outside of NZ, not within."
(3) "A lot of people . . . just see New Zealand made, not necessarily Alpha-made . . . if we had a disparity in products from New Zealand, Alpha would suffer if New Zealand forestry manufacture is not perceived as being environmentally friendly."
(4) "It helps to reduce our cost. If Beta are supplying only us with a specialty chemical, the price is much higher than if they are developing huge volumes." (The small market size combined with overcapacity, means that the marginal benefits from increased production volumes are higher than they would be otherwise.)
(5) Alpha will receive the [specially developed] chemicals at one price, its competitors will receive it at a higher price."

*The impact of industry concentration.* The concentration of the NZ chemical industry in just two players, Beta and Gamma, exemplifies the finding of Ratnayake (1999: 1041) that "NZ manufacturing industries are more concentrated than those of most other countries." Ratnayake also discerns a declining trend in industry concentration over time indicating that the liberalization of the NZ economy has had an impact.

The relatively small size of the domestic market and the need to realize economies of scale, especially in capital-intensive, process flow industries such as the manufacture of chemicals, compound industry concentration. Chemicals are characterized by low ratios of value to weight as well as the need for specialized handling, both of which push up freight costs as a percentage of value. Thus, NZ's geographical isolation, coupled with short shelf lives of at least some chemicals, aggravates concentration in the chemicals industry by forestalling exports of chemicals. Beta (and Gamma) can instead supply only local forestry companies, which account for less than 1% of the global market. As a result, both Beta and Gamma struggle to meet ROI criteria. Industry concentration also manifests in the NZ forestry industry, albeit to a lesser extent because of the focus on exports.

Industry concentration impacted the present partnership in at least three respects:

(1) Beta was reluctant to be the sole supplier to Alpha because that would create a monopoly due to Alpha's size relative to the whole NZ forestry industry ("it would mess up the market, the winner would get a huge share of business and the loser would chase the rest"); by "taking advantage of a monopoly situation, Beta would leave itself wide open for a new player, and would no longer be forced to continue to develop, to be innovative, to look for cheaper TC and cheaper chemical solutions for our customers."

(2) Other manufacturers actually moved to "correct the imbalance", being "comfortable with between 60/40 and 50/50 [split of market share]."

(3) Alpha had to cease procuring chemicals from Gamma in such a way that it had "minimal effects on the supplier that we were leaving. If we had to go back at sometime in the future [which was more likely in an industry that was concentrated and not diffuse], then there wouldn't be any bad feelings because of the way that we had exited from the previous supplier arrangement."

*The role of corporate citizenship in partner selection.* One of Alpha's considerations in the eventual choice of partner was the impact of the choice on local communities, such as redundancies made by the unsuccessful candidate. Despite being tiny by global standards, both companies were major employers in their vicinities, and wished to be perceived as good corporate citizens. Thus, Beta's continued use of Omega reflected its wish "to use locals wherever we can . . . both in the broader NZ sense as opposed to overseas suppliers, but also within Beta's local community."

# CONCLUSION

Our case study illustrates the need to distinguish between partnerships that are located in discrete-part fabrication/assembly contexts and those that are situated in process industry contexts. The changed role of supplier proximity and the relative insignificance of physical asset specificity and EDI appear to proceed directly from the nature of the industry. Improved waste management as well as improved control of obsolescence of chemicals through the vendor's management of consignment stock are benefits that are likely quite particular to vendor-manufacturer partnerships in process industry contexts.

This case study has also highlighted a number of aspects that are unique to the New Zealand situation, particularly with regard to the small domestic market. For example, the polygamous relationship between the vendor-partner and the manufacturer (whereby the vendor, Beta, supplies even the competitors of the manufacturer, Alpha) is, intriguingly enough, viewed favorably by the manufacturer. To cite another illustration, the manufacturer needs to reckon with a whole host of knock-on effects of the move to a single supplier strategy, such as the possible need for the unsuccessful candidate(s) to downsize in a country where the importance of manufacturing is waning, factory closures are widely publicized, and industry concentration is high.

It might be argued that only one vendor-manufacturer partnership has been studied in our case analysis, and therefore the results are not necessarily indicative of other vendor-manufacturer partnerships in process industries and/ or the New Zealand context. In response, we highlight the growing recognition (e.g. Yin, 1994) that the potential for generalization of case-study findings should not be interpreted in statistical terms. Rather, the potential for extrapolation should be construed in relation to the cogency of the theoretical reasoning.

In the present study, the findings have been rigorously induced from case data with recourse to formal coding techniques. Further, the interpretation of the findings is conceptually coherent with reference to, for instance, the impact of the New Zealand situation and of the manufacturing environment. Therefore the theoretical insights engendered by the present case evince the potential for generalization to other similar partnerships.

## REFERENCES

Bensaou, M. (1999). Portfolios of buyer-supplier relationships. *Sloan Management Review, 40*(4), 35–44.

Bensaou, M., & Venkatraman, N. (1995). Configurations of inter-organizational relationships: A comparison between U.S. and Japanese automakers. *Management Science, 41*, 1471–1491.

Bowersox, D. J., & Closs, D. J. (1996). *Logistical management: The Integrated Supply Chain Process* (Intl. ed.). Singapore: McGraw-Hill.

Bryman, A. (1989). *Research Methods and Organization Studies*. London: Routledge.

Carr, C., & Ng, J. (1995). Total cost control: Nissan and its U.K. supplier partnerships. *Management Accounting Research, 6,* 346–365.

Chase, R. B., Aquilano, N. J., & Jacobs, F. R. (1998). *Production and Operations Management: Manufacturing and Services* (8th ed.). Boston: Irwin/McGraw-Hill.

Cusumano, M. A., & Takeishi, A. (1991). Supplier relations and management: A survey of Japanese, Japanese-transplant, and U.S. auto plants. *Strategic Management Journal, 12,* 563–588.

Dyer, J. H. (1996a). Specialized supplier networks as a source of competitive advantage: Evidence from the auto industry. *Strategic Management Journal, 17,* 271–291.

Dyer, J. H. (1996b). How Chrysler created an American Keiretsu. *Harvard Business Review, 74*(4), 42–56.

Dyer, J. H. (1996c). Does governance matter? Keiretsu alliances and asset specificity as sources of Japanese competitive advantage. *Organization Science, 7,* 649–666.

Dyer, J. H., Cho, D. S., & Chu, W. (1998). Strategic supplier segmentation: The next "best practice" in supply chain management. *California Management Review, 40*(2), 57–77.

Dyer, J. H., & Ouchi, W. G. (1993). Japanese-style partnerships: Giving companies a competitive edge. *Sloan Management Review, 35*(1), 51–63.

Ellram, L. M. (1995). Partnering pitfalls and success factors. *International Journal of Purchasing and Materials Management, 31*(2), 36–42.

Glaser, B., & Strauss, A. (1967). *The Discovery of Grounded Theory: Strategies for Qualitative Research.* Chicago, IL: Aldine.

Holmlund, M., & Kock, S. (1996). Buyer-dominated relationships in a supply chain – a case study of four small-sized suppliers. *International Small Business Journal, 15,* 26–40.

Kalwani, M. U., & Narayandas, N. (1995). Long-term manufacturer-supplier relationships: Do they pay off for supplier firms? *Journal of Marketing, 59,* 1–16.

Kumar, N. (1996). The power of trust in manufacturer-retailer relationships. *Harvard Business Review, 74*(6), 92–106.

Kumar, N., Stern, L. W., & Anderson, J. C. (1993). Conducting inter-organizational research using key informants. *Academy of Management Journal, 36,* 1633–1651.

Lambert, D. M., Emmelhainz, M. A., & Gardner, J. T. (1996). Developing and implementing supply chain partnerships. *International Journal of Logistics Management, 7*(2), 1–17.

Langfield-Smith, K., & Greenwood, M. R. (1998). Developing co-operative buyer-supplier relationships: A case study of Toyota. *Journal of Management Studies, 35,* 331–353.

Leverick, F., & Cooper, R. (1998). Partnerships in the motor industry: Opportunities and risks for suppliers. *Long Range Planning, 31,* 72–81.

Lincoln, J. R., Ahmadjian, C. L., & Mason, E. (1998). Organizational learning and purchase-supply relations in Japan: Hitachi, Matsushita and Toyota compared. *California Management Review, 40*(3), 241–264.

Lofland, J. (1971). *Analyzing Social Settings.* Belmont, CA: Wadsworth.

Macquet, C. (1997). Evaluating, selecting and implementing successful supply chain management solutions. *Proceedings of the "Logistics – for the forest industry" conference,* Rotorua, New Zealand, November 3–5. Rotorua, NZ: Liro Ltd.

Maller, J. (1998). Supply systems are based on relationships. *The National Business Review,* April 24, 70.

Martin, P. Y., & Turner, B. A. (1986). Grounded theory and organizational research. *The Journal of Applied Behavioral Science, 22,* 141–157.

Miles, M. B., & Huberman, A. M. (1994). *Qualitative data analysis* (2nd ed.). Thousand Oaks, CA: Sage.

Mudambi, R., & Helper, S. (1998). The 'close but adversarial' model of supplier relations in the U. S. auto industry. *Strategic Management Journal, 19*, 775–792.

Newman, K. (1998). Customer service emphasis 'lacking.' *The New Zealand Herald*, March 31: D6.

Nishiguchi, T. (1992). *Strategic Industrial Sourcing: The Japanese Advantage*. Oxford, U.K.: Oxford University Press.

Nooteboom, B. (1993). Research note: An analysis of specificity in transaction cost economics. *Organization Studies, 14*, 443–451.

Porter, M. E. (1980). *Competitive strategy: techniques for analyzing industries and competitors*. New York: The Free Press.

Ratnayake, R. (1999). Industry concentration and competition: New Zealand experience. *International Journal of Industrial Organization, 17*, 1041–1057.

Silver, E. A., & Peterson, R. (1985). *Decision Systems for Inventory Management and Production Planning* (2nd edition). New York: John Wiley

Silver, E. A., Pyke, D., & Peterson, R. (1998). *Inventory Management and Production Planning and Scheduling*. New York: John Wiley.

Spekman, R. E. (1988). Strategic supplier selection: understanding long-term buyer relationships. *Business Horizons, 31*(4), 75–81.

Strauss, A., & Corbin, J. (1990). *Basics of Qualitative Research: Grounded Theory Procedures and Techniques*. Newbury Park, CA: Sage.

Swamidass, P. M. (1991). Empirical science: new frontier in operations management research. *Academy of Management Review, 16*, 793–814.

Waters-Fuller, N. (1995). Just-in-time purchasing and supply: a review of the literature. *International Journal of Operations and Production Management, 15*(9), 220–236.

Yin, R. K. (1994). *Case Study Research: Design and Methods* (2nd ed.). Beverly Hills, CA: Sage.

# ABOUT THE CONTRIBUTORS

**Nicole Woolsey Biggart** is Professor of Management and Sociology at the Graduate School of Management, University of California, Davis where she has taught courses on corporate strategy, innovation, and social theory. Her recent research has concerned the social structural bases of organized economic activity. She is author of *Charismatic Capitalism: Direct Selling Organizations in America*, *The Economic Organization of East Asian Capitalism* (with Marco Orru and Gary Hamilton), and "Developing Difference: Social Organization and the Rise of Automotive Industries in South Korea, Taiwan, Argentina, and Spain", *American Sociological Review*, 1999, with Mauro Guillen. She has also published in *American Journal of Sociology*, *Administrative Science Quarterly*, *American Journal of Economics and Sociology*, and *Social Problems*. She has served as chairperson of the Organizations, Occupations, and Work Section of the American Sociological Association 1999–2000, and is on the Organizing Committee of the new Economic Sociology Section of the ASA. She has also served on two National Research Council Committees, and several editorial boards including *Organization Studies*, *Organization*, *Journal of Applied Behavioral Science*, and *Administrative Science Quarterly*. She received her Ph.D. in Sociology at the University of California, Berkeley.

**Margaret Brindle** is Associate Professor in The Center for Health Policy, Research and Ethics at George Mason University, teaching strategic management, leadership and organizational behavior in health care. She is also co-director of the Summer Leadership Institute on Capitol Hill. Professor Brindle has authored several books, the latest of which is *Managing Management Fads* with Peter Stearns, Quorum-Greenwood, 2001. Her research interests combine organizational theory, history and health care. Her Masters and Ph.D. degrees are in applied history, health management and organizational theory, from Carnegie Mellon University.

**Debra A. Cantelon** graduated from Trinity Western University. She currently lives in Toronto and works as a writer.

**Judith A. Claire** is an Associate Professor at Boston College. She received her Ph.D. from the University of Southern California. Her current research interests are in exploring new forms of employee-organizational relationships, crisis management, and how individuals manage their organizational identities.

**Kimberly D. Elsbach** is an Associate Professor of Management at the Graduate School of Management at the University of California, Davis. She received her Ph.D. in Industrial Engineering from Stanford University. Her research focuses on the perception and management of individual and organizational images, identities, and reputations. Professor Elsbach has studied these symbolic processes in a variety of contexts ranging from the California cattle industry and the National Rifle Association to radical environmentalist groups and Hollywood screenwriters.

**Tal Elyashiv** is a Vice President of Information Technology at Capital One Financial Corporation, Falls Church, Virginia. He is also the CEO of Navion, a software development company in Shanghai, China. Elyashiv graduated from Bar-Ilan University in Mathematics and Computer Science and has an MBA from the University of British Columbia.

**Lance B. Kurke** is Associate Professor of Management at the John F. Donahue Graduate School of Business at Duquesne University, and is an adjunct Associate Professor at the H. John Heinz School of Public Policy and Management at Carnegie Mellon University. He holds MBA, MA, and Ph.D. degrees from the Johnson Graduate School of Management at Cornell University, and has served on the faculties of the Graduate School of Industrial Administration at Carnegie Mellon University, the Babcock Graduate School of Management at Wake Forest University, and the International Management Center at the Central European University in Budapest, Hungary. His research interests are primarily in the areas of strategy, history, and leadership. Professor Kurke is President of Kurke & Associates, Inc., a strategic planning firm, and President of the CEO Club of Pittsburgh.

**J. Keith Murnighan** is the Harold H. Hines Jr. Distinguished Professor of Risk Management in the Department of Management and Organizations, Kellogg School of Management, Northwestern University. His research, on negotiation, groups, and interpersonal interaction, has appeared in a variety of organizational behavior, social psychology, and experimental economics journals. Professor Murnighan's books include *The Dynamics of Bargaining Games*, *Bargaining Games*, and *Social Psychology in Organizations*. Along with John Mowen, he is currently writing a book on decision making.

**Christine M. Pearson** is a Research Professor at University of North Carolina, Chapel Hill. She received her Ph.D. from the University of Southern California. Professor Pearson's research examines the "dark side" of organizational life.

**Gayle Porter** is a member of the Management Faculty at Rutgers University, School of Business, in Camden, New Jersey. Her industry experience includes technical work in the oil and gas industry, finance and accounting with a Fortune 500 company, and consulting on training programs and employee development. Professor Porter received her Ph.D. in Business Administration from The Ohio State University. At Rutgers she teaches courses in organization change and development, leadership, social responsibility of business, and organizational behavior. Her research interests focus on employee potentials, particularly related to team interactions and personal factors that may inhibit employee development efforts.

**Jayaram (Jay) Sankaran** is an Associate Professor in operations management at the Department of Management Science and Information Systems in the University of Auckland at Auckland, New Zealand. He received his Ph.D. in management science from the Graduate School of Business, University of Chicago. His research interests lie primarily in modelling and field research on operations management, especially logistics and supply chain management. He has co-authored a book with Suchi Mouly on organizational ethnography, and has published over 20 research articles.

**Peter N. Stearns** is Professor and Provost at George Mason University, and was formerly Dean of the College of Humanities and Social Science at Carnegie Mellon University. Professor Stearns has authored over 60 books and is founder and editor of the *Journal of Social History*. His latest books are a history of modern consumerism and *An Encyclopedia of World History*. Stearns holds Ph.D. and undergraduate degrees from Harvard University.

**Terence Wilson** is a Scheduling Implementation Analyst with Carter Holt Harvey Ltd, a New Zealand-based diversified manufacturer. Prior to this he was Production Planner with Fletcher Challenge Steel Group Ltd. He holds a Master of Commerce with Honours in Management Science and Information Systems, and a Bachelor of Commerce in Marketing and Operations Management, both from the University of Auckland, New Zealand. His article in this volume is based on his Masters thesis in operations management.